The Unknown Freud:
Five Plays
and
Five Essays

Robert L. Lippman

IPBOOKS.net
International Psychoanalytic Books

Copyright © 2016 Robert L. Lippman
Published by IPBooks
(International Psychoanalytic Books)
25–79 31st Street Astoria, NY 11102

Quotations from VIRGIL (1983). *The Aeneid.* Translated by Robert Fitzgerald, used by permission of Random House.

Cover illustration: Pablo Picasso, *Portrait of Daniel-Henry Kahnweiler* (1910). Courtesy Art Institute of Chicago.

All rights reserved. This book may not be reproduced, transmitted, or stored in whole or in part by any means, including graphic, electronic, or mechanical without the express permission of the publisher except in the case of brief quotations embodied in critical articles and reviews.

ISBN: 978-0-9969996-3-2

*This book is dedicated
to the memory of
my parents,
Irving and Molly Lippman*

My deep engrossment in the Bible story (almost as soon as I had learned the art of reading) had, as I recognized much later, an enduring effect upon the direction of my interest.
—Sigmund Freud (1925; added 1935). *An Autobiographical Study*

If this mad effort's to your liking, then
Consider what you must accomplish first....
A tree's deep shade conceals a bough whose leaves
And pliant twigs are all of gold...
No one may enter hidden depths
Below the earth unless he picks this bough...
So lift your eyes and search, and once you find it
Pull away the bough. It will come willingly,
Easily, if you are called by fate.
If not, with all your strength you cannot conquer it,
Cannot lop it off with a sword's edge.
—Virgil, *The Aeneid.* Book VI. R. Fitzgerald (1983) translation

CONTENTS

The Plays

1. *Freud in Rome: It Takes a Little Courage* 1

2. *Ann and Aaron Look on as Freud on his Deathbed Turns the Pages of Balzac's* **La Peau de Chagrin** 113

3. *Freud at the Crossroads in Rome* 161

4. *Ann and Aaron Pore Over Freud's Fainting Spells in Jung's Presence* 171

5. *"The Struggle is Not Yet Over."* 199

The Essays

Author's Note 265

1. Freud's Botanical Monograph Screen Memory Revisited 267

2. Freud's Dream Castle by the Sea 285

3. Freud's Failure to Recall the Surname of Julius Mosen 291

4. The Aliquis Lapse: Preparing the Ground With Minna 301

5. Freud's "Disturbance of Memory on the Acropolis" Revisited 313

Author's Other Relevant Papers 325

Selected Bibliography 327

One night, after failing to choose this book's lead play, I dreamt that a woman was dancing, more like jumping, on a park bench trying urgently to get my attention. Her features and colorful outfit suggested a Gypsy, not unlike Miss Portero, a character of my creation in one of the plays. With the lead play 'chosen,' the four others fell into place.

Ah, the lights are lowering . . .

Enjoy,
Robert L. Lippman

Freud in Rome:
It Takes a Little Courage

A Two-Act Play

Michelangelo's *Libyan Sibyl* (c.1511–1512),
Sistine Chapel, Vatican

FREUD IN ROME: It Takes a Little Courage
A Two-Act Play

... there is plenty of evidence that the fulfillment of this great wish [to visit Rome] was opposed by some mysterious taboo which made [Freud] doubt if the wish could ever be realized.
—Ernest Jones, Sigmund Freud's official biographer.

We can now understand why heroes visit the underworld, the dwelling place of the dead. They do so in order that they may return from the dead as gods.
—Lord Raglan, *The Hero.*

CHARACTERS

Sigmund Freud	Age 45, impeccably groomed, he is wearing a 3-piece suit, a blue gardenia in his lapel.
Miss Portero	Attractive, about Freud's age, with long dark hair parted in the middle. Her blouse and full-length skirt would have been in fashion in classical antiquity.
Lucina	Miss Portero's African maid in her twenties of uncommon beauty. Regal bearing, she's wearing a huge turban, a bright loose-fitting outfit, and one huge gold earring.
Prosecutor	Groomed and dressed like Freud, he can pass for him.
Vittorio	Miss Portero's pajama-clad five-year-old son.
Freud's Brethren	Five actors play ten Jews of all stripes.
Freud's "Julius" or "Julian" Line	Males and Females: all ages, races. (The Actors who play Freud's brethren also play members of this line.)

SETTING

All scenes take place in the living room of Miss Portero's Rome hotel apartment overlooking St. Peter's Square. The room doubles as an artist's studio. It is a large, dark, book-lined room with several lighted candles. On

3

the left side are artifacts and paintings of ancient Rome, including deities (e.g., Janus; Pan; Jupiter), pottery (urns; flower-pots; an ink-well), and also a painting of Garibaldi. On the right side are works of art with Christian, especially Roman Catholic, subject matter, including a picture of Virgin nursing Child. A large, crude crucifix is over a fireplace. On the right-rear are double glass doors leading to a terrace. Center-stage there is an oblong table between a sofa and a comfortable armchair in earth tones.

Behind the couch and chair and to the left, is a curtained area, a 'stage'. The curtain is made of violet, purple, and scarlet yarn. On its center is a gold Sphinx, the mythological monster with a woman's head, the body of a lion, and wings. Directly over the Sphinx, in Greek, is the legend, "Know Thyself." On each side of the Sphinx is a gold sheaf of five ears of wheat. The curtain is bounded by a gold cord.

The set is multi-leveled for enacted projections from Freud's mind, including flashbacks.

AT RISE:

About 9:30 P.M., Wednesday, September 4, 1901. It is storming. There is a powerful peal of thunder and brilliant lightning.

ACT I, SCENE I

> FREUD and MISS PORTERO are re-entering the room from the terrace which has hanging plants. MISS PORTERO has several clipped roses in her hand as well a pruner. Her face is partly in the shadows, designed to give an eerie effect. FREUD is closing the doors against strong resistance. Shutting the door with a forceful hip movement, MISS PORTERO, smelling the roses, goes to the buffet.

MISS PORTERO

It is miserable outside.
> (She pours water into a vase on the buffet with care; arranges the flowers.)

FREUD

> (Spotting the Sphinx on the 'stage' curtain, he takes a doily from the chair and goes to Sphinx. He carefully puts the doily over his own hair to make it a kind of Sphinx hair. Suddenly, he mimes the Sphinx: his hands and arms braced against an imaginary object, his back arched, with fearsome visage.)

Like an oriental despot.

> (MISS PORTERO look up; smiles, almost breaks out in laughter, in spite of self.) (Straightening up, FREUD spots the Greek Legend.)

"Know Thyself!"

> (Backing away, wipes brow with his handkerchief, and returns the doily.)

MISS PORTERO
> (Setting the vase in front of and then to the side of the marble figurine of Venus.)

And the Mother of Cities, does she meet your expectations?

FREUD
Ah! An incomparable city. . . Today, my brother and I took in the National Museum. It's a jewel—

MISS PORTERO
I understand your brother Julius is always with you.

FREUD
What?! I have no brother Julius.

MISS PORTERO
> (Getting the wine carafe.)

Some wine?

FREUD
No, thank you . . .
> (And to self:)

Roman red wine, that's all I need.
> (Climbing the library ladder, HE studies the titles.)

MISS PORTERO
> (Pouring self a drink.)

In the National there is an immediacy. Even the Lares, the household gods of long ago, they spring to life—
> (FREUD, slipping off a rung, almost falls off ladder.)

THE UNKNOWN FREUD: FIVE PLAYS . . .

(Hearing Freud slip, MISS PORTERO turns—)

LUCINA (Offstage)

Ha!

(Then LUCINA laughs heartily, mockingly, as though Freud is the butt of a joke.)

(FREUD is unnerved.)

MISS PORTERO

I should have cautioned you.

FREUD

After we left the museum, I had an unsettling experience of another kind. Alexander and I took a carriage tour and got off at the Capitoline Hill overlooking the Forum. I am standing on the hill, taking everything in . . .

(HE looks down, across the room: Astonishment!):
Just as we learnt it at school, the Roman Forum is real!

(Climbs down.)

MISS PORTERO

But surely you must have known that the Forum is not a mere myth. How then can you account for this momentary disbelief in its physical reality—?

FREUD

Standing on the hill signified I had risen higher in the world than my father. You see, Miss Portero, I was guilty of the crime of excelling the father.
(Studying the marble Venus.)
That's why—

MISS PORTERO

The Mother of Rome won't bite.—
(Taking a cigarette from a silver case.)

FREUD

(Handles Venus delicately.) (To self:)
And Rome seemed out of reach. All it took was a little courage.

MISS PORTERO

Filial piety, guilt, then, spoiled your pleasure—?
(Lighting her cigarette with a candle.)

FREUD
Right! My momentary astonishment or disbelief in the objective reality of the Forum was my way of punishing myself for having risen higher in the world than my father—
> (Returning Venus to her spot.)

MISS PORTERO
Your father Moses?

FREUD
> (He almost drops Venus.)

Moses? My father's name was Jakob.
> (Relieved that he didn't drop Venus, he returns her to her spot; his eyes lingering.)

MISS PORTERO
> (Swats a mosquito)

One less bearer of malaria . . .
> (Crushes the mosquito with her fingers.)

Not that it is cause to rejoice. The miserable pests are as thick as the locusts of the Bible story.
> (FREUD takes a cigar from his vest.)
> (Deciding a brass ashtray isn't good enough, SHE hands him a crystal one instead.)

Tell me, what do you hope to find in the Eternal City?

> (Cutting an orange in half, SHE places one half on a plate so that it 'mocks' the Dome of St. Peter's, which can be seen from the apt.; then she quarters it with two strokes. With her nails she peels the 'quartered' Dome.)

> (FREUD, oblivious, is studying the crystal's fire.)

> (MISS PORTERO has realigned the four quarters in the shape of St. Peter's Dome, and, tapping him, offers FREUD, who gives a start, a quarter from the plate. FREUD takes it.)

FREUD
> (Somewhat taken aback by the uncanny symbolism, HE says to self:)

Quartering St. Peter's should be that easy.

> (With silver cigar clipper, HE cuts cigar. As HE is about to light the cigar, spotting a large painting of Garibaldi on his horse, HE goes to it abruptly.)

On his deathbed my father looked like Garibaldi.

> (Lighting his cigar, HE has a flashback:
> *Sigmund, 7, is being rebuked by his father, Jakob, 47, in the parents' bedroom.*
> *His mother, Amalie, 27, is in her nightgown. There is a fire in the fireplace.*
> HERE, WE JUST HAVE THE VOICES OF BOTH FREUD and MISS PORTERO AS IF IN AN ECHO CHAMBER:
>
> —*Amalie, that boy will come to nothing*
> —*Jakob, he's but a child!*)

MISS PORTERO
> (Tapping Freud with an orange branch.)
> (FREUD jumps; his *FLASHBACK* fades.)

For urinating on his bed you expected your papa to hand you a medal?

FREUD

I was only seven—

> (White-faced, as if he had seen a ghost, he abruptly turns to her.)

How?!—(High-pitched!)

> (From a shelf MISS PORTERO gets *The Interpretation of Dreams*; hands it to him.)

My Egyptian dream book. (Relieved.) Some ticket to immortality!

> (Taking out a train ticket, HE knocks on wood 3 times . . . HE looks at the ticket.)

The first time I saw my mother naked was on a train . . .

> (Putting the train ticket in the Dream Book in the manner of a bookmark.)

In two years only about two hundred have been sold.

> (Takes puff.)

MISS PORTERO

Then I am fortunate?

> (Dips quill in inkwell for inscription.)

FREUD IN ROME: IT TAKES A LITTLE COURAGE

> FREUD
> (Taking out his pen he writes with a flourish. Blowing on inscription, he coughs.)

I once quit for fourteen months . . . (Pats heart.) Trouble is, without my cigars work is impossible.

> MISS PORTERO (Reads)

"To Miss Portero, my Roman reader, the best of dreams."
> (SHE blots it carefully with a framed blotter.)

Revolutionary ideas are often resisted. . . Who has the courage to own his sleeping thoughts and desires? . . .
> (Replacing the blotter, SHE walks to the book case while turning to Title Page . . .)

Virgil gave you your motto, "If I can not bend the higher powers, I'll move hell."

> FREUD (Looking at the books.)

Whatever it takes. . . compulsions, phobias, dreams . . . the repressed breaks through.

> MISS PORTERO

"If I can not bend the higher powers, I'll move hell."
Sounds like a battle cry.

> FREUD

In a way it is. The discoveries there will (Turning over a large hourglass.) disturb the sleep of mankind.

> MISS PORTERO

A peculiar people, you Jews. If you are not reading the Book, you are writing it.
> (From a bookshelf, SHE gets a faded pink book with gold lettering. FREUD and MISS PORTERO are on opposite sides of the ladder. SHE offers him the book.)

> FREUD

The Aeneid?
> (SHE nods. As HE goes around the ladder to get the book, SHE smiles. HE puts his cigar down and wipes his hands on a handkerchief before taking *The Aeneid*. HE feels the title, sits in the armchair and puts his face in the book.)

                    MISS PORTERO

It was my father's.

                    FREUD

My father chided me for spending money on books. You see, for this bookworm, the smell . . . the taste of books . . . reading, is sensual.

        (Perhaps since it is acted out, FREUD needn't say the above.)

As a schoolboy I read The *Aeneid* for pleasure and in Latin. (From memory:) "*Arma virumque cano* . . ."
  "Of arms and the man I sing..." Colored plates!

        (LUCINA enters.)
        (SHE's carrying a tray holding a pot, two cups, a creamer, cheese, and crackers. Placing the tray on the oblong table, SHE pours coffee.)

                    MISS PORTERO (To Freud.)

Cream?

                    FREUD
        (Oblivious of both Lucina and Miss Portero, HE reads:)
"In the perilous underworld the golden bough renders the hero invulnerable."—

        (LUCINA pours Miss Portero a cup of coffee, with cream and sugar. She then approaches Freud.)

        (FREUD, upon seeing Lucina, jumps; and indicates that it's fine: no sugar, no cream.)
        (LUCINA exits.)

        (FREUD's eyes follow Lucina out. He is about to drink when—
        (LUCINA, off-stage, laughs heartily, a mocking quality.)

        (FREUD, startled by LUCINA'S laughter, spills some coffee; then examines book.)
The coffee didn't get on *The Aeneid*. I'd never forgive myself.

        (MISS PORTERO dips a linen napkin in water and starts to wipe him.)

        (Her attention makes FREUD uncomfortable; taking the

> napkin from her, HE wipes himself. Seeing the blood-red wine stains on the napkin, HE quickly discards it.)

Thanks . . . (To self:) Since making this pilgrimage, my foot, my hand, even my mind, they've all slipped. Can my heart take it, my mad task?
> (Returning to *The Aeneid* and Miss Portero)

Virgil and the Greeks were my teachers. . . I named my brother Alex after Alexander the Great.
> (*A projection: little Sigmund beaming as his parents, Jakob and Amalie, make over him for having chosen the baby's name.*)

MISS PORTERO

You named your brother? How old were you?

FREUD

Ten. . . . My parents liked my suggestion—

MISS PORTERO

Ten? Even then a Mesmerist. (BOTH smile.) Thank goodness you didn't name him after your one-eyed hero of your school days, the relentless Semite who almost vanquished Rome—
> (SHE pats Dream Book.) (BOTH laugh.)

FREUD

I don't think I could have pulled it off . . . Imagine! Hannibal, get off your elephant and pass the salt..
> (Accidentally knocking over a salt shaker, he tosses salt over his left shoulder.)

We're like a book, the brothers, the covers; the five sisters, the pages.
> (HE smiles; turning the pages.)
> (*A Mental projection: We hear them sing at the Passover Seder.* FREUD joins in:)

"Da-da ye-nu, da-da ye-nu, da-da ye-nu, da-ye-nu, da ye-nu!"—
> (Catching self.)

Miss Portero, you say you're troubled by a series of dreams?

MISS PORTERO
> (Seats self on couch, smoothes out her garment behind her; extends her left hand.)

I believe they are on common ground.

FREUD

Would you like to work on one?

MISS PORTERO

Not now, later perhaps. . . Your right hand.
> (Across the oblong table, FREUD reluctantly gives her his hand, conveying an impression that he doesn't like being touched, very reserved, uncomfortable in this area.)
> (FREUD watches her examine his hand, palm up. Both of her hands handle his hand, very sensual.)

Keep it still! Don't help me!
> (SHE examines his hand intently; still sensual. Freud, looking at his hand and catching himself getting pleasure, tightens hand, withdrawing it some. She pulls it back, straightening his fingers.)

Your birth?

FREUD

1856. . . May 6th. The great French-Jewish General, Marshall Massena, was born that day, exactly one hundred years earlier. In my toy soldier days Napoleon's "favored child of victory" and I crossed the Alps together many times.
> (*Flashback: Freud, about, 8, on the floor placing names on the backs of toy soldiers.*)
> (Not getting a response from her, FREUD, annoyed, blurts out:)

Am I boring you?
> (Still no response from Miss Portero, who appears engrossed. He moves his hand to get her attention. She pulls it back.)

I was born in a caul, a membrane on my head . . .
> (*A Projection from Freud's mind showing his mother in the scene he relates below, Infant Sigi is in a wicker cradle. Initially, for a moment, the slide does not find the right place and Freud's mother is projected on Freud himself.*)

A Moravian peasant-woman told my mother, who was only twenty, that she had brought a great man into the world . . . Even today this shabby old Jew is her *goldener Sigi*.

MISS PORTERO

Hm! the 6th of May, the day of your birth, is, of course, the anniversary of the Sack of Rome, long ago, in 1527. The Holy Father scurrying to the Castel

FREUD IN ROME: IT TAKES A LITTLE COURAGE

Sant Angelo. . . can you imagine?
>> (Miming the scurrying with her fingers.)
>>>> FREUD (To Self, as he looks at his hand.)
When I show my hand, the Holy Father won't have a thatched hut to escape to.
>> (MISS PORTERO gives him back his hand.)
Well, . . . shall I have a long life?
>> (In a mocking tone, in a manner of an unbeliever. But he is deeply curious.)

MISS PORTERO

Your father had the gift of prophecy.
>> (Rubbing her palms together, SHE shows him the blackish epidermis scales.)
In the end we all come to nothing. . . . What do Mcravian peasant-women know?!

FREUD

>> (At first he doesn't know how to take this. He thought she had been reading his future. He softens as he notices a playful mischievous smile, although one mixed with sadness.)
I'd better go. Tomorrow is a big day.—

MISS PORTERO (Lifting *The Aeneid*)

When it came to essential matters my father would consult the oracle . . .
>> (Raising her gown, SHE scratches her left leg.)

FREUD (Averting his eyes.)

The practice of Virgilian lots?
>> (Intrigued, but feigning disdain.)

MISS PORTERO

With eyes closed, Father would select a passage.
>> (Demonstrating with her left forefinger.)
And it had to be with his special pointer.
>> (With her left hand, she feels in the drawer of the oblong table. Then she looks in the drawer, bending down: nothing. She looks around the room. She throws her arms out in frustration.)
Uncanny how it returns, the exasperation as father and I searched—

THE UNKNOWN FREUD: FIVE PLAYS . . .

                FREUD
           (Walking to the antiquities side of the room to an unfinished painting. By the palette he spots a thin bright pointed metal rod about a foot long with gold leaves. The painting has a burning house in the background; in the foreground is a man in ancient attire carrying an elderly man on his back and holding a boy by the hand. They are fleeing. The grandfather is holding the household gods.)
           (Lifting the bough, FREUD speaks to it:.)

Right next to Aeneas escaping his homeland, Greek-besieged Troy, with his father, Anchises, and his son, Julius Ascanius.
           (MISS PORTERO looks up; surprised.)

You believed golden Sigi wouldn't find and pluck you? Some careful concealer!
              MISS PORTERO
The scientist and intuition.—
              FREUD
I'm a conquistador!
           (Testing the bough as one might a sword. Suddenly, he slashes the air in the direction of St. Peter's.)

              MISS PORTERO
You come to plague-ridden Rome!
           (Lifting the Dream Book, SHE squashes a mosquito; scrapes it off the book.
           Trying for another, SHE misses.)
           (The first slam startles FREUD. Inspired, with the bough HE slashes the air, barely missing her nose. This frightens MISS PORTERO: 'has he lost control'?
           HE shows her an imaginary mosquito he picked off in flight.)

           (Regaining HER composure—)
Had your pleasure—?
           (SHE Reads passage from Dream Book:)
For a long time to come, no doubt, I shall have to to continue to satisfy my longing for Rome in my dreams; for at that season of the year when it is possible for me to travel, residence in Rome must be avoided for reasons of health.

FREUD IN ROME: It Takes a Little Courage

(SHE puts the Dream Book down.)
A fool, a knave, or just simply brave, the firstborn son risking a plague.

FREUD
(Uneasy, and wanting to get off the topic, FREUD quickly re-aligns large chess pieces but accidentally drops the white queen. He strokes the white queen; examines her in detail. She isn't chipped; relieved, HE returns her to the board.)

When I was fourteen I played Brutus to my nephew John's Julius Caesar. He's the son of Emmanuel, my half-brother from my father's first marriage. We both loved and hated one another.
(Takes a puff and coughs.)
Through my self-analysis, I've come to understand that I've always needed an intimate friend and a hated enemy.
(With a black and a white pawn he 'mocks' wrestling and boxing; their shadows are on the back wall.)
When we were kids, poor John played both roles. . . . We were like brothers. When he was 17 or 18 he left home and hasn't been heard from since.
(To self:)
It's as though, like Julius, John had never lived.

MISS PORTERO
(Taking the golden bough and playing the stabbed Caesar incredulous, with sadness, SHE faces Freud:)
"Et tu, mon fils?"

(FREUD bites his lips at *"fils"*)

(Feigning pondering, MISS PORTERO asks:)
Why does the poet have Caesar call Brutus. "son"?

FREUD (Arms folded, glaring at her.)
Out with it! You're up to some—!

MISS PORTERO (As if she hadn't heard him.)
Oh well, . . . for your reward consult Virgil . . . (Offering golden bough.)

FREUD (To self.)
You're too jumpy. Collect yourself! (He replaces the chess pieces.)

MISS PORTERO

When in Rome . . .

                  FREUD (He takes the bough.)

Which Rome? . . .

        (Pointing HIS left arm at the wall opposite him, the 'classical antiquity' wall.)

The pagan

        (Pointing the bough in HIS right hand at the 'Christian' wall behind him.)

or the Christian?

                  MISS PORTERO (Lifts a porcelain Madonna.)

My taste is too Catholic.

        (BOTH laugh; FREUD despite himself.)

                  FREUD (Turns Madonna away.)

Nothing Catholic is funny . . .

                  MISS PORTERO

And these, my Catholic legs, are they funny?

                  FREUD

I had a Catholic nanny. God, was she ugly—
        (Smiles as he catches self saying "God.")

                  MISS PORTERO

Ugly as sin?— (Handles beaded necklace a la Rosary.)

                  FREUD (*Touche:* He nods to her.)

Resi told me a great deal about God, heaven, and of souls burning in Hell . . .
        (Looking at the fire-place, over which is a crucifix.)

This was in the Catholic town of my birthplace, Freiberg in Moravia. Just two percent were Jews.

        [A FLASHBACK (using a series of slides): 2 year-old Sigi 'telling' his parents about God and Heaven and Hell. Enjoying him, they act terrified when he throws sticks into the fireplace. Jakob is smoking a cigar.]

After Mass at the Church of the Nativity of Our Lady I preached to my parents how the Lord Jesus conducted His affairs. . .

(Crosses self with cigar.)
Miss Portero, it's all a waste! All the coal needed for hell-fire.
(HE throws 'sticks' at the slides which become encircled with hot red lights, as if burning.)
It'd be so much better to follow the usual procedure, condemn the sinner to so many hundred thousand years of roasting, then lead him to the next chamber, and just let him sit there. In no time the waiting would become a worse punishment than being actually burned—

MISS PORTERO

This wisdom, may I pass it along? Or perhaps you prefer a private audience with Pope Leo?—

FREUD

What this Godless Jew has to say to the Holy father, believe me, Miss Portero, the Holy Father wouldn't want to hear ... When I was two-and-a-half they let Resi go. (Tinge of sadness.)

MISS PORTERO

For seducing you?—

FREUD

For seducing me?

MISS PORTERO (Looking up at the Crucifix.)

Into the faith.

FREUD

They dismissed her for stealing ... money, even my toy soldiers.
[A FLASHBACK: Little Sigi is handing nanny some coins and his toys, including toy soldiers.) ...] (He 'comes back'.)
Strange that her name, like an un-laid ghost, should come back to me ...
(Puts rod down.)
Frantic, I searched for Resi all over, even in the cupboards.—

MISS PORTERO

Virgil is waiting.
(SHE holds out the bough in an apparent no-nonsense way.)

FREUD

I take no stock in oracles, even Virgil, much as I love him—

THE UNKNOWN FREUD: FIVE PLAYS ...

MISS PORTERO

Consult the magician, and, unbeliever, Venus (pointing to the figurine) is yours. What have you to lose? . . . As you say, tomorrow is a big day.

(Nonchalantly, SHE playfully holds on to it.

When FREUD applies some 'pull', she lets it go. Not expecting this, Freud is propelled back in his chair. She smiles and, in this instance, HE seems to appreciate her toying with him.)

So much for your intuition.

FREUD

You thought I wasn't infallible?!

(An accusation!: this way HE places the blame on her.)
(SHE smiles but there is concern behind the smile.)

So, now, we cast our lot! (Heartily.)

(Quickly but gently HE opens *The Aeneid,* randomly selecting a page and extending palm as a surgeon might for a scalpel.) (MISS PORTERO places it in his palm.)

Let it fall where it will!

(Eyes closed, FREUD selects a passage. Opening his eyes he reads silently, turns pale and becomes frozen in space, the pointer fixed to the passage.)

MISS PORTERO

(Taking *The Aeneid* from him, SHE looks at the lot; then at Freud.)

Ah! The Sibyl of Cumae's advice to Aeneas who has just arrived in Italy to enter the underworld to visit his father's shade.

(By heart)

If you are still bent on this mad task you must first find the Golden Bough.

Only those favored by fate can pluck it free.

(FREUD spots a portrait of a Sibyl with a striking resemblance to Miss Portero studying a large book. Wiping and replacing his glasses, he studies Miss Portero's face, and for a better view, he starts for the portrait—)

(SHE taps FREUD on the shoulder with the golden bough. HE jumps.)

This was father's favorite passage. It virtually opens on its own.

(SHE demonstrates)

See! The spine, it is cracked.

FREUD IN ROME: It Takes a Little Courage

> FREUD
> (Looking again at Miss Portero's face and that of the Sibyl, HE retrieves *The Aeneid,* which flies open to the page. Relieved, his confidence restored, He jokes:)

If I were superstitious, I'd see this as an omen.

> (SHE smiles but there is concern behind the smile.)
> (HE re-tests and, again, it opens to that page.)

So, again, we cast out lot! (Heartily)

> (Again, HE turns pale and becomes frozen, with the pointer fixed; this time, at a new passage. And, again, SHE takes *The Aeneid,* fixing her eyes on the lot.)
> (In a trance-like state, FREUD recites from memory:)

. . . And there Aeneas tried three times
To throw his arms around his father's neck,
Three times the shade untouched slipped through his hands,
Weightless as wind and fugitive as dream.

> (While reciting, HE gestures with his left hand, trying to hug space: anguish at not being able to touch his father.)
> (If possible a holograph could be used as FREUD tries to touch his father and nothing's there.)
> *(A mental projection: a slide based on an actual photo of Sigmund Freud, at age 8, with his father. In that photo, Jakob is seated, with a book in his lap; and little Sigi wearing a suit stands beside his father to his left. But here the slide of little Sigi is projected on the back of Freud while that of Jakob is projected higher on the wall, like a god. The projection is in sepia hues)*
>
> (Coming to, FREUD retrieves *The Aeneid* from Miss Portero and checks its spine.)

No crack! (To self). . . . It's uncanny. I've been to the underworld . . .

> (Returning *The Aeneid* to Miss Portero, he goes to the painting of Garibaldi on his white horse. Garibaldi's head is radiant.)

Daily after my father's death. . .

(Long silence as though FREUD blacked out momentarily—there is pain here. With his fingers he closes his eyes as he might have his father's on his deathbed. Then with his left fore-and middle fingers he presses his forehead just above the eyebrows.)

A father's death has to be the most poignant loss of a man's life. . . Where was I?

MISS PORTERO
(Looking at Garibaldi picture.)

Burying your papa who looked like our glorious freedom-fighter—

FREUD

He was a very happy man with a peculiar mixture of deep wisdom and fantastic light-heartedness. . . .Whenever I was too much on my high horse

(Mocking holding the reins of a horse.)

he'd admonish me:

There are more things in heaven and earth than are dreamed of in your philosophy . . .

For a moment, the lot seemed his way of tweaking me.

(He twists his nose.)

"Remember, my brilliant son"! . . . After his death—he died in November 1896, five years ago—I felt uprooted . . . . I studied, analyzed, myself, by my dreams . . .

(pointing the bough at Dream Book.)

I became my most interesting patient—

. . . . (Glancing at the Aeneas painting.)

[There is a projection from Freud's mind: He is seated at a desk with artifacts. It is night. Freud has a cigar in his left hand and a pen in his right. Behind him is a bookcase from which Janus, the 2-headed god, looks down. Adjoining the bookcase is a table with more of his collection of antiquities behind those figurines, and on the table, against the bookcase, is a large portrait of Michelangelo's Moses, but only the tip of the head is visible. The rest of Moses' head is hidden by the figurines.]

(A peal of thunder and brilliant light startle FREUD)

MISS PORTERO (She looks out the terrace.)
Michelangelo could have made this storm.
    (The golden bough in his right hand, FREUD approaches, as if drawn to it, the now gleaming full-figured statue of JANUS on his throne. With his left hand Freud fondles the key in Janus' left hand. A sceptre is in JANUS' right hand.)

                        FREUD
Janus' two stone faces look down on me very haughtily.
    (Looking up at JANUS, FREUD gives him a haughty look back.)

                      MISS PORTERO
    (Looking at Janus' key held by Freud:)
Janus clubs those who trespass, but then Janus is also the god of new beginnings . . .
    (FREUD eyes St. Peter's Dome while tightening HIS hand around the key.) (SHE caresses Janus' sceptre sensually.)

                        FREUD
He forgets my golden bough—
    (A private joke, or so he thinks—)
    (With the golden bough he starts to parry Janus' sceptre. Suddenly JANUS's left head glows, radiance as though straight from EXODUS 34:29–35. Looking up at the terrible glowering face, FREUD, experiencing awe and terror, tries to cover his eyes. The bough falls from his hand. He faints, falling away on his back.)

                    MISS PORTERO
    (Rushing to him, she cradles him.)
My little Sigismund, you've come home—

                        FREUD
    (Coming half-to, he catches himself as he about to suckle her breast—)
Resi?

                    MISS PORTERO
Yes, my darling, Resi. Our warm baths together, do you remember? Such pleasure we—

                    FREUD (Crying, as though a little boy.)
I just wanted Julius to go away—

                         MISS PORTERO
Hush, my son, Julius is with Jesus in Paradise
          (Humming a lullaby, SHE comforts Freud, as he drifts off.)

          (Outside there is a loud peal of thunder and brilliant light. For a brief moment St. Peter's Dome is visible through the terrace doors.)

          END of ACT I, SCENE 1

ACT I, SCENE 2

A few minutes later. FREUD is lying on the sofa. An earth-colored pillow is under his head and his face is buried in one of the throw pillows. He is more on his side than on his back. An earth-colored quilted cover is partially over him.

MISS PORTERO watches the dead-like Freud with concern and yet she's afraid to wake him.
FREUD, coming to, looks around and sees Miss Portero. From the supine position with a wonderful calmness, he says:

FREUD
How sweet it must be to die.

MISS PORTERO
So, you come to die!
(Without warning, SHE removes the cover!)

FREUD
(HE sits up quickly. Not knowing how to take her words and action for only he can joke about his own death! FREUD opts to cloak his anger.)
If I must rest in a grave, let it be an Etruscan one.
(MISS PORTERO tosses both the pillow and the cover into the armoire.)
(Noticing he doesn't have his shoes on, FREUD starts to put them on. But he takes his socks off first and then begins to put a shoe on when he catches self.)
My feet are burning.
(HE pours himself a glass of water.)
I've had these attacks before . . . I suppose the heart rebelled . . .
(HE looks around for Miss Portero, who has exited.)
Miss Portero? Where the devil is she?—
(HE now hears VOICES coming from behind the Sphinx curtain.)

(FREUD warily approaches the "stage" curtain.)
(The "stage" curtain lifts and FREUD comes face to face with the PROSECUTOR, who, dressed and groomed like Freud, can pass for him. FREUD is horrified!)

My double . . . I'm about to die!
>(Clutching his heart.)
Collect yourself! It's just a superstition! (To self!)

PROSECUTOR

>(In one hand the PROSECUTOR holds a yellowing legal folder with a blue ribbon around it. With the other hand he gestures with FREUD'S gold-handled walking stick for Freud to address the others on the "stage," a JURY OF JEWS.
>
>The JURORS are seated on stone benches, but scattered about. The same actor can play more than one Jew. More than bewildered, FREUD is terrified. The JEWS are of all stripes: some in religious garb; workers; craftsmen; professionals; socialists: a cross-section. They are seated. A catacomb effect is aimed for. There is a large gold Menorah with blue flames.)

PROSECUTOR

Well, we haven't all day! Tell the boys the best of what you know!

FREUD

No, you tell me! And I'll take my cane! (Grabbing his walking stick.) Now, what's all this about?!

PROSECUTOR

>(HE waves the legal folder at FREUD.)

Make your suit!

>(He gestures for FREUD to sit in a leather armchair in the center.)

FREUD

Where's the witch?!

PROSECUTOR

Take the chair!

>(Michelangelo's *MOSES* now appears. HE's seated on his Throne, with the Tablets.)

FREUD

Moses!

>(Seeing *MOSES*/MOSES startles FREUD; he wipes his forehead with his handkerchief. As he does so, his cane's gold

handle falls to the ground. Freud, in vain, tries to re-attach the handle.)
The handle's got to go on! . . . Damn!

PROSECUTOR

Make your accusation!
    (HE points to *MOSES*/MOSES)

(FREUD doesn't want anything to do with this initially. But when he looks at the Jews and notes their seriousness and concern, he takes the stand, discarding his stick and handle.)

THE JEWS

An accusation? Against Moses! What?! Yes, Reb. He blames Moses. For our misery. No?! Who is he? A doctor. An alienist. From Vienna. An unbeliever. He says. And he was named after. His zayde. Reb Shlomo. A chasid. From Galicia—Of blessed. Memory.

FREUD (To self.)

Uncanny. How can they <u>know</u> about me, about my grandfather?

PROSECUTOR (To Freud)

Make your plea to your brethren. Or haven't you the courage, the moral courage? . . . It is still miserable outside.
    (Handing Freud his Dream Book.)

FREUD

(Pointing his Dream Book at *MOSES,* he speaks with a mixture of love and hate for Moses.)

We owe Moses so much. This great man raised our self-esteem by assuring us that we are God's chosen people. This has made us confident, optimistic, even proud. Yes, it is to that great man that we owe our tenacity of life, but it is to him also that we owe, ultimately, the hostility we have experienced and continue to experience, the miserable anti-Semitism.
    (All the time *MOSES*/MOSES glowers at FREUD.)

OLD JEW

Blasphemy!

YOUNG RELIGIOUS JEW

I say stone him.

THE UNKNOWN FREUD: FIVE PLAYS . . .

OTHER JEW

Judas!

OTHER JEW

You'll wish you never set foot in Rome.

OTHER JEW

Herr professor, on the couch did you analyze away your conscience?

RABBI

Moses is not to blame for our misery. The seed-bed of anti-Semitism is the Church. On Good Friday, for an example, the little ones are instructed that we, *"perfidi Judaei,"* perfidious Jews, had killed Jesus.

FREUD (With respect.)

Rebbe, the loving Christians hate us because we <u>gave</u> them Jesus.

ONE JEW

That doesn't make sense!

FREUD

The Christian hates being a Christian—

ANOTHER JEW

Of course! He'd rather be a Jew! (Laughter.)

ANOTHER JEW

You have lost me. What happened to the anti-Semite, Moses?

FREUD

One fact and one fact alone is behind the undying enmity of the Christians. It's that Paul, Peter and the apostles, all Jews, handed them their cross, Christianity. And behind——

ANOTHER JEW

What nonsense now?

FREUD (Faces *MOSES*/MOSES.)

And behind Paul and the others is the figure of Moses, himself—

ANOTHER JEW

Herr professor, yet have I to hear a Christian say that Christianity is his Cross. It's their Salvation—

FREUD IN ROME: It Takes a Little Courage

FREUD
That's my point! Not having the courage—the moral courage—to face that he hates his repressive religion, the good Christian displaces his hatred for Christianity onto us, his jailers . . . . And with a vengeance!

ANOTHER JEW
So that is why they detest us so!

FREUD
How else account for the recent bloody pogroms in Romania and Russia? Or the long life of the centuries-old blood libel –

ANOTHER JEW
Leopold Hilsner—

FREUD
Sentenced to death three years ago for allegedly killing a 19-year-old Christian girl to bake the Passover matzos with her blood. That young Jewish shoe-maker could be any one of our sons—

ITALIAN ARMY COLONEL
That's Czechoslovakia. It can never happen here!

FREUD (Approaching the COLONEL.)
Hate, my dear Colonel, has a keen eye. Just one national crisis and, like that, you'll see the true worth of your proud medals—
       (FREUD polishes the Colonel's medals with his elbow.
       Before the COLONEL can react, FREUD salutes smartly.)
Former Austrian Senior Army Surgeon Freud requesting permission to brief you on the infallible deliberation of the French General Staff in 1894—

JEWS
Dreyfus. Captain Dreyfus. The miserable Dreyfus Affair.

FREUD (AS A FRENCH GENERAL)
Gentlemen, one of our officers is selling our military secrets
to the Germans. It cannot be, heaven forbid,
       (Makes the sign of the Cross with a cigar.)
one of us, a Christian. It's got to be Captain Dreyfus, the one Israelite
on our staff.
       (HE 'wipes' his hands)

FREUD
And, like that, the good Christians ship Dreyfus off for life to Devil's Island—
A JEW
With the shouts of "Death to the Jews!" ringing in his ears.

ANOTHER JEW
Here, it's an open secret that from his office the Vatican Secretary of State Cardinal Rampolla directs the anti-Semitic campaign of the Royalists in France.—
FREUD
That's Christian of him!
ANOTHER JEW
He has even counseled a diplomat that it's the duty of every good Catholic to support the French Premier in his anti-Semitism campaign.—

FREUD
Colonel, are you lending your Roman brothers your ears? . . . That good cleric just happens to be the strongest supporter of the ever popular mayor of Vienna, "I say who is a Jew!," Karl Lueger,
> (Posturing like Lueger, hitting his own chest with right fore-finger.)

Three years ago, Easter, not far from here, in one of the caves of St. Cangian near Trieste, I spotted Herr Doktor Lueger.
> (Freud's area darkens.)

It was Dante's Tartarus itself.
> (Using a large stone as a prop.)

Then and there, in the pitch dark, I should have lifted that good doctor, and, just before pitching him over the iron rail, whispered, "I am a Jew."
> (We hear echoes of "I am a Jew" as Lueger falls to his death, including the splash as Lueger hits the water.)

Alas! He's still the Fuhrer of Vienna . . . To think I let pass that golden opportunity.
ANOTHER JEW
When the white smoke next rises from the Sistine Chapel chimney it will probably signal that the Cardinals have chosen Rampolla Pope.
FREUD
And that good news doesn't trouble you? The noose round our necks is tightening.

FREUD IN ROME: IT TAKES A LITTLE COURAGE

ANOTHER JEW

And you are certain that so long as there is Christianity, there will be anti-Semitism?

*(A projection: **"Freud"** bound by the phylacteries and the Torah Scroll to the Cross: Christianity is the Jew's Cross. The two rollers of the Scroll are positioned to make the Cross to which **"Freud"** is bound. The phylacteries are wrapped around the twisted Scroll enveloping "Freud" who is in full religious garb, including full-length prayer shawl.)*

FREUD

The Torah, the root cause of our misery, must go!

PROSECUTOR

(Bending back his fingers, one at a time:)
No Torah; no Judaism; no Christianity; no miserable anti-Semitism. . . Elegant.

ANOTHER JEW

The destruction of our Tree of Life! The misery I'd rather suffer, thank you!

ANOTHER JEW

Some deliverer!

ANOTHER JEW

But why does it fall to him to deliver us?—

RABBI

Brethren, I, too, see increasing darkness for our nation. Not a day passes without dreadful visions intruding, even during sleep—visions I dare not relate. But only Jehovah can redeem us—not him!—
(pointing at Freud)
not Herzl!

ANOTHER JEW

Oh! But to be a wall on the Berggasse Street
When the two Messiahs first they meet.

(Wearing Freud's straw hat and swinging his walking stick, the PROSECUTOR encounters another bearded Jew, handsome, aristocratic, wearing a black suit and a top hat, THEODOR HERZL. Both bow.)

FREUD

Herzl! *(High-pitched, as though seeing a ghost.)*

"HERZL"

If not now, when?

"FREUD"

If not us, who? (They tip hats; each goes his 'way'.)

FREUD (Collecting self; to the Jews:)
And just what, my scornful brothers, has Jehovah done for us lately?

ANOTHER JEW

A plague on both your houses!

FREUD

My hat please—
(Removing his straw hat from the PROSECUTOR's head)
He's done nothing because He exists only in our, er, in your minds.

ANOTHER JEW (Points to the heavens.)
May Yahweh strike down your firstborn son!
(With considerable effort, THE PROSECUTOR and OTHERS keep FREUD from charging the above Jew.)

PROSECUTOR

Collect yourself! (to Freud)... Brothers, please. (To the Jews, who quiet down.) Continue with your plea.

FREUD

Look! Our ignorant desert fathers were all alone in a world of natural forces, terrible forces beyond their control and understanding. Out of their childlike helplessness, they longed for, and got, a powerful father, God the Father, a comforting illusion.

ONE JEW

The *philosophe* not only psychoanalyzes man but God, too! . . . Tell me, does He make a deep impression . . . on your couch, I mean?

ANOTHER JEW

Without the Law, without the fear of the Almighty, man is an animal.

FREUD (Gesturing with Dream Book.)
The time for religious superstition is over. . . New generations who've been brought up in kindness and taught to value reason won't need the fear of God to make a socially just and decent society.
(Bats fly by, startling Freud.)

ANOTHER JEW

He is blind. Pity him.

STONE-THROWER

Pity him?!   (Spits in Freud's direction.)
I say stone him!

FREUD

Because they'll listen to the voice of the intellect, they'll *choose* to set the same aims as those whose realization you expect from God—

ANOTHER JEW

Dreamer, face reality. There will never be such a splendid race of men—

FREUD

Self-knowledge will give them a handle on their own emotions and behavior. They won't throw
> (He moves his left fist down his chest; then he 'throws' with left hand.)

their own asocial qualities or tendencies onto others—

ANOTHER JEW

Such as the greedy Jew pervert.

FREUD

They'll identify with others. And with mutual identification comes the possibility of, of—why should I be ashamed to say it?— comes the possibility of love—

ANOTHER JEW

At long last, the Golden Age of brotherly love.

ANOTHER JEW

How shall I love thee? Let me count the ways—(He plays a Jew's harp.)

FREUD

Leaving heaven to the sparrows, their liberated energies concentrated into this life on earth,
> (With his right hand picks up some earth.)

they'll succeed in achieving a state of things in which life will become tolerable for everyone and civilization no longer oppressive to anyone.
> (If possible, the mockery below can be acted out; there can even be the sound of a violin.)

ONE JEW
And the wolf shall dwell with the lamb.

ANOTHER JEW
And the leopard shall lie down with the kid.

ANOTHER JEW
And a little child shall lead them.
> (A spot-light brightens the face of A JEW who is lying on his back, curled up. He makes out he is being blinded by the light. With his hand, he struggles against the light as if it were a caul.
> Hovering over this Divine Babe are THREE JEWS.)

JEW 1
He's born in a caul!

JEW 2
Ah! A Great Man has been brought into the world!

JEW 3
Already a Moravian peasant-woman has told his pretty young mother it's a sign her *Goldener* Sigi is destined to become a great man.

JEW 1
The biblical prophecy has come to pass. Behold the "Star out of Jakob."

JEW 2
How shall we honor this little *pisher?*

FREUD
> (With each sarcasm, HIS right hand tightens more and more; earth correspondingly slips away from the hand. . .
> HE throws the remains on the ground.)

Moses and the Law must go!

A JEW
He going to attack Moses! Stop him! —

FREUD
> (The PROSECUTOR steps in his path, as do, also, the STONE-THROWER and a BUTCHER.)

Out of my way!

FREUD IN ROME: It Takes a Little Courage

PROSECUTOR (Pointing above Freud's head.)
Ah, wicked bookworm, it has managed to find you.
    (A large black book, The Philippson Bible, floats down.)
    (As FREUD reaches for it, the PROSECUTOR motions for The STONE-THROWER and BUTCHER to leave.)

FREUD
(He quickly turns to the inside cover and sees his father's inscription below.)
Where did you get this?! (High-pitched and white-faced.)

PROSECUTOR
"There are more things in heaven and earth—"

FREUD
(A projection of Jakob Freud giving Freud the Philippson Bible on his 35th birthday and inscribing it.)

Ten years ago, on my thirty-fifth birthday, my father presented me this, our family bible.

PROSECUTOR
And the birthday boy, was he able to read his papa's Hebrew inscription?
    (FREUD: Mental projection: Sigmund Freud as a Bar Mitzvah boy.)
    (FREUD closes the Bible; glares at the PROSECUTOR.)
It's still miserable outside. And much worse is to come.

FREUD
Tell me something new.
    (He re-opens the Bible, reads:)
When you were seven years old, the Spirit of God—

PROSECUTOR
From the beginning.

FREUD
My dear son, Schlomo—
    (To the PROSECUTOR.)
Now, only my dear old Hebrew teacher, Professor Hammerschlag, calls me Schlomo . . . I named my daughter, Anna, after one of his girls. . . I'm always his son—

PROSECUTOR

Pity he's not here. Continue: "When you were seven . . ."

FREUD

When you were seven the spirit of God began to stir and said, study my Book . . .

[A mental projection: Jakob Freud is seated with young Sigismund standing beside him. This had been in Scene 1. But now we see that the book in Jakob's lap is the Philippson Bible. Perhaps we see its frontispiece lithograph of Moses with the Tables of the Law. This can be a series of slides in quick succession, leading to close-up of the Bible.]

from which lawgivers have drawn the waters of their knowledge—
(Holds back tears.)
You get the gist.

PROSECUTOR

Continue would-be lawgiver!

FREUD ('Far away'.)

For many years, the Book, like broken tablets,
(His voice starts to crack: He's out to break the Tablets, destroy the Law!)
has been lying in my closet. Now, on your forty, er, thirty- fifth birthday I have brought this same Bible out from retirement, and, in a new leather cover,

(Finding a phylactery in his hand, HE jumps. It seems to have come out of nowhere.)
A phylactery! ... (He wipes his face with his sleeve.)

PROSECUTOR (Taking phylactery from Freud.)

Ties that bind. Continue.

FREUD

and, in a new leather cover, send it to you as a token of love. From your father who loves you forever, Jakob, son of Schlo. . . . son of Rabbi Schlomo Freud. In the Capital of Vienna, . . . the 29th of Nissan in the year 5651.

ONE JEW

Look! He is moved.

ANOTHER JEW

He's breaking down—

FREUD IN ROME: It Takes a Little Courage

ANOTHER JEW

It's his bad conscience—

ANOTHER JEW

He can still back out—

(With the Bible FREUD heads towards *MOSES*/MOSES.)

ONE JEW

He is going to tear up the Torah, the five books of Moses—

ANOTHER JEW

Stop him!

PROSECUTOR

No! Brothers, please.

(Trying to restrain the enraged brethren who are blocking the determined Freud.)

Our father Moses doesn't need our help.

(An ARK behind *MOSES* opens, revealing a dust-covered Torah scroll.) (The PROSECUTOR addresses Freud:)

Legend has it that it dates back to the time of he who is called the Second Moses, Ezra the Scribe—

(The PROSECUTOR gently dusts off the Scroll.)

But once the dust clears we see it is as dazzling as ever.

(FREUD for a moment is blinded by the brilliance of the Torah's gold breast-plate, which is engraved with the two Tablets of the Law.)

(The Ark resembles Miss Portero's armoire.)

An exchange is in order, wouldn't you say?

(THE PROSECUTOR hands FREUD the Scroll while taking Freud's Bible.)

FREUD

Out of my way!

PROSECUTOR

Wait! Won't you consider wearing a *tallith* and *yarmulke*, perhaps even binding the *tefillin* on your arm and forehead?—

FREUD

(Shouldering aside the PROSECUTOR, FREUD approaches *MOSES*/MOSES.)

[*MOSES*/MOSES begins to rise, his terrible, supernatural radiance emanating from his face: brilliant orange-red light with splashes of violet, purple and scarlet. (Cf. EXODUS 34:29–35.)]

Moses' radiance! (FREUD covers his eyes with the Scroll.)

ONE JEW
Look! The wretch is cringing!
ANOTHER JEW
And shielded by the Torah Scroll yet!

ANOTHER JEW
Some hero.
ANOTHER JEW
So much for this unbeliever's glorious self-knowledge.

(*MOSES*/MOSES laughs: it's LUCINA's mocking laughter.)

FREUD
(FREUD peers out, only to see the mocking LUCINA remove the *MOSES* mask from her face.)
Lucina! . . . That miserable hag. Wait'll I get my hands on her!
(As though about to strangle someone.)
(Swinging around, FREUD addresses his Brethren.)
By what right?! . . .
A JEW
"By what right?!" . . . Now, that, brothers, *that* is what I call *chutzpah*!

ANOTHER JEW
Another moment and we'd find you prostrate reciting the *Shema* . . .
"Hear, O Israel, the Lord is our God, the Lord is One."
(Making out he is davening.)

FREUD
Never!
(The CHURCH BELLS peal twelve times.)
(The first bell startled FREUD. Anxiously, he listens.)

PROSECUTOR
Ah! The hour when ghosts are abroad.

FREUD IN ROME: IT TAKES A LITTLE COURAGE

(The 'stage' is now dark. We hear *Kaddish*)

FREUD

Kaddish? The prayer for the dead?
>(We see MISS PORTERO as AMALIE FREUD grieving over BABY JULIUS in her arms. She is wearing a dark hooded cloak.)

Julius! Julius! Julius! (High-pitched.)
>(There is a SHOFAR BLAST.)
>(FREUD jumps, still holding the Scroll. Before HE can reach them, JULIUS and AMALIE disappear; *Kaddish* is over.)

Jesus! Jesus! Jesus!
>(Pounding his head on the Torah.)

A JEW

He's defiling the Torah! —

FREUD

Julius, if I could just change places with you. (Sinking to the ground with the Torah, which will support him.)

A JEW

Such suffering—

ANOTHER JEW

What should we do?—

ANOTHER JEW

And that impious Cain, he doesn't deserve it?—

PROSECUTOR

Silence!

FREUD

Julius... Julius... Julius... If there is a God in heaven would He have let you die... cause me to suffer so?
>(Startled by these, his words, FREUD sits straight up. For this 'return of the repressed' holds a terrible truth, below:)

THE JEWS

Look! He can't. Believe. He said. This . . . He. Now. Knows. That. The germ. Of his. Atheism. Sprang from. The. Death. Of his. Brother. Julius . . . That. It came. Not from. His Head. But. From. His. Heart. His. Heavy. Heart.
>(Now ALL in unison:)

No. Longer. Blind. Better. Our. Brother. From. Vienna. Who. Has. Lost. His. Way. Should. Give. Up. The. Ghost . . . Moses. We. Mean! And not. Sacrifice.

Martin. His firstborn. Son . . . . There. Are. More. Things. In. Heaven. And. Earth. Than. Are. Dreamed. Of. In. His. Philosophy.

END of ACT I, SCENE 2

FREUD IN ROME: It Takes a Little Courage

ACT I, SCENE 3

Apparently several minutes later. We hear FREUD twisting and moaning.

When the lights return we see FREUD lying covered on the couch as in Scene 2.

MISS PORTERO is seated on the armchair observing, smoking. A half-full wine glass is on the oblong table; also a game of solitaire, as well as Freud's dream book, *The Interpretation of Dreams*.

FREUD
Julius wake up. It's your play.
(Flips wrist as if tossing a playing card.)
He'll visit Naples, too? You know what they say, "See Naples and die!" One day, Julius, I've got to meet your famous brother, Arthur . . . You're not preparing for surgery now. Make your play. It's only a game.

MISS PORTERO
(SHE approaches Freud.)
Sigi, who is this Julius with the playing cards? (In a whisper.) This is Resi.

FREUD
He is baby Julius come back to me.

MISS PORTERO
"Baby Julius"? Tell me more—

FREUD
Julius . . . Julius . . . (HE's "coming to") . . . Miss Portero? . . .

(Seeing JANUS startles him.)
What time is it?

MISS PORTERO
Just past eleven.

FREUD
What?! Why didn't you wake me?! (Putting on his shoes.)

MISS PORTERO
(Placing smelling salts under his nose.)
This strong perfume didn't rouse you. Were we to bludgeon you?—

FREUD
We? Who's we?

MISS PORTERO
Why just Lucina and I, of course. (Placing the cover in the armoire.)

FREUD
I'm sopping wet.

MISS PORTERO
(From a silver case, SHE removes a cigarette, lighting it by lifting a candle to her face.)
You cried out, "Julius."

FREUD
(He turns white as though he had seen a ghost; he's obviously agitated.)
"Julius," I did?!
(Strangled, high-pitched voice.)
Anything else?

MISS PORTERO
No, "Julius" was all.

FREUD
(HE's distressed, but his analytical side comes to the fore.)
I must have been dreaming of Julius Caesar.

MISS PORTERO
"Julius Caesar"? But the cry, it arose from the ground of your very being.—

FREUD
Look, this is Rome, isn't it? Who else could it have been but Caesar?

MISS PORTERO
Yes, who else, indeed? There are those who claim to have seen on the Ides of March at the Forum, where the Senate stood, the broken ghost of Caesar, his blood oozing onto his linen toga—

FREUD
Spirits, I'm afraid, suspend their activities when I am around.

FREUD IN ROME: It Takes a Little Courage

MISS PORTERO

Perhaps you've not visited the right spot at just the right moment.
>(Swallowing a cracker like a Communion Wafer, followed by a gulp of wine.)

FREUD

Well, when that happens, Miss Portero you'll be the first to know.

MISS PORTERO

And not you, impious son?

FREUD

Leave my father out of this!—

MISS PORTERO

Your papa, he will not so easily give up the ghost. . . . Despite your wishful dreams.
>(Lifting Freud's Dream Book.)

FREUD (Grabbing the Dream Book.)

These are the dreams troubling you? . . . My dreams of my father?. . . I didn't come to Rome to be played with. My things! (Looking for his things!)

MISS PORTERO (Handling the Golden Bough.)

The troubling dreams, they are not the ones of your papa Jakob. They are the ones of your papa who is as cold as stone —.

FREUD (To self:)

"As cold as stone"? The witch knows. . . Collect yourself! I carefully concealed the statue.

MISS PORTERO

Would-be patricide, Moses won't be killed off so easily. He is not a wax manikin. He will not melt before your eyes. He is hard as stone.
>(With the Golden Bough raised over her head and murder in her ice-cold eyes, SHE rushes at FREUD, who, terrified, raises Dream Book to shield self. Suddenly wraithlike, SHE returns to the table the Golden Bough, which HE quickly grabs, dropping the Dream Book.)

FREUD

My hat and stick!

      (Rushing to pull-rope, HE pulls so hard it comes loose; HE flings rope across room.)
Lucina can bring my things to my room. (HE looks at his key.)
Room 51... Ha! 51.
      (HE superstitiously believes he'll die at age 51; this comes out in Act II.)

      MISS PORTERO (Lifts his Dream Book)
Including your Egyptian dream book?
      ("Egyptian" gets FREUD'S attention, almost a startle response; biting his lips he moves towards the door.)

      LUCINA Enters:
      (Silently, SHE hands FREUD his straw hat and gold-handled cane. LUCINA leaves but not before giving him a hard look. Out of sight, SHE laughs, which startles Freud.)

      (Facing an object which is cloaked by a scarlet-red canvas, MISS PORTERO says:)

At the Capitoline, filial piety poisoned your pleasure. But the papa in question is not your papa Jakob. Here, wicked son, is the actual papa in question:

      (MISS PORTERO quickly unveils a bust of Michelangelo's *MOSES* holding the two Tablets of the Law.)

      (There is brilliant lightning and thunder.)
      (Seeing *MOSES* with his lit up face, terrifies FREUD. With his Dream Book, he covers his own face. Recovering, HE is angry, enraged at her but also disgusted with himself for not having been able to contain himself. HE's about to leave.)

As I am ambitious, I slay him!

      (With the golden bough SHE stabs *MOSES* in his right eye, where it remains. Facing *MOSES,* she lifts her wine glass and toasts:)

Moses is dead, long live the new Moses, the little *pisher,* Sigmund Freu—

FREUD
No! You must not utter my last name!
> (Lunging at her, HE covers her mouth with his right hand; his left hand is on the back of her struggling head. SHE didn't anticipate this. HIS superstitious side is excited. Terror is FREUD's basic emotion, but there is rage as well, for SHE is putting him and HIS secret mission at risk. There is also a trace of lust: FREUD, touching her, experiences sensual pleasure. Catching himself, HE backs away.)
>
> (He realizes he could have seriously harmed her.)

Over four years to prepare and I come unglued like this! (To Self) . . . I must ask your forgiveness.

MISS PORTERO
> [Wipes wine from outfit. (SHE, too, had experienced lust.)]

Do not muzzle me again!

FREUD
> (FREUD picks up his hat and cane, which had fallen in the struggle. The cane's gold handle came off. An omen? It's by the painting of Aeneas. FREUD looks at Aeneas, and picks up the handle, holding it the same way Aeneas' father, Anchises, holds the household gods. HE stares at the bright handle; then at the Sphinx curtain.)

It's coming back. In the dream, the handle came off . . .
(To Self:) I can't still be dreaming?!
> (As if his life depends on it, HE struggles to replace the handle, but can't.)

MISS PORTERO (Wiping herself.)
You, the man of science; you, whose god is Reason; you, who lusts for fame, for glory, for immortality; you, the great Sigmund Freud, still fears names. For names, carry souls. And my coupling
> (Pressing her snake bracelet together, so that the head meets the tail. Or, SHE could, with the thumb and forefinger of each hand, link her hands—)

your name with that of the great man of your people, well, just the thought of that, it horrifies you, doesn't it? For Moses, then knowing where you are, would appear—

FREUD
It's got to go on! Damn!

MISS PORTERO
(Watching Freud as he tries re-attaching cane handle.)
An omen, Golden Sigi? (Still wiping herself.)

FREUD
Some Golden Bough!
[HE throws handle across the room. HE then breaks cane over his knee. One piece is longer than the other. As if knifing someone, he forcefully 'stakes' the larger piece into a planter. Then, unconsciously, he 'attaches' the smaller piece to larger piece at a 45 degree angle: Root (Moses) and Branch (Jesus).]

Root and Branch! Ha!
(Laughing uncontrollably, as if HE's just realized something: a joke—a joke that's on him.)
Jesus.
(HE flips, with disdain, the smaller piece into the fireplace: but no added blaze.)
Moses.
(Standing tall, HE looks at crucifix, and, as Zeus/Jupiter would a thunderbolt, hurls the larger piece (Root) into the fire. There is a brilliant, crackling fireplace blaze. HE's transfixed.)
It should be that easy.
(Meanwhile, to contain herself, MISS PORTERO places a red record on a hand- operated phonograph: Prelude to *Don Giovanni.*)
(FREUD is startled)
No! No! No!
(Rushing to the phonograph, HE removes the record.)
Music moves me too much!

MISS PORTERO
(Picking up the cane handle, SHE points it at Aeneas.)
A recurrence of the past, no?

FREUD (Face turns white.)
A recurrence of the past? (High-pitched.) . . .

MISS PORTERO
To find a home for his uprooted and wandering nation, the hero must, with his golden bough,

FREUD IN ROME: It Takes a Little Courage

(Using the gold handle to 'light the way'.)
descend into the perilous underworld and, there, face his papa—

FREUD (Collecting self.)
I've had it with the father ghost business!
(HE picks up his hat; then grabs the handle from her and heads for door.)

MISS PORTERO
Leave and —

FREUD
And what?! Tell the world I'm a Jew boy from Vienna?—
(His hand on the door knob—)

MISS PORTERO
Something far more damning . . .
(SHE goes to Pan and whispers to him while playfully fondling his horns.)
See that miserable Jew boy?
By father-murder at Rome
He, brother-murder, would atone —

FREUD
What the hell are you getting—?
(When HE looks back at her he sees his "double," who seems to have materialized out of thin air. Actually, it's Freud's reflection in a mirror. Turning pale, FREUD backs away, covering his eyes with his hat, while clutching his heart.)

My double. . . I'm about to die! (High-pitched, to self.)

MISS PORTERO
You, the great Sigmund Freud, you, who would rid the world of religious superstition, you, the would-be Messiah of the Jews who would usher in a Golden Age grounded in Reason, you are the most superstitious of creatures, believing that names conjure ghosts and in the old fish wives' tale that each of us has a double who appears when we are about to die! And who knows in what else?! Some hero! Some careful preparation you have made for your baptism in Hell, that is to say, the gloomy chamber of Michelangelo's *Moses*, in the Church of San Pietro in Vincoli . . . Moses and Jesus need not, it seems, lose any sleep over this the latest comer . . .

45

(SHE grabs the hat, which still covers his face, out of Freud's hands.)

Hero, it is safe to unveil your face. For your terrible double is but your own pitiful reflection.

FREUD

(FREUD looks at himself in the mirror. Disgusted with himself, HE bites down on his lips. There's a howling wind; the terrace doors fling open; St. Peter's Dome is visible; Gregorian chants are heard, a boys' choir; HE covers his ears; the mirror shatters into many pieces before his eyes. HE jumps. Collecting himself, and, as though drawn there, HE goes to the terrace. HE looks out at St. Peter's Dome.)

How proudly it rears its golden head to heaven, that lie of the salvation of mankind.

MISS PORTERO

(SHE's by what remains of the mirror, trying on Freud's straw hat.)

In 15 years, Hannibal, with all his men and large-tusked elephants, was not able to storm the city gates. And, yet you, you who are terrified of your own image, you would crush the new Romans, the Holy Roman Catholic Church!?

FREUD

It's a question of arms.

(HE picks up an old clay pot which has touches of gold.)

MISS PORTERO

Then you have the arms? (With Freud's golden cane handle, SHE tilts the hat.)

FREUD

I have the arms.

(With his hands, as one might an egg, HE breaks the pot. HE looks at it and at the Dome. HE pulls a shard from his left hand, using his handkerchief to staunch the bleeding.)

MISS PORTERO

That's good. (Satisfied with the way the hat looks.)
Well, hero, what do you think? (Referring to the way the hat looks on her.)

FREUD

I think it's time to go.

(HE grabs his hat and gold cane handle.)

It's been an experience—

MISS PORTERO

(SHE blocks the way; in her hand is an orange branch with oranges still attached.)

Tell me, which of us belongs in the Manicomio, our brilliantly lighted lunatic asylum?

FREUD

Move witch!

MISS PORTERO

Leave and I nip your line in the bud.

(Her right thumb and forefinger are poised to pinch an orange from the bough.)

FREUD

You threatening my kids?

(Letting go of his hat and cane handle, HE grabs her by the shoulders.)

MISS PORTERO

Your biological children, no. Your enlightened line, yes.

FREUD

Enlightened line? Just what the hell are you talking about?

MISS PORTERO

One can be a Moses without fathering a people who will be a light unto all nations? That is news to this *goyische kopf*.

(Lighting a cigarette.)

FREUD

If the arias you sang at La Scala are as silly as the things you say, then there is a merciful God after all.

(HE is about to bend over to pick up his cane handle and hat—)

MISS PORTERO

My singing days, they may be over, but I can still speak. And were I to mouth my silly idea that you intend to destroy both Judaism and Christianity, there would be no receptive ground to scatter your seed . . . now would there? And, poof, there goes your longed-for line, your longed-for *redemptive* line.

(Pulling off two small oranges SHE drops them into his hat.)

(FREUD looks at the oranges. Then HE takes the cane handle and lifts it in a menacing manner, as though about to cudgel her with it.)

You haven't the stones. (Rolling the oranges across the floor.)

Now, Castrato, you may kiss the nun . . . (Handling her beaded necklace as Rosary beads, which now sparkle.)

("Losing it," FREUD begins to choke MISS PORTERO, who, biting his left hand, won't let go. FREUD, finally freeing his hand, grabs a couch pillow to smother her.)
(LUCINA's laughter off-stage brings FREUD 'back'.)

FREUD
(HE looks down in horror at his homicidal hands squeezing the pillow over the face of the now barely struggling MISS PORTERO whose beads are scattered. He lets her go.)
I could have killed her!

(There is a loud peal of thunder and brilliant light. The crude crucifix lights up. FREUD looks at it; then, at his bleeding hand; then back at the crucifix and becomes frozen in his posture.)

(A mental projection: This time on FREUD'S face and hands: CHRIST's face on FREUD's face and the bloody stigmata on FREUD's hands.)

(For a brief moment, St. Peter's Dome is visible through the terrace doors.)

(Note: The crucifix is a crude work, and just plain wood; not painted, making the stigmata projection more powerful.)

(LUCINA's laughter, again, is heard.)

END of ACT 1, SCENE 3

FREUD IN ROME: IT TAKES A LITTLE COURAGE

ACT I, SCENE 4

A few minutes later. MISS PORTERO is pouring herself wine; periodically rubbing her neck.
A bandage on his bitten hand, FREUD is placing her necklace beads on a large seashell.

FREUD

I could have killed you.

MISS PORTERO

In your gloomy sleep you mouthed more than "Julius."

FREUD (Knocking over the seashell.)

Then you lied to me!

MISS PORTERO

And, dissembler, you can reproach me? . . .
(SHE holds up his Dream Book; reads:)
"My politeness is a cover." Take note: I am not your common reader. This much is clear: your brother Julius, he is behind your pilgrimage to Rome . . . It remains miserable outside . . . And time, it is running down.
(Turning over the hourglass.)

FREUD

What I am about to say—

MISS PORTERO

(With her ringstone MISS PORTERO "seals" her lips . . .)
Well? Your confession?

FREUD

(A mental projection: Two year-old SIGI sees young mother, Amalie, nurse Julius.)
I was jealous of Julius, hated him—This is difficult . . . I wanted my mother for myself.
(Mental Projection: Mama, und Ich?! Mama, und Ich?! ["Mama, What about me?!" "Mama, What about me?!"])

My hateful thoughts, I believed, had killed him . . . thoughts of knocking him from her breast and kicking him in the head, over and over again... Well, I got my hateful wish.

MISS PORTERO

Just south of here, where so-called Civilization has yet to come, the people believe in the magical power of words— words can heal, words can kill.

FREUD

Julius's death left the germ of guilt in me.—
>   (Lifting a clay figurine of a seated boy, FREUD projects: Holding her dead infant, AMALIE FREUD looks for answers into JAKOB'S eyes—"WHY? WHY?"—as JAKOB tries comforting her.)

MISS PORTERO

The idea that you had rid yourself of Julius—that you had murdered him—this tormenting Cain phantasy, it is your scar.

FREUD (Replacing the figurine)

I couldn't account for my deep depressions and debilitating migraines . . . Deluding myself, making myself believe it was pure scientific research, I experimented with the active ingredient of coca leaves, cocaine.
>   (Takes a sip of water.)

And like that (Snapping fingers), my migraines vanished, were washed away. And I've got to say it made me quite gay and confident.
>   (Miming 'gay" and "confident.")

I must tell you, it seemed a magical substance.

MISS PORTERO

Seemed? Then this self-cure you discontinued?

FREUD

I convinced a close friend and colleague to take this magical drug for his morphia addiction, but he got addicted to it instead. Six years later he was dead . . . .
>   (Wincing, HE rubs the heel of his left hand into his forehead.)

MISS PORTERO

Dead like Julius . . .

FREUD

When Hannibal was nine,
>   (Freud's shadow is on a screen on the back wall. It is smaller than Freud, making him the size of a child. HE postures as Hannibal, below, before the family altar.)

his father, Hasdrubal, made him vow, with one hand on the sacrificial lamb to take vengeance on the Romans. Well, in my later school years, I vowed to take vengeance against the new Romans, the Holy Roman Catholic Church!
>   (Opens his Dream book to motto:)

"If I can not bend the higher powers, I'll move hell."

FREUD IN ROME: IT TAKES A LITTLE COURAGE

MISS PORTERO

Your battle cry!

FREUD

Until my self-analysis, I didn't know Julius's death was behind it.—
(Claw-like, FREUD snaps book shut.)

MISS PORTERO

That in actuality it was your vow to Julius.

FREUD

Yes, ultimately, Miss Portero, it was—and is—my vow, my secret vow, to Julius . . .

(FREUD projects; We hear his voice, and possibly there is an image reflecting Freud, tormented, below:)
Julius to you I vow to do away with the miserable Church and institute an enlightened world, a brotherly world, where, my dear Julius, children like you, children of our detested and homeless race, are free to develop their talents and satisfy their needs. A peaceable, secular world in which anti-Semitism is unknown— and all can move freely across frontiers.

MISS PORTERO

Can I get you anything?

FREUD (He sits down on the chair.)

I'll just have to ride it out.

MISS PORTERO

The name of Hannibal's papa was Hamilcar, not Hasdrubal. Hasdrubal was the name of Hannibal's brother . . . his *younger* brother—An apt slip, no?

FREUD (Writes in note pad)

Yes, Miss Portero, an apt slip. I'll make that correction in my Dream Book.
(And to self:)
Provided I'm not wheeled out of that gloomy church tomorrow.

MISS PORTERO

Your design is clear. Institute a better world for other, future little Juliuses, and you make an atonement for killing Julius—

FREUD

But Miss Portero, Julius is not dead.
(Picking up some playing cards, he studies the designs. Deals cards, fast, adept.)

THE UNKNOWN FREUD: FIVE PLAYS ...

MISS PORTERO
To your heart, no. For it won't relinquish him—
(Arranging the cards dealt her.)

FREUD
Saturday afternoons I sit down to play a lively game of taroc with Julius.

MISS PORTERO
What?! (Putting cards down!)

FREUD
Yes, my all-knowing Sibyl, my brother has come back to me in the form of another Julius, Julius Schnitzler. (Arranging his cards.)

MISS PORTERO
You sense that this Julius is little Julius reincarnated . . . a *revenant*? . . .

FREUD
He's a brilliant surgeon and not a bad taroc player.

MISS PORTERO
(Lies on couch; mimes Freud dreaming.)
"It's your play, Julius." –

FREUD
You got it! And I'm the one who would lead the world—

MISS PORTERO
Hush!
(Still on the couch, pondering.)
Unable to acknowledge that his brother is dead once and for all, this tormented Cain senses that the card-player Julius is little Julius . . . But, of all the Juliuses, why
(Putting one picture card on another.)
fasten little Julius on this, this Julius Schnitzler? Ah!
(Tossing the cards in the air.)
Sometimes you merely have to ask the question . . .
(SHE gets up.)
May I intuit? . . . Julius Schnitzler's older brother is the renowned writer, Arthur Schnitzler—

FREUD
Right! The playwright is his older brother. So?

FREUD IN ROME: It Takes a Little Courage

MISS PORTERO
(Gets up and touches Janus' left head.)
So this! Your mystical head senses that Arthur Schnitzler is your double.

FREUD
(Sits on the edge of his seat, engrossed in an imaginary stage-play:)
How can Schnitzler *know* so much about the unconscious, . . . about the instinctual forces driving humankind?!. . . I could have written his stage plays . . .
(Enumerating with fingers.)
He's also a Jew, was born in May, and like me even started out as a neurologist.

MISS PORTERO
And if that born psychologist is your double, then, of course, his younger brother Julius must be your brother Julius come back to you. For, as we know, names, they carry souls—

FREUD
(Spotting the Golden Bough, HE raises it.)
And I would lead humanity to the Promised Land of Reason!

MISS PORTERO
Only someone like you, one with the moral courage to look deeply into his heart and examine his soul in detail can instruct man about himself, about what drives him . . . If anyone can found a line as prophesied by Virgil for Aeneas' son Julius, a line like the Latins of the Golden Age of ancient Latium, you can.
(SHE points to Julius Ascanius in the painting; putting the cards down, she hands Freud *The Aeneid,* open, to the verse.)

FREUD (By heart:)
. . . A line that is just—
Not by constraint or laws, but by choice.

MISS PORTERO
"A line that is just . . . by choice." An apt description for your longed-for Julius or Julian line . . . your brotherly line upon which you pin your redemption—

FREUD
(Again, HE studies the painting of a Sibyl with a striking resemblance to Miss Portero.)
Who are you?

53

MISS PORTERO
(Shows his Dream Book inscription.)
Why, your Roman reader . . . Such a short memory . . .
> (FREUD, as if HE is drawn to it, heads for the painting of Aeneas.)

If you can pull it off (eating a grape), if you can conceive this brotherly line, you would, in effect, undo, cancel, that terrible crime, the murder of Julius, wouldn't you?

FREUD
(Bending, FREUD looks at Aeneas's boy, Julius.)
(A Projection: FREUD'S Voice):

Aeneas, you have your Julius line, the Romans. But one day, my classical double, I'll have my own Julius line! Only instead of being like yours, a battle-hungry line, my Julius line will be a brotherly one. And through this enlightened line my little brother Julius will come back to life.

MISS PORTERO
(SHE taps him with the Golden Bough. Startled, FREUD grabs it from her.)

May I intuit yet again? You have yet to meet Arthur Schnitzler. For to meet one's double means that one is about to die. Die prematurely and your vast ambition, well, it goes up in smoke.

FREUD (Turns to her.)
I dread my afternoon walk, especially when Theodor Herzl is back in Vienna—

MISS PORTERO
The father of modern Zionism? But of course!
(Hides behind a pillar, before taking first tentative steps.)
Death could be around the corner—in the form of that other would-be Moses of the Berggasse, Theodor Herzl, another felt double, who, too, has a solution to the miserable anti-Semitism: a Jewish homeland. That you leave your own home at all is a wonder.

FREUD (Heading for picture of Garibaldi.)
Why do you think I work out of my home?
(HE says this in a way that makes her wonder if he is serious.)
Herzl was also born in May and his father's name happens to be—

MISS PORTERO
Jakob?

FREUD

Jakob.
> (Removing his red tie, HE lays it flat on the oblong table, like a carpet.)

Even before the Dreyfus Affair made him realize assimilation was hopeless, Herzl had come up with a way to save the children,
> (Picks up two White Pawns)

mass baptism of all the Jewish children.

MISS PORTERO

No?! When was this?

FREUD

1893.

MISS PORTERO

The year before Captain Dreyfus's court-martial!

FREUD

He'd strike a bargain with Pope Leo.
> Help us against the anti-Semites and I will start a great movement for the free and honorable conversion of Jews to Christianity.
>> (HE places the Pawns on the 'carpet' in front of two Black Castles which seem connected, like closed double doors. The Castles are not on the 'carpet.')

MISS PORTERO

In Rome, you go to one papa, and he to the other papa. How nice.

FREUD (Gives her a 'look!')

Once the pact with the Holy Father was made, there would be a grand procession, made up of the elders and the little ones, to that relic from the Middle Ages, St. Stephen's Cathedral in the heart of Vienna.
> (Projection from Freud: Herzl and Jewish elders lead Jewish children to entrance of St. Stephen's Cathedral, completed in the 15th Century.)

Naturally, Herzl would be the pied piper . . . God, how like me!
> (Holds a Black Bishop in left hand.)

If the Pope couldn't be there to greet them, then Herzl
> (White Knight in right hand)

would settle for the Archbishop of Vienna.
> (FREUD puts one Black Bishop aside; lifting the other Black Bishop, HE places it between the "children" and the

Black Castles. The Black Bishop is not on the "carpet"—not just yet. Freud adds other "children," two-by-two; still holding "Herzl," a White Knight, in his hand.)
At noon, on a Sunday, probably Easter Sunday, to the pealing of church bells, the procession would arrive at that Gothic horror, and Herzl and the brethren would stop at the entrance . . .

> [FREUD puts 'Herzl' at head of procession; Freud pulls 'carpet', with 'Herzl' and 'children' on it, to the Black Bishop who is before the 'Church doors' (the Contiguous Black Castles). 'Herzl' steps aside; the Black Bishop takes Herzl's place. The 'doors' open. Freud pulls the 'carpet' through the 'doors'; the Black Bishop, now on the 'carpet,' leading the way.
> Now, the Black Castles, again positioned as double doors, are closed.
> The White Knight, 'Herzl', stays for a moment; then leaves, looking back one last time.]

the last Jews on earth!. . . .

> (If the above chess piece action won't "play," then Freud could play Herzl walking, leading an imaginary procession to the terrace doors facing St. Peter's.)

MISS PORTERO
Such an imagination!

FREUD
He's a playwright, remember! Fortunately, his newspaper publisher talked Herzl out of it. . . . Don't get me wrong! I admire Herzl. His wife, by the way, is named Julie—

MISS PORTERO
Tell me, hero, shouldn't you have gone out of your way to meet, to make contact with both Herzl and Arthur Schnitzler, seeing as you are in the Eternal City to face your ultimate double?!

FREUD
Ultimate double? . . . Good Lord, Moses! (A realization.)

MISS PORTERO
"Good Lord"!? Some careful preparation! Make your pilgrimage to Moses, the terrible desert father who conceived and shaped you and every Jew—and, impious *Jew boy* from Vienna, you die!

(Before Freud knows it, SHE 'stamps' his forehead with a head phylactery. Enraged, FREUD grabs her hand; the phylactery cord "veils" his face.)

(Mental Projection: slide of MOSES' radiant face on FREUD's face.)

(We hear LUCINA's laughter.)

END of ACT I, SCENE 4

THE UNKNOWN FREUD: FIVE PLAYS . . .

ACT II, SCENE 1

> A few minutes later.
> MISS PORTERO is emptying the crystal ashtray.
> FREUD is by the picture of Aeneas holding his son Julius's hand. FREUD'S rubbing his forehead with his right palm.

FREUD
My self-analysis made me realize that my guilt over Julius's death had impelled me to make decisions, take actions—
> *(A mental projection: 'Freud' and pregnant wife, Martha, about 30, with their three children, a girl, Mathilde, 4, and two boys, Martin, 2, and Oliver, 1. This can be a slide. The children are heard; including baby Oliver crying.)*

> (FREUD's head is tilted as if looking at slide.)

The choice of our first home, an apartment . . . The first three of our six children were born there. Commissioned by Emperor Franz Joseph, it was built on the site of the ill-fated Ringtheatre. (HE looks at the fire.)
Four hundred, most if not all Jewish, burned to death.
> (Not conscious of doing so, he picks up a deck of Tarot cards.)

The rent is used to provide for their children.

MISS PORTERO
You would somehow make up for killing Julius.

FREUD ("Killing" stings him.)
> (Holding back tears.)

The apartment house is known as the House of Atonement . . . I was driven, driven to find a way to atone for killing Julius.

MISS PORTERO
And once the terrible memories surfaced you understood this?

FREUD
Memories and feelings . . . After that, I was open to anything . . . even a pact with the Devil. (Mocks cutting his wrist and writing with his blood.)

MISS PORTERO
> (SHE starts to fall way; catching herself, SHE rejects FREUD's help.)

I can support myself, thank you!
                              FREUD (Holds up the Dream Book.)
"If I can not bend the higher powers, I'll move hell." ...What had I to lose?...
            (HE grimaces as if a migraine is coming on.)
My inner torment? Nothing human is alien to me! . . . Nothing! . . .
            (More to self.)
Not with time running out.

                      MISS PORTERO

But a compact with Lucifer!
                            FREUD
If I couldn't save the children, then I'd, I'd lose the strength to live . . .
            (His right hand grasps ribs on his left side, placing him in the posture of a particular wretch Michelangelo's *Last Judgment,* one who knows he's doomed.)
            (MISS PORTERO starts to fall away again.)
            (This time FREUD catches her.)
Miss Portero, are you all right?!

                      MISS PORTERO

I am fine . . .
                            FREUD
You sure?
                    MISS PORTERO (SHE pours herself wine.)
I am sure. . . But exchange your soul for what?

                            FREUD
For that indefinite something which attracts men. . . and time. . . I didn't pluck my golden bough any too soon.

                    MISS PORTERO

Then you didn't—?
                            FREUD
This Godless Jew was that close, believe me —
            (HIS left thumb and fore-finger almost touching.)

                    MISS PORTERO

So, hero, just how did you happen to pluck this godsend?. . . It's still miserable outside.
            (FREUD is before the picture of Garibaldi; he momentarily blacks out; then 'comes back'.
            HE 'seals' his lips with his wedding ring.)

(MISS PORTERO, getting the message, 'seals' her lips with her ringstone.)

FREUD

I remembered being sexually jealous of my father and wishing he were dead so I could take his place with my mother . . .

(HE studies the marble Venus; then looks at his train ticket.)
The train ride to Leipzig . . . (HE is back there:)

[FREUD projects: A slide of Botticelli's The Birth of Venus *is projected. Freud's lips and tongue move. The slide then lands on Freud. Freud reaches up to touch his own breasts. (Venus' breasts are superimposed on his.)]*
(HE fondles his breasts, catching himself before passion overwhelms him.)
(A big moment: there could be music.)

MISS PORTERO

(Noticing he is 'away,' she sensuously touches his thigh.)
Where were you?

FREUD (HE jumps.)

On a train, long ago . . .

MISS PORTERO

(SHE sets an orange half on plate, so that it looks like the Dome. 'Quartering' it, she offers him a slice. HE refuses. SHE eats it, with pleasure.)
Lusting for your mama?

FREUD

Right! I was younger than three . . . about two and a half. . . . All boys experience this.

(He studies Venus.)
Here, Miss Portero, is the source of God . . .

MISS PORTERO

The boy's passion, you say, is the source of God?
(VITTORIO Enters)
(VITTORIO drifts in, surprising Freud, and also, apparently, Miss Portero. As if sleep-walking, VITTORIO is holding a large stuffed frog by one of its legs.)
Vittorio!

(Carrying him to the couch, SHE places VITTORIO's head

                on her breast, and hands him an orange slice. Eyeing Freud,
                VITTORIO eats it.)

This angel?—
                            FREUD
That angel.
                        MISS PORTERO
Vittorio, this handsome gentleman is Dr. Freud. (In Italian.)
                (SHE squeezes Vittorio's cheeks; he grimaces.)
Ever see such a *punim*? Kiss me my little Oedipus. (In Italian.)
                (VITTORIO kisses her. SHE plants a kiss on a cheek; hands
                him the rest of the orange. VITTORIO offers FREUD a
                piece. FREUD takes it, and ruffles VITTORIO'S hair.)

                (VITTORIO indicates it's all right for FREUD to handle
                the frog, whereupon FREUD and the frog begin to hop on
                the floor, amusing Vittorio.)

                (LUCINA, in a nightgown, enters; seeing the jumping
                Freud, she laughs.)
                (Embarrassed, FREUD becomes the dignified *Herr
                Doktor.*)

                (Once she collects herself, LUCINA makes apologetic ges-
                tures re: VITTORIO intruding . . .)
                (VITTORIO and LUCINA EXIT as hopping frogs.)

                            FREUD
My kids don't often get to see that side of their father, except—
                (We hear LUCINA's laughter, again rattling Freud.)
except when we're on vacation collecting mushrooms.

                        MISS PORTERO
The way Vittorio holds himself, just like Bernard, his father.
                (When SHE says this it's with some pain.)

                            FREUD (Before the picture of Garibaldi.)
Vittorio loves and admires Bernard, but he also hates him. To Vittorio,
Bernard is the most powerful and wisest creature in the whole world . . . A
model to imitate and . . . to get rid of—

THE UNKNOWN FREUD: FIVE PLAYS ...

                      MISS PORTERO

To take his place with me in bed. . . . My empty bed. (To self; shivering.)

                      FREUD
            (He projects: JAKOB and AMALIE are in bed, as above. A knife in his hand, JAKOB is about to ATTACK his little rival. who is not actually in the scene: it could traumatize a child actor.)

That charming little fellow is afraid that Bernard will castrate him.

                      MISS PORTERO.

That he'll be stoned for his impious intentions? (Removing a plum pit.)

                      FREUD

Stoned?

                      MISS PORTERO

To stone an animal is to castrate him.

                      FREUD (Writes it down on pocket pad.)

That gruesome expectation makes Vittorio abandon his wicked ambition.

            (A projection: AMALIE, the mother, is giving little ANNA her bath, and young SIGI 5, sees ANNA, 3, naked.)

The sight of my younger sister, Anna . . . without a penis. (To self; shudders.)

                      MISS PORTERO
            (SHE hands Freud an orange bough. HE pulls off an orange; smiles; and offers bough to MISS PORTERO who pulls off another orange while FREUD still holds bough: *'Touche!'* HE puts it back in planter; lights a cigar.)

And God, He comes from this, this, family romance?

                      FREUD

"Family romance"? (HE writes it down on pocket pad.)
            (MISS PORTERO smiles, shakes head:
            'This he *must* write down *now*?')

God the Father once roamed the earth in bodily form. He's nothing but the young boy's idealized perception of his father magnified a thousand times.
            (Mimes the exalted oedipal father.)

                      MISS PORTERO

God was fashioned from the little boy's magnified image of his father?

FREUD IN ROME: It Takes a Little Courage

FREUD

Right! Long ago this the overvalued exalted father of boyhood, this all-knowing, all-powerful, superhuman creature was thrown out onto the universe and became God. . . . *Gott in Himmel* is a hollow wish fulfillment, pure and simple.

MISS PORTERO
(About to light a cigarette with a candle—)
And the terrible Yahweh, just how is He a wish fulfillment?!

FREUD
(HE now heads to statue of Jupiter who has an eagle on his shoulder and a thunderbolt in his right hand.)
The ways of the Lord are dark, but seldom pleasant—(Smiling.)

MISS PORTERO

What?!

FREUD

Just a joke . . . Look! . . . Like the earthly father, the Heavenly Father rewards and punishes His children, doesn't He?

MISS PORTERO

His Mercy and His Justice, yes, so? . . . Ah! I see how He can be seen as a wishful illusion. God cares for and protects us and our families . . . Famines, plagues, wild beasts will not harm us—All we need do is obey His Will. (She re-lights her cigarette.)

FREUD

Now, to our ancestors the inner storms of lust and rage are, er, were just as terrifying as—

MISS PORTERO

The blowing winds and thunderstorms without . . . Now it's even more clear.
(SHE offers him grapes. FREUD takes a small bunch.
SHE pulls off one of his grapes and eats it.)
The fathers yearned for a caring but dreaded father, the fear of whom would keep them and the others from acting on their murderous urges and illicit sexual desires.
(SHE licks his ear.)
FREUD (Spits out pits; brushes her away)
And a comforting illusion, God the Father, was born.

MISS PORTERO

A Merciful and Just Father . . . .

FREUD
(Takes two walnuts from the horn of plenty.)
And the prototype of God's terrible Justice is—

MISS PORTERO
The dreaded castration . . . By strength of hand. (SHE reaches for his crotch.)

FREUD (Brushes her hand away.)
Are Roman women all like you? . . .
    (With his hands, HE cracks the walnuts. HE offers her the meat. SHE takes a piece.)
You know, you'd make a good psychologist.

MISS PORTERO
You, too.

FREUD
When it came to me I felt an extraordinary clarity.
    (HE removes a "veil" from eyes; looks at 'fire' in crystal ashtray. Then eats the nut.)

MISS PORTERO ('Blows' horn of plenty.)
You wished to trumpet this divine revelation but you hold back, say nothing about it in your Egyptian dream book. For first Golden Sigi must be seen as the authority on the psychology of so-called civilized man.

FREUD
(Another projection: He is receiving the Nobel Prize.)
If only. (To Self)

MISS PORTERO
Today, preach about God's humble beginnings and psychoanalysis would be dismissed as but a Jewish science. (A wave of the hand.)

FREUD
I can't risk psychoanalysis succumbing to anti-Semitism, of it being seen as just another Jewish national affair, like Herzl's political Zionism.

MISS PORTERO
You'll need Christian comrades—

FREUD
They'll find their way to me against great inner resistances and will be

all the more valuable for that. Rest assured, if my name were Oberhuber, psychoanalysis would have met with far less resistance.

MISS PORTERO

And the world is ready for the good news that God is an impotent old man? (Caressing Freud's leg.)

FREUD (Removing her hand.)

Men can't remain children forever; they must in the end go out into 'hostile life.' The world is not a nursery!

MISS PORTERO

You are not afraid of me, are you?

FREUD

Sexual excitement is of no use to me.

MISS PORTERO

Not even in the Mother of Cities with my painted sisters? (Mocks a painted lady soliciting a client.)

FREUD

You want me to continue or not?!

MISS PORTERO

I'm all ears.

FREUD

Men who, from childhood onward,
  (Places his open right hand about 18 inches from the floor.)
are educated to reality will be able to live without that sweet poison, the pap of religious illusion.—

MISS PORTERO

Pap? (Smiling) You desire me, don't you?

FREUD

You make too much of yourself.
  (HE gets up; heads for a large globe.)
Knowing they're on their own, these new men will use their intelligence to cultivate their small plot on this earth so that it supports them . . . They'll have no alternative—(HE spins the globe.)

MISS PORTERO
And at long last the Golden Age of brotherly love emerges. And all this arising from your fevered head, it is not a fantasy?

FREUD
A poor girl may suffer from the delusion the her prince will come and marry her. And if a prince, indeed, comes along and does marry her, then it is no delusion.

MISS PORTERO
Similarly, if an ambitious Jew boy believes he is destined to become the Messiah of the Jews, and does indeed become the long-awaited Messiah, then that too is no delusion.

FREUD
Less probable, but, Miss Portero, still possible.

MISS PORTERO
Especially if that ambitious Jew boy from Vienna was born in a caul, and so is destined to become a great man. Of course, my charming prince, your golden bough (Handling it), it promises too much for it not to be suspect—

FREUD
And I haven't wrestled with that?!

MISS PORTERO (Extending one finger at a time)
The destruction of the hated church; the deliverance of your people from the miserable anti-Semitism; immortality, by replacing both Moses and Jesus as the new moral authority with your one command, "Know Thyself"; and, of course, the grandest promise of all: the undoing of having played Cain to Julius's Abel—for so long as your "Julius" line lives, Julius lives!

FREUD
How can you know this?! (More to self)

MISS PORTERO
Face it, hero! Your dazzling revelation (Raising the Golden Bough)
very well may be, itself, what you claim God to be, a hollow wishful illusion.

FREUD (Raising his Dream Book)
Look! If there is a God in heaven, would He have let Julius die?!
(A deeply troubling insight: 'my atheism stems from Julius's death'!)

FREUD IN ROME: It Takes a Little Courage

MISS PORTERO

In the morning I will send for a carriage to take you and your brother to the railway station—(looks at railway schedule)
One leaves for Vienna at nine.

FREUD

Don't you understand?! If I turn back, I'd lose the will to live.

MISS PORTERO

An exchange then is in order.
(Taking his Dream Book from him, SHE, in turn, hands FREUD *The Philippson Bible.*)
One sacred text for another.

FREUD

(Quickly, HE looks inside; he's relieved: there's no inscription.)
The Philippson Bible. How'd you know this was the Bible I had when I was a boy? Was I hypno—?

MISS PORTERO

Some question. Your father would have handed you Luther's Bible? . . . It's yours, here, to tear leaf by leaf, law by law.

FREUD

My memory is fuzzy I fainted before Janus, didn't I?

MISS PORTERO

Yes, you fell away just as a thunderbolt occurred, one that Michelangelo could have made.

FREUD

(Putting the Bible down, HE removes his jacket; folds it neatly; places it on couch and lies down on the floor, on his back, by JANUS.)

No movement, no apparent consciousness . . . . I appear dead, don't I?

MISS PORTERO

Yes, like a corpse. So?
(Smelling his blue gardenia.)

FREUD

This bit of hysteria, my deathlike swoon, signifies my death.

MISS PORTERO

Go slow.

(Putting Freud's jacket over her shoulders.)

FREUD

I wanted Moses dead. I wanted to take his place—

MISS PORTERO

And now you are dead, taking that Great Man's place? (Hands up: puzzled.)

FREUD

The death wish was redirected towards me . . . a fitting self-punishment.

MISS PORTERO

I see! You should die for wanting Moses dead so as to succeed him . . . Filial piety, guilt, then, and not the fear of God, is your Achilles heel.

FREUD (Getting up.)

I've had four years to work on my fear of *der Liebe Gott*. I believe I have a handle on it . . . But the old man means, er, meant a great deal to me.

MISS PORTERO

So, "Conscience makes cowards of us all"—even golden Sigi.
   (FREUD takes his jacket from her!)
   (A SHOFAR BLAST startles FREUD. The Sphinx 'stage' curtain rises: *MOSES,* played by an actor, is on a hill.)

FREUD

What is this?!

MISS PORTERO

Let's just say it's a rehearsal, a dress rehearsal . . . .
   (As SHE tries putting a head phylactery, on him, FREUD takes it from her.)

FREUD

That's not Lucina, is it?

MISS PORTERO

Does that Great Man look like Lucina? For safe passage in the underworld Aeneas relied upon his guide, the Sybyl of Cumae. Well, this evening to your Aeneas I play the Sybyl of Rome. Do not worry, I shall not be in a corner of the gloomy church whispering, "Take courage, take heart." That task, that

FREUD IN ROME: IT TAKES A LITTLE COURAGE

mad task, in the netherworld is yours to accomplish alone—

FREUD
Life has no value, no value, if I don't go through those doors. (To self.)

MISS PORTERO
It's still miserable outside. If not you, who? Your younger rival, the other would-be Moses of the Berggasse, Herzl? . . . ?
    (FREUD retrieves the Bible.)
Your glorious Hell's Charm, it is unsheathed?

FREUD
[HE heads for, and halts before, *MOSES*;
face-to-face. Containing himself, HE opens the Bible, to tear it.
The divine radiance (Cf. Exodus 34:29–35.) now emanates from *MOSES'* face: radiant orange-red light with splashes of violet, purple and scarlet.]

[*A mental projection: Voice of God, a voice like Morris Carnovsky's:*

VOICE OF GOD
Sigismund Schlomo. "No man shall see my face and live!"]

FREUD
Moses' radiance! I'm doomed!
    (HE cringes as if he were before a wild, raving beast . . .
    Blinded by the radiance, FREUD, terrified, tries to see his hand.)
I can't see!
    (A SHOFAR sounds; there is thunder and lightning, and smoke. Then, total darkness . . . . Freud, in the dark, recites the *Shema,* the Jew's declaration of faith in God.)
Shema yisrael, adonai elohainu adonai eh—
    (Some light returns. HE catches self as he's about to kiss the phylactery.)
I lost it ! (Self-disgust!)
    (The rest of the 'stage' is still blacked out.)
    (Sounds of long ago return, sounds of bed boards creaking.)
    (And Freud now witnesses: His grey-haired papa JAKOB in bed, gazing up at his naked and voluptuous young WIFE.

> THEY embrace. The bed has red satin sheets and pillows. There is a brilliant fire in fireplace. A gown identical to Miss Portero's is at the foot of the bed.
> Dropping the Bible and phylactery, FREUD, enraged, grabs fireplace poker and rushes at Jakob. JAKOB gives him a hard look, one of scorn and furious wrath.
> Dropping poker, FREUD covers his genitals with one hand; then holds out his arms to JAKOB, who starts to hold, to comfort him.
> FREUD, catching himself, is, again, disgusted with himself.)

How can I hope to contain myself in the damn Church?! ... Some great concealer! (Self-disgust.)

> (MISS PORTERO and LUCINA now emerge from the dark. They are adjusting Miss Portero's gown as if it had just been put back on; they also readjust her hair. All this is done to confuse Freud.)
> (Seeing Miss Portero, FREUD does a double-take.)

Was that you? (The 'stage' is blacked out.)

MISS PORTERO (She mimics Freud.)

"*Shema yisrael,* ... Hear O Israel, the Lord is our God, the Lord is One." And, hero, you expect to stand fast before His messenger, Moses? Such careful preparation!

FREUD (Turning to the 'stage')

But how can you know?

MISS PORTERO

Rather, how can I *not* know?! Thank you, Lucina. (In Italian)

(LUCINA Exits.)

You intend to kill that great man to supplant him. (Fondling Janus' key.)

(LUCINA's mocking laugh is heard.)

The situation just begs for a re-awakening of the feelings you had when you wished to kill your papa to take his place. ... Only this time the mama you wish to possess is Mama Earth. We are hitting bedrock, no?

(FREUD does not appreciate the pun.)

Sorry. (Referring to pun.) Coming face-to-face with Moses tomorrow will be your attempt at purging yourself of the emotions which originated in the family romance.

> (From the bookcase she gets an 1896 journal. In it is Freud's essay, "The Aetiology of Hysteria")

FREUD IN ROME: It Takes a Little Courage

This is still the way you cure troubled souls, isn't it?

                        FREUD (Opens to ribbon marker; reads:)
>We lead the patient's attention back from his symptom
>to the scene in which and through which the symptom
>arose. And, having thus located the traumatic scene,
>we remove the symptom. (HE puts journal down.)

Only by a fresh high tide of the childhood passions can the symptom be resolved and washed away . . . (Lights cigar.).
And, Miss Portero, just what's my symptom? (Takes puff. Coughs.)

                        MISS PORTERO (Retrieves journal.)
Submission to the Will of the Papa, be he Moses or Jehovah . . . or your beloved gray-haired papa, Jakob (She reads:)
>We remove the symptom by bringing about, during the
>reproduction of the traumatic scene, a subsequent correction
>of the psychical course of events which took place at that time.

Of course, just now, no self-cure occurred. You merely became once again that budding Oedipus.—
            (As she did with Vitttorio, SHE pinches FREUD's cheeks—
            only forcibly, enough to inflict pain.)

Such a *punim!*
                                  FREUD
        (Removing her hands from him! and checking the impulse
        to leave—after all, she could sabotage his project—HE
        goes to JANUS and touches its right head.)
A part of my ego has got to be detached, be free to observe and understand what's happening—
                            MISS PORTERO
Like Janus, moment-to-moment you must be on guard, ever vigilant—

                                      FREUD
I've got to stay in the immediate present, not be pulled back into the past. Otherwise, it's all over.
                      MISS PORTERO (Looks at Garibaldi painting.)
As the thoughts, feelings, and attitudes in regard to your father, Jakob, return, you must recognize—and in that very instant—that they belong to long ago—

                                    FREUD
As they wash over me I can't let them overwhelm me.

MISS PORTERO

Prevail over them and you rob the feelings and impressions of their charge, of their power. (SHE grabs a handful of clay.)

FREUD

(With phylactery in his hand, HE goes to the crucifix)
Especially the passive-masochistic attitude, that of the dutiful boy sacrificing his will, his life—to the Will of the powerful father
(HE looks at the crucified Jesus.)
I can't, I won't, identify with that sacrificial lamb!

MISS PORTERO

As you may know, in Michelangelo's Bible, the Vulgate, the Hebrew word for "rays of light" was mistranslated as horns. Accordingly, Michelangelo
(SHE now crowns *Moses* with 'horns', handling them sensually.)
crowned Moses with horns.—

FREUD

Your point?

MISS PORTERO

It is ironical that one and the same feature—this crown of horns—symbolizes the terrible radiance of Moses and calls up the dreaded retribution, castration.
(Like a bull with horns, head down SHE charges Freud; he is not amused.)

FREUD

(HE looks at her; decides to 'open up'.)
In the Vienna Academy of Fine Arts there's a large plaster cast of *Moses*.
(He goes to "stage" curtain Sphinx.)
Before that pale copy, I repeatedly experienced what I can only describe as an uncanny feeling.

MISS PORTERO

An uncanny feeling?

FREUD

A sense of dread . . . with horror—creeping horror..The feeling was familiar but I couldn't place it. On one visit *Moses'* angry scorn seemed directed at me. And, as I was trying to hold my ground,
(Trying to hold his ground before the Sphinx.)
I had the delusion that Moses was about to rise up and strike me down with the Two Tablets of the Law.

FREUD IN ROME: It Takes a Little Courage

(A mental projection : The SPHINX's TALONS seem poised at Freud and it now has the FACE OF MOSES: a slide of MOSES' FACE can be superimposed on the Sphinx.)

(FREUD backs away, wiping his brow with his sleeve.)

MISS PORTERO
This was after plucking your golden bough, that is, your dazzling discovery of how the idea of God the Father came to be?
(Eats plum; discards nut.)

FREUD
What do you think?! . . . The room became dark. There was just Moses and me, and his towering shadow. And in the half-gloom his huge stone seat started to move ominously, first on one corner, then the next.
(HE puts up his hands to protect himself from the tilting seat.)
It looked like it was about to topple over . . . on me. Never in my life have I sweated so much. . . It seemed that all I was, was terror, wild terror.
(A Shudder goes through him.)
My heart felt as though it would explode. I almost passed out . . .

[A mental projection: 'FREUD', played by a double, before MOSES; there are others as well viewing MOSES. FREUD hears their comments:

VOICES
I hear Michelangelo struck Moses' *knee with his hammer demanding that Moses speak.*
To the Jews in Michelangelo's day, the statue was something divine, as though it is Moses himself or his shade.
It was said that, like God, Michelangelo breathed into his creation the breath of life.
Just think what it must be to stand before the original!
More terrifying than facing the Golem
It would be worth going to Rome just for that.
Not for this sinner! (Laughter.)]

(The VOICES fade. FREUD realizes he is alone with *MOSES*; he takes a step back; then another step back; wipes his forehead, and flees. We hear the hollow echo of his steps.)

FREUD

Then and there, I understood I must board the train for Rome.
>(He looks at his railroad ticket.)

MISS PORTERO

>(SHE swallows a cracker as if it were a Communion Wafer; then gulps wine.)

Ah! Yes, your all-important pilgrimage! . . . If bread can be Jesus (Italian pronunciation), then marble, stone, can be Moses.
>(SHE wipes her mouth with a white linen napkin; some of the blood-red wine stains it. She eyes the stain.)

(LUCINA's laughter is heard.)

END of ACT II, SCENE 1

FREUD IN ROME: It Takes a Little Courage

ACT II, SCENE 2

(A few minutes later, FREUD is studying Dante's death mask. MISS PORTERO is pouring coffee.)

FREUD

I've just six years to live.

MISS PORTERO

Six years?

FREUD

If I can hold out that long.

MISS PORTERO

Your heart?   (SHE hands him a cup.)

FREUD

Fifty-one is a critical age. . . . You see, that's when men are likely to die.

MISS PORTERO

(Puts cup down.)
What?! Your classical double, Aeneas, must be behind your believing this fatal age nonsense.
(Picks up *The Aeneid*.)

FREUD

There's nothing about how old Aeneas was when he died.

MISS PORTERO

But of the magician there is.

FREUD

(Grabbing *The Aeneid* from her, HE opens it to the biographical note:)
Born October 15, 70 BC . . . died September 21, 19 BC.
(HE turns white; sits down.)
In three weeks Virgil would have been fifty-one!

MISS PORTERO

(While reading, SHE was figuring Virgil's age with her fingers.)
It was stored in your subconscious mind . . . Don't you see? You've time to prepare.

FREUD (Points to grey hairs in beard.)

You see these grey hairs?! (HE pulls one out.)

75

THE UNKNOWN FREUD: FIVE PLAYS . . .

Not a day, not one day, goes by that I don't think about my death.

       (MISS PORTERO holds his hand while looking at the hair; then she takes the hair, looks at it in her palm; and blows it away, watching it go.)

       (FREUD musing)
A man does his best when he has no alternative.
       (HE comes back to her.)
Napoleon died at fifty-one.
       MISS PORTERO
       (Postures, with disgust, as Napoleon.)
Now, you're Napoleon! (Disdain). Your Berlin friend Dr. Fliess should stick to the nose and throat!
       FREUD
You know Wilhelm?!
       MISS PORTERO
And his crazy fatal ages numerology, yes. A tenor in our company had recommended him. He washed my tonsils. Much good it did. He then suggested I consult you in Vienna. Instead, I consulted your dream book.

       FREUD
Our 14-year friendship is about over. At our last "congress", an outing where we discuss our ideas, Wilhelm called me a "thought-reader."

       MISS PORTERO
And, "thought-reader," in your Hell, the dark chamber of Moses in the gloomy Church of San Pietro in Vincoli, your heart, it will not rupture?

       FREUD
It's not my heart I'm worried about . . .
       (There is another projection: 'Freud' is trying to strike MOSES/MOSES *with his walking stick, as* OTHERS *try restraining him. HE's now on his back, kicking the others: manic energy. Italian police or guards are nursing their wounds.*
       To one side is an attractive woman with a torn yellow-gold blouse covering her breasts: Freud's fear of loss of control of both his sexual and his aggressive impulses.)
I just might crack up, have a psychotic breakdown.
       (Looks at his wedding band.)

FREUD IN ROME: It Takes a Little Courage

> *(Another projection: His WIFE and FIVE of their SIX children observe 'Freud', disheveled, with toy soldiers on the floor, and tearing paper. His sixth child, ANNA, almost six, enjoys playing with '**Freud**',who could be wearing a French Army officer uniform, with an officer's hat beside him.*

After all, the whole enterprise seems a bit crazy, doesn't it?

> *(HE walks around aimlessly, agitated. HE stops at Astraea, the Greek goddess of Justice. Then he goes to Jupiter with thunderbolt and eagle on shoulder.)*

For me to think that I can pull it off, that 1,
> *(Projection: '**Freud**' with Dream Book in his hand and eagle on his shoulder, is standing facing Jew and gentile alike, who look up to '**Freud**'.)*

a Jew boy from the miserable streets of Vienna, can institute a brotherly world, that I can take possession of the field . . . of Mother Earth.

MISS PORTERO

Perhaps you are of that rare, dangerous breed, the Hannibals, the Alexanders, the Cromwells of this world who can turn their big dreams into reality . . . Your *landsman,* Herzl, may belong to that race. In just four or five years his Zionist movement has taken hold and his followers, they are not just *schnorrers.*

FREUD

Against the rising tide of virulent anti-Semitism a sovereign Jewish state is a finger in the dyke. Worse, it's a retrogression, a return to the physical ghetto . . . of our own making. In my Promised Land, on the other hand, *der Kinder* will be able to move freely across frontiers.

> *(Stepping boldly across room.)*

MISS PORTERO

But Herzl's example was a spur for you—

FREUD

> *(Taking aim with the telescope, HE 'fires'; then HE puts it down.)*

Don't get me wrong! I admire that fighter for the human rights of my people. But if one person is responsible for my boarding the train to Rome, it is Emile Zola!

> *(Another mental projection: A full-faced portrait of **Zola**, with his bold open letter, "I Accuse!" as background.)*

THE UNKNOWN FREUD: FIVE PLAYS . . .

MISS PORTERO
Zola? . . . His bold defense of Captain Dreyfus?—

FREUD
(HE projects: The step-by-step public degradation of CAPT. DREYFUS with 'Freud' as Dreyfus. He is stripped of his honors; his sword is broken in two.
The MOB is jeering (mime: "Death to the Jews!")

*[If slides are used, they show Freud as Dreyfus and flash very quickly on a screen wrapped around the back wall. Either way, **slides** or not, **HERZL** is a troubled onlooker. (He reported on the degradation for the "Neue Freie Presse.")]*

Zola kept me breathless.... Now there is a *mensch!* If he can take on the French army and stand up to the contempt and hatred of his nation, I can face my own people—

MISS PORTERO
But first there is the task set for you by Pope Julius—

FREUD
May I finish?! The miserable plight of Dreyfus and the mushrooming of vicious attacks on Jews throughout the Land of the Declaration of the Rights of Man are sobering. For they signify a return of the Middle Ages when my race was blamed for all epidemics. Hear me, Miss Portero, these are but rehearsals, much worse is to come—

MISS PORTERO
Unless your Promised Land is realized.

FREUD
And soon! Otherwise the children are doomed.
(By the chess board with large marble pieces.
With a White Castle, HE 'takes' a Black Castle.
As He does so, the shadow of Freud's Castle is
superimposed upon the Dome of St. Peter's.)
(Thunder and lightning.)

MISS PORTERO
(On 'stage', when the smoke clears, MOSES
appears played by a physically imposing actor. MOSES

is looking down at FREUD. MOSES is holding the Tablets
so that they face Freud: 'Here they are, shatter them!')
Ah, . . . Your dreaded double, the Great Man in the flesh, with calling cards in hand.

(SHE holds out a yarmulke and a tallith.)
What have you to lose? Your inner torment?

FREUD
(Reluctantly, He puts on Yarmulke and recites the ritual blessing for placing the prayer shawl around him.)

Baruch ata adonai elohainu melech ha-olam asher kidshanu d'mitzvotav v'tzivano l'hit –atef b'tizitizti—

MISS PORTERO
Now, pretender, make your plea!
(Points with her right forefinger on which there is a gold ring with a large green stone.)

FREUD
(A brilliant flash from the ring stone gets Freud's attention. HE is now in another state: he was mesmerized by the flashing light.. There is thunder, lightning and smoke.)

(With fear and trembling, FREUD, with his Dream Book, heads for MOSES.)
A SHOFAR BLAST startles him. FREUD turns towards it and sees:
ZOLA and, in the background, a huge front page of ZOLA'S "I ACCUSE!"

Zola!

FREUD hears a SHOFAR BLAST from another direction. Zola is blacked out.
HE sees HERZL with his grief-filled eyes.

Herzl!

FREUD hears another BLAST. Herzl is blacked out. HE sees GARIBALDI.

Garibaldi!

FREUD hears another BLAST. Garibaldi is blacked out.
HE sees AENEAS plucking the Golden Bough.

Aeneas!

Another BLAST. Aeneas is blacked out.

THE UNKNOWN FREUD: FIVE PLAYS ...

>FREUD sees young HANNIBAL with his
>father, making the oath of vengeance.

Hannibal! ...
It's now or never!

>(Summoning courage) (Planting himself before MOSES, who seems about to strike, FREUD contains self, holds his ground despite his emotions.)

Moses, if Yahweh exists, why hasn't He shown His strong hand? His Chosen People, they haven't suffered enough? Moses, it is with a heavy heart that I say this to the Great Man who has shaped me and every other Jew, and to whom we owe so much, The Torah, it is your people's Cross, and so must be destroyed. There is no alternative—to save the children, The Law, Judaism, must be sacrificed. You look down at me with scorn, but, Moses, I will not cower or fall away before your wrathful gaze. The time for Jewish martyrdom is over!

>(As FREUD starts to remove the Prayer Shawl and Skull Cap, there is a series of SHOFAR BLASTS as on *Yom Kippur.*)
>(Brilliant lightning and a thunderclap occur.) (Blinding light now emanates from MOSES' head.)

>The radiance! I'm doomed!
>(Clutching his heart, FREUD shields his face with his Dream Book.) (The floor shakes and smoke rises, as if from a fiery pit.)

>*[A mental projection: "They, and all that appertained to them went down alive into the pit"; then a SLIDE of Botticelli's The Punishment of Korah, Dathan, and Abiram (Numbers: 16-35), which depicts Moses with rays emanating from the top of his head calling down Yahweh's wrath on these Hebrews who rebelled against his, MOSES', authority.]*

>(The radiance of Botticelli's Moses is superimposed on FREUD.)

>(MISS PORTERO, moved, anxious for FREUD, reaches for him from her spot. Clutching her heart, SHE starts to shake, and sinks to the floor, convulsing before passing out. FREUD is oblivious of this.)

FREUD IN ROME: It Takes a Little Courage

(MOSES' radiance causes Dream Book to smoke . . .)

Moses, I love you . . . . But I've got to kill you.
    (Removing the prayer shawl and Yarmulke, FREUD strikes the Tablets with the Dream Book, turning his head away: guilt. When FREUD again faces MOSES, HE sees that MOSES is about to fall off the 'cliff'.)

Moses! . . . If I touch him, I'd die. But I can't just leave him.
    (Carrying MOSES the way Aeneas, in the painting, carries his father, Anchises, FREUD lays MOSES, still holding the Tablets, on the sandy ground. Rolling up his jacket, HE makes a pillow for MOSES, lays his head on MOSES' bosom, next to the Tablets, and sobs quietly. Laying MOSES' hands on his head, HE cries:)
Bless me! Bless me! Bless me!

    (The Tablet letters bleed, dark red.)
    (FREUD closes MOSES' eyes.)
    (The *mana*—the divine and terrible radiance which had been transferred from Yahweh onto Moses on Mt. Sinai [Exodus 34: 29- 35]—emanates from FREUD'S face, but, for now, Freud is unaware of this.).
    [In *Group Psychology and the Analysis of the Ego,* Freud, 1921, refers to the *mana* of Moses.]

    (JEWS now make a great lamentation, expressing deep grief. SOME, armed with stones, now approach Freud.)
My B'nai B'rith lodge brothers! Go ahead! I deserve to be stoned to death!

    (Seeing FREUD's glowing face, his BRETHREN back away in terror, their hands covering their eyes.)

    FREUD (to self:)
They back away from me, even Alexander, as though I've got a fatal, contagious disease.—
    (HE tries surmounting his patricidal sense of guilt by justifying to himself his having killed Moses. All the while, HE is in a fugue state.)
I had to kill him! He had to die!
    (To backing away BRETHREN . . .)

(FREUD has a hunch; limping, HE rushes to a window; HE sees his shining face.)

The radiance. No wonder they're backing away. It was transferred on to me . . . I've died!. . . I'm, I'm Moses! Moses with a limp. Well, It's no sin to limp.

(HE spots the shattered Dome of St. Peter's.)

And St. Peter's Dome. That golden egg—that lie of salvation—is cracking!

(We now hear SOUNDS like that of bats flying. But it's the shuffling of cards.)

The shuffling of cards? It's Julius! . . . Julius! Julius! Where are you?

(JULIUS Appears.)

(JULIUS is in the form of a handsome middle-aged Jew in a white surgeon's outfit. He tosses the playing cards, one at a time.)

Julius! You've come back to me.

(Deeply moved, He presses hand against chest; then picks up the cards at his feet; kisses them.)

(FREUD now sees JULIUS with his right arm around little VITTORIO. JULIUS is holding the Dream Book in his right hand. With his left arm and hand, JULIUS tosses seed into air.)

[There is now the sound of JOYOUS MUSIC, maybe of a lyre and tambourines. FREUD is startled.

DANCERS now appear: healthy, erotic, intellectual, well-balanced, all ages and races. They dance around Maypole with *'Freud'* in the center on an elephant whose trunk holds a golden branch: Freud is the new totem, the new primal father. *'Freud'* has the Dream Book (now in marble) and on his shoulder is an eagle. His head is crowned with a string of acorns. His face glows. The dancers each hold either of the two: a sheaf of wheat (symbol of fruitfulness) or a gold-tinted oak branch .]

'JULIUS LINE' (Pointing to Dream Book.)

Turn it and turn it again. For everything is in it, the new Torah!

FREUD IN ROME: IT TAKES A LITTLE COURAGE

[The dancers have cymbals, castanets, and musical instruments from biblical times. There are golden acorns all over, out of which emerge healthy, energetic children. (The golden acorns are the counterpart to the to the gold Dome of St. Peter's. It is the children, remember the golden line, who would make the difference!)
(The streamers are made of the brilliant "stage" curtain colors—purple, violet, scarlet, gold.)].

FREUD
(From a height, an Olympian!)

I am Hercules!

(HE's holding and swinging an orange branch as Hercules might his club. Caught up in the gaiety and with a display of manic energy and exultation, FREUD 'lets go': scooting across the floor like a bull charging, dancing backwards; circling, kissing and petting pretty girls; wrestling with the men, hugging, spinning and throwing the children in the air; putting on a crown of acorns.)

(One of the dancers is LUCINA. She has Freud's hat and his gold handled cane.
LUCINA and FREUD play out an erotic fantasy to music, a ballet but with the sound of drums.)
(Slides can be used for much of the above, plus actors playing various roles.)

Ah! Fair moment! . . . Linger awhile.

[The PLAYERS DISAPPEAR. There is brilliant lightning, with a tremendous peal of thunder. FREUD, blinded, his hands protecting his eyes, falls away on his back. There is light. (A strobe-light can be used).
On his back, still blind, FREUD *has a terrible vision, prefaced by the sounds of a train, including track squeals—A mental projection:*
Naked, pale, emaciated dead Jews, strewn in the harsh light of the sun, many on their back, an actual photograph of hovering scavenger birds are part of this projection as are, also, the sounds and shadows of ferocious guard dogs. Whips are also heard.]

THE UNKNOWN FREUD: FIVE PLAYS...

What's that stench? (He is gagging.) . . . . Like burnt flesh . . . . The children! Martin! Martin! Martin! My firstborn son where are you?! It's me, papa! Answer me! Answer me! . . . Anna, Ernst . . .

>(HE crawls, gropes, trying desperately to find, to save, his little ones.)

My babies where are you? Answer me! Answer me! It's papa. Mathilde! Sophie! Oliver! My little ones, where are you? Answer me! Answer me! Tell papa where you are!

>(Extending his hand through a 'hole'.)
>
>(MISS PORTERO is startled by his screams but remains unconscious.)
>
>(FREUD comes out of fugue state but is still blind, and he no longer possesses the *mana* or radiance.)

The visitations, they've begun! (Horror.)

>(HE gropes in his blindness.)

Miss Portero! Miss Portero! Miss Portero!

>Now, there is a powerful peal of thunder and brilliant lightning. Suddenly HE can see. . . HE spots his jacket on the floor, rolled up. Reaching down, He feels the blood on his jacket. The gardenia is blood-stained.
>
>HE touches the blood on the floor left by the Tablets, and moves his hand to his face to make sure it's blood. Recoiling in horror, HE almost throws up.
>
>HE turns and sees Miss Portero on the floor. HE's near panic.)

Did I actually kill her?

>(FREUD approaches her. HE wipes his hands on his pants. HE feels her neck.
>
>She is alive. HE goes to armoire to get a cover for her. When he opens the door, he is startled. On a hanger is a Garibaldi outfit, complete with red blouse, felt grey hat plumed with ostrich feathers, trousers and sword. HE covers Miss Portero, looking fondly at her. HE looks back at the Garibaldi uniform.)

MISS PORTERO

>(Unconscious, desperate, SHE clutches Freud, holding on to his arms.)

Don't go! Don't leave! . . . Don't leave! Bernard! Bernard! Don't leave me!

(FREUD, anguished, comforts her.)

END OF ACT II, SCENE 2

ACT II, SCENE 3

A few minutes later. MISS PORTERO is on the couch, coming to.

MISS PORTERO
Some wine, and I'll be all right.

FREUD (Pointing to his bloody jacket.)
Did I kill anyone?!

MISS PORTERO
(Backs away from the stench.)
How would I know? . . . (Still coming to.)

FREUD (Shaking her violently.)
What happened? What did I do?
(MOSES appears in his seat.)

MISS PORTERO
(SHE points to MOSES.)
It seems you didn't kill anyone, anyway in objective reality.

FREUD
(HE rushes to MOSES)
I need to know!
(MOSES vanishes.)
(FREUD tries to find MOSES: futile.)

MISS PORTERO (SHE gets the wine herself.)
There is no more to be said.

FREUD
Don't you think I should be the judge of that?!
(HE shakes her again.) . . .
It's my life!
(Removing his hands, MISS PORTERO wipes wine from her outfit. Then SHE picks up his jacket and throws his blue gardenia in a woven waste basket.)
(HE's angry still, but respects her.)
I've got to hand it to her. She stands her ground. (To self.)

FREUD IN ROME: IT TAKES A LITTLE COURAGE

                    MISS PORTERO
          (As FREUD places his wallet and notebook on the oblong
          table, SHE gestures for his bloodied vest. HE hands it to her.)
Lucina will sponge the clothes.
          (SHE opens a door and puts clothes and cover outside.)
Lucina!
          (FREUD heads for the armoire, now open.)
          (MISS PORTERO follows him.)
One of Garibaldi's red shirts wore this during the siege of Rome in 1849 . . . .
He was shot there.
          (SHE points to a pant leg. FREUD notices blood on his own
          pant leg. Placing the Garibaldi hat on her head, SHE looks
          out the terrace.)
It happened in the street-fighting, just before the exodus from Rome to the
mountains . . . From the Square, Garibaldi made his glorious plea for volunteers:
          I am going out from Rome. Let those who wish to continue the
          war against the stranger come with me. I offer neither pay, nor—

                    FREUD
          (Looking at picture of Garibaldi.)
nor quarters, nor provisions. I offer hunger, thirst, forced
marches, battles and death. Let him who loves his nation
in his heart and not with his lips only, follow me!

                    MISS PORTERO
          (Offers the hat to FREUD, who handles it as if it's sacred.)
"Let him who loves his country," Garibaldi cried.
  Not, "Let him who loves his nation."

                    FREUD
I'll own that error . . . Garibaldi possessed what God, er, nature, had not
granted me— that indefinite something which attracts men.
          (FREUD continues holding and looking at the hat, meditating. Then he returns the hat.)

                    MISS PORTERO
The father, he may have looked like Garibaldi, but the son, he is Garibaldi.

                    FREUD
What did you say?

MISS PORTERO (Taking Dream Book.)
You are re-living the symbolic castration of your father, aren't you?

FREUD
(A projection: Jakob Freud's fur hat, his Shtreimel, being thrown in mud by a CHRISTIAN; JAKOB meekly going into the gutter and picking it up: not taking up himself.)

His words on that Sunday stroll around Vienna when I was ten . . . Even now they are painful to remember . . .
(FREUD acts out the terrible event.)
—*Schlomo*, one *Shabbos* when I was a young man in your birthplace, Freiberg, a Christian came up to me as I was walking and with a single blow he knocked my new *Shtreimel* from my head into the mud and shouted, "Jew! get off the sidewalk!"
—And, Papa, what did you do?
—I went into the roadway and picked up my cap.

(FREUD, as Sigismund Schlomo, ashamed of Jakob's unheroic behavior, holds back tears.)
The strong man holding my hand changed before my eyes . . .
As if God Himself had died. (To self.)
(HE recovers.)
Well, when my boys look back, they'll have a different picture of their father. Just before Alexander and I left for Rome an ugly incident occurred. We were on vacation near Salzburg, in my so-called fatherland. My sons, Oliver and Martin, were on the lake fishing when they were jeered by Christians, grown men. The good Christians accused the "dirty little *Yid Jew boys*" of stealing fish . . . With that can one live?!—

MISS PORTERO
How can people be so cruel?
FREUD
They are only ten and eleven.—
MISS PORTERO
About the age of you with your father.—

FREUD
Well, later that afternoon, Martin and I chanced on those good Christians. The trash made way, let me tell you!
(Takes Golden Bough; flails it.)

FREUD IN ROME: It Takes a Little Courage

And Martin was at the ready.
> *(A projection: young Martin, 11, prepared to fight with oar as club.)*

MISS PORTERO
(Opens *The Aeneid:*)
Son learn fortitude and toil from me . . . When before long you come to man's estate be sure that you recall this . . . let your father arouse your courage.

FREUD
My boys won't need to look for models, . . . for fathers.
> (MISS PORTERO offers him Garibaldi's hat.)
> (FREUD puts hat on. It is a bit large. HE puts it on at an angle.)

MISS PORTERO
Not a bad fit for a conquistador.

FREUD
Even for one with a limp?

MISS PORTERO
Especially for one with a limp.

FREUD
Just let some good Christian try to knock this from my head!

> (MISS PORTERO takes Golden Bough from him; hands him sword instead.)
> (There is lightning. HE goes to terrace. St. Peter's Dome is whole.)

Now all I need is—

MISS PORTERO
Garibaldi's white horse.

FREUD
I was going to say., "Garibaldi's brave *Pasionaria,* his beloved Anita, beside me."
> (In the background of the Garibaldi picture is his brave young wife, Anita, in the same uniform.)

MISS PORTERO
(Beside him; deeply moved; holds back tears.)
That's my name.

FREUD
I know. (Laughs; pats her knee-thigh; he doesn't notice her tears.)

But instead of Garibaldi's white horse, I'd prefer Hannibal's elephant, his white elephant.

                    MISS PORTERO (Yells down:)

Golden Sigi is at the gates!

                    FREUD (Does her one better:)

Golden Schlomo is at the gates!
           (With angry edge; sword overhead.)

                  MISS PORTERO
          (Tears come; wipes eyes; keeps Freud from knowing.)
          (FREUD's caught up.)

Look at them squirm. There, the Holy Father is scurrying to his fortress, the Castel Sant' Angelo for shelter.
          (FREUD brandishes sword.)

He's not afraid of that. (Pointing to sword.)

But of your special something, your golden stream of baptismal wine, his drowning in it, . . . The little pisser comes of age.

                  FREUD (shakes head, appreciating her.)

My dream of the Open-Air Closet, you broke it?!

                  MISS PORTERO

Of course! You think we do things here half-assed?
          (SHE swings her hip into his; this makes his sword stands
          upright. BOTH laugh.)
          (Looking in the Dream Book.)

Its meaning is crystal clear. Your pissing on the Open-Air seat, which reminds you of Italy, must signify your pissing on the Papal Seat, no?

                  FREUD

A Herculean task.

                  MISS PORTERO

A labor of love.

                  FREUD

And of hate! I'm a good hater!

                  MISS PORTERO

Ah! Here it is, your veiled allusion to the Papal Seat, "The museum of human excrement."
          (We hear a GREGORIAN CHANT: a boys' choir)

FREUD IN ROME: It Takes a Little Courage

FREUD
(HE swats a mosquito on his neck.)
The stinking seeding ground for pious anti-Semites . . . .
(Momentarily lost in wonder as HE looks at St. Peter's.)
Still, it's so hauntingly beautiful.

MISS PORTERO (Looks through spyglass.)
Over the centuries they came, messianic pretenders, arrayed in rags, and stationed themselves there, (pointing) by the bridge leading to the Castel Sant' Angelo.

FREUD
And the misery continued . . .

MISS PORTERO
Each one living out the Jewish legend that within the gates of Rome the Messiah will reveal himself. Romantic personages, one and all.
(Hands Freud the spyglass; directing his gaze.)

FREUD
To think that I'm different from those deluded *schnorrers!* (To self.)

MISS PORTERO
In one dream you view this very bridge, the Ponte Sant' Angelo. Of course, you do not elaborate. Excuse me—
(As SHE physically directs the spyglass at St. Peter's—)
But, my finely attired pretender, that is not a windmill but a formidable power!

FREUD (Looking thru spyglass)
A poisonous power!

MISS PORTERO (Pours self wine; toasts:)
"Moses is dead, long live the new Moses, Sigmund, er, *Schlomo* Freud!"
(FREUD's caught off-guard but stays in control.)
(SHE claps!)
Well, well. There is hope for you yet.

FREUD
I almost lost it again.

MISS PORTERO
Because names carry souls your non-rational head
(Caressing JANUS' left head.)
believed Moses would be conjured up, but this time
(Caressing JANUS' right head.)

your rational head prevailed.

FREUD

Garibaldi's motto was "Rome or death!" You could say mine is "Hell or death."
(HE hands Garibaldi hat back to MISS PORTERO, who begins to place it on table.)

MISS PORTERO

It will be the battle of your life!

FREUD

It's the battle for *my* life!

MISS PORTERO

Ironical is it not? The more you try to break free of Moses, the more his impress shows: the intellectual boldness, the single-mindedness of purpose, the quest for peace and social justice through an enlightened line—

FREUD

(HE heads for the Aeneas painting)
It's as though I'm living out a myth.

MISS PORTERO

But only up to a point. In order to save his homeless people, Aeneas, once in Italy,
(Mimes Aeneas with Golden Bough.)
enters the underworld to *receive* instructions from his father, Anchises. On the other hand, in order to save your people, you, on your third morning in Rome, enter the underworld to *destroy,*
(Mimes Aeneas/Freud with the Dream Book as shield.)
ultimately, the Instructions from your father Moses, the Torah. (Taking defiant stand before bust of *Moses.*)

Which begs the question, Presuming that you succeed at this "mad task," that is, you do not flee, nor faint, nor come apart, but contain yourself before Moses in his gloomy chamber—
(Miming standing strong.)
do you sincerely believe that you will then have surmounted, once and for all, your dread of Yahweh, of His terrible Justice?—

FREUD

Nothing can erase the instruction repeated year after year at the Passover Seder:

FREUD IN ROME: It Takes a Little Courage

[*FREUD has a mental projection: The Passover Seder: JAKOB FREUD is at the head. SIGI, 5; his sister, ANNA, 3; and his MOTHER, AMALIE, are at the Feast. There is an empty chair and wine cup for the Prophet Elijah. SIGI (played by the child actor who played Vittorio) is mouthing the Passover question, "Why is this night different . . . ?" But the voice is from long ago and off-stage.*]

YOUNG BOY'S VOICE
Mah Nishtanah halailah hazeh, mikol haleilot?

FREUD
(Simultaneously, HE also recites:)
"*Mah Nishtanah halailah hazeh, mikol haleilot?*"

[*JAKOB FREUD dips his right forefinger into a silver wine cup and with his finger drops wine onto a saucer which already has some wine on it: The Finger of God. The LITTLE BOY is enthralled. JAKOB is acting out the 8th Plague, the LOCUSTS: miming locusts gobbling everything. For the LOCUSTS we can have a LIGHT SHOW such as a rock group might put on, with appropriate SWARMING SOUNDS . . . We see horror on the boy's face, as he covers his ears. . . . Then, we can hear the FAMILY of long ago.*]

Da-da ye-nu, da-da ye-nu, da-da ye-nu, da-ye nu, da-ye!]

MISS PORTERO
And should catastrophe befall any of your loved ones, you would hold yourself responsible.

FREUD (Shaken up.)
To Martin, especially (More to himself.)

MISS PORTERO
Of course! That is your greatest fear. Martin, your firstborn son, paying for his father's rebellion. For, having spared, that first Passover, the firstborn sons of the Israelites, Yahweh has a special claim on Martin.

FREUD
(Reaching for the head phylactery on the table, HE presses

it to his forehead, as though one of his migraines is about to come on.)

Exodus 13: 15 . . . "but all the firstborn of my children I redeem"—It's up to me to redeem Martin, my firstborn son—

MISS PORTERO

By obeying, not trespassing, Yahweh's Commandments—
(FREUD places the phylactery and hat on table. With the hat, he accidentally knocks over VENUS, shattering her, and bends to pick up the pieces.)
(MISS PORTERO sits on floor.)

I'm afraid there's no help for Venus.
(SHE has FREUD hand her the Venus pieces, which she places in her lap.)

According to you, so-called accidents are purposeful. By shattering Venus, you sacrifice your ambition to take possession of Mother Earth—and so avert disaster from befalling your loved ones, Martin, especially.

FREUD

But what kind of a life would Martin or any of my children have here on earth—a Christian earth?
(Helping her up.)

MISS PORTERO

Thank you.
(Placing the Venus pieces in the woven waste basket, SHE pours herself a drink.)

Some wine? . . . (HE shakes his head)
Are you sure? You may need it!
(SHE hands him a photo from her desk drawer.)

FREUD

This is Bernard beside you? (Pointing)

MISS PORTERO

Yes, Vittorio's papa, Bernard.

FREUD

(Looks at self in mirror and back at photo.)

Uncanny. We could be brothers.

MISS PORTERO

Or *doppelgangers, no?* When I first saw in Dr. Fliess's office the photograph of the two of you, I almost fell away . . . Bernard was as removed from his people as one can be. And yet—

FREUD

And yet?

MISS PORTERO

On Sunday morning, January 6, 1895, the day after Captain Dreyfus's ceremonial degradation, Bernard, awakening to the pealing of bells, begins to come out of a dream. Rather, it was more a *tableau vivant,* a frozen image. He and Theodor Herzl are marble pillars supporting a platform, in the center of which is a golden Star of David—

FREUD

The wish instigating the dream-image seems to be transparent.

MISS PORTERO

And, Bernard, he hears loud and ever more threatening echoes of the bloodthirsty mob on the parade ground, *"A la Morte les Juifs"*—"Death to the Jews."—Emerging from the dream, he is changed—a transformation, a change so profound that, for a moment, I feel once again I am on stage preparing for a new role, a challenging role . . .

> *(Projection: BERNARD'S VOICE: Freud's voice with a French accent):*
> *Anita, an irresistible feeling of solidarity with my threatened people has mounted within me—Dearest one, I must tear myself away from you and our joy, Vittorio, to devote myself to Theodor Herzl and his Divine Dream, a sovereign homeland for my threatened, defenseless people.*

Some of Bernard's newspaper pieces—

> (SHE holds out clippings to FREUD, who takes, and studies, them intently.)

The disgusting behavior of his 'brother' journalists pained Bernard deeply—not only did these 'guardians of truth' champion the fraudulent conviction of Dreyfus! They gleefully incited the bloodthirsty rabble—especially after Zola's "bomb" hit the streets three years later.

FREUD

Bernard is French?

MISS PORTERO

Bernard is dead.,...

FREUD

Dead, how old was he?

MISS PORTERO
Excuse me. (Lies down on couch.)

FREUD
(HE sits, wipes his glasses and reads to self a passage from the article.)
(A projection: We hear BERNARD'S VOICE, which sounds like Freud's with a French accent.):
A French Army officer is selling our military secrets to our enemy, the Germans. Naturally troubled, the Army sets out discover the traitor.. Ah ha! Of course! It's plain as the nose on his Israelite face: Dreyfus is the Judas. But I must be fair. The Jewish Captain was not without guilt. His sin was in believing that in the Republic he and his children have a fatherland.

Bernard, (FREUD, looking again at Bernard's photo.)
we could have gotten on. You did not blind yourself.

MISS PORTERO
(Opening her eyes, SHE seats herself)
Vittorio was not yet two and, Bernard, his Jewish soul awakened, sacrifices us for a dream, a "Divine Dream." Dr. Luzzatti said Bernard had worn out his heart. But in my bones I know this: Herzl with his "Divine Dream" killed Bernard.
(SHE gestures for the photo.)
(FREUD hands it to her.)
FREUD
It was trash, human trash, that killed Bernard!

MISS PORTERO
Tomorrow, it will be two years.
('Circling' the photo with her finger...)

FREUD
Tomorrow?

MISS PORTERO
Yes, your big day....Sensing a bond between Bernard and you—
(Catching herself, she places the photo on the table.)

FREUD
Let me see . . . By gaining insight into me—Bernard's "double"—you'd then

understand Bernard? What had driven him?

                    MISS PORTERO
What was driving him. He was still alive . . . wasting away but alive—

                         FREUD
Incredible!! That you would go through this whole business of getting me here—
            (HE waves her posted letter to him.)

                    MISS PORTERO
More incredible than making a pilgrimage to one's totem?
            (Taking the letter from him, SHE studies it, and throws it in the fireplace.)
After agreeing to write you for an appointment, Fliess showed me the copy of your dream book that you had sent him.
            (With Dream Book, SHE mimes:)
   He relates and interprets his own dreams!
   I must obtain a copy!
Repeatedly, I pestered my bookseller.

                         FREUD
But the book was published after Bernard had already died.

                    MISS PORTERO
I needed to know what drove him. Surely, you understand this.
            (SHE 'mocks' eagerly opening the Dream book skipping pages.)
   I shall begin with this short dream, the dream of the Botanical Monograph.
            (Looks up dictionaries; takes notes.)
   Ah ha! So That's the dream wish!
            (SHE goes before her bust of *MOSES*.)
No more! No more will you or your Law, the Torah, control my life!

                         FREUD
But I carefully concealed the statue. How?

            (HE goes to her desk; examines her thick books.)
Simple dictionary decoding?!

                    MISS PORTERO (Reads from Dream Book:)

THE UNKNOWN FREUD: FIVE PLAYS . . .

The thoughts corresponding to the . . . dream consisted of a passionately agitated plea on behalf of my liberty to act as I chose to act and to govern my life as seemed right to me and me alone.

But who or what can keep a grown man, a Jew, from governing his own life? Anti-Semitism? Yes. On the other hand, there is the Mosaic Code, the Law.

FREUD
The dream just shows that I wished to become my own person—

MISS PORTERO
On the surface, yes. But Dr. Freud, surely you must know that mortals are not meant to keep a secret.
(Sensuously, SHE fondles JANUS' key.)
Michelangelo's *Moses,* whom you have so carefully veiled, was the master key to unlock your dreams of Rome.
(From the desk drawer SHE removes a sheaf of papers bound with a purple ribbon.) (FREUD reaches for them—)
(MISS PORTERO unties the ribbon, letting the pages fall.)
Voila!, the veil, it lifts, only to reveal that the world's greatest representation of Moses is not but a mere prop for you to deliver yourself from the Law. Rather, it is a symbol in the same manner that the bread Jesus of the Eucharist is a symbol for faithful Catholics, which is to say, Michelangelo's terrible *Moses* is Moses himself, possessing all of his qualities, including the terrible, divine radiance.
(FREUD begins lifting the pages)
(SHE puts her ear to JANUS' left mouth) —
'If bread can be Jesus, then stone, marble, can be Moses,' exactly! Yes, his bloody nun of a mother instructed him well . . . Unfortunately, you just remain stone.
(Patting JANUS' left head, SHE 'returns' to Freud.)
Because you are obsessed with your secret messianic ambition to save your nation, it, like a (Miming with the ribbon that had bound the dreams) thread, runs through your dreams.
FREUD (Looks at a lifted page)
Castle by the Sea. (HE reads silently.)

MISS PORTERO
Here your isolated nation is being besieged. And you are next in rank to take Moses' place, a volunteer yet! . . . With your pointed, rapier-sharp questions
(Thrusting the golden bough)

you kill Moses, and wonder if you should inform der *Oberkommando, Yahweh,* of your impious deed.

FREUD (Flips page)

Dissecting My Own Pelvis.

MISS PORTERO

Here you must confront your personal totem, Michelangelo's *Moses—the* dreadful task left you by Pope Julius the Second, that warrior-pope who had commissioned Michelangelo to sculpt *Moses* for his tomb. Ironic is it not—

FREUD (Flips page.)

This is unbelievable. Uncle with the Yellow Beard.

MISS PORTERO

Here you identify with paternal uncle Joseph who broke your grey-haired papa's heart— (Miming fondling a beard.)

FREUD

He was imprisoned for being in a counterfeit ring.

MISS PORTERO

And you cannot but wonder if you, too, like uncle Joseph, are dispensing false coin—and will also, like him, be punished for breaking the law—in your case, for breaking Divine Law, Yahweh's Law, the Torah.

FREUD

Did you tell anyone . . . Fliess?—

MISS PORTERO

Not a soul!

FREUD
(Troubled, HE flips the pages quickly .)
My Son, the Myops (flips); Hollthurn (flips); Count Thun . . .
(Before throwing them in the fireplace, HE looks at them one last time.)
If you can read me, that means others can!

MISS PORTERO

How can Bernard just discard us . . . sacrifice us. Nothing mattered, except his and Herzl's messianic mission— not Vittiorio, not me—

FREUD
And Vittorio, he's not a Jew boy? Just try selling that to the good Christians in Vienna or Paris or Kiev or Algiers or Bucharest—

MISS PORTERO
But Vittorio needs, needed him. . . .
> (With a finger, SHE "circles" the photo; catching herself, she hands it to Freud, who again studies it.)

FREUD
After Bernard died that's when your singing difficulties began?

MISS PORTERO
No. When he left . . . . Why sing, why *live,* if there's no reason?!

FREUD
And Vittorio, (Pointing to where Vittorio had exited) this precious child, he's not reason enough!

MISS PORTERO
Bloody fool!
> (With the ribbon that had held his dreams, SHE tries strangling Freud.)

It is to bring me back to life that you are here . . .
> (FREUD, struggling free, keeps the ribbon.)

Venus couldn't have loved her love-child, Aeneas, more.
> (SHE gets several Venus fragments.)

I am now no more Vittorio's mother than this broken Venus . . . Just as your nanny became your mama after Julius had died, Lucina is now Vittiorio's mama—

FREUD
> (Taking the Venus fragments from her, HE flings them in the basket, and takes her firmly by the shoulders.)

Listen to me! For this Venus there is help!

MISS PORTERO
> (She rubs his left hand still on her shoulder.)

I fear you make too much of your Roman reader.

FREUD
No, too little. Bernard was blessed.—

FREUD IN ROME: It Takes a Little Courage

MISS PORTERO
(Looking at him, decides to tell:)
I told Dr. Fliess's housekeeper that we are lovers.

FREUD (HE lets her go.)
What?! You said what to Flora?!

MISS PORTERO
I made this 'confession' to pore over your correspondence with Fliess. Flora relented when I pleaded with her: (miming)
    Flora, for Vittorio's sake, I must know his true intentions.
    Vittorio had already lost one papa.
From my stage appearances, I have learned that one can depend upon the sentimentality of the Germans. In this regard, Flora didn't disappoint. And when Fliess and his wife, Ida, were away vacationing, I, thanks to my papa's example, like a Talmudic scholar pored over your letters. And from them, I learned much—

(Miming this at her desk, turning pages of a pad.)
5 May 1897
"Another presentiment tells me. . . . I am about to discover the source of morality."
Hm! Is not God "the source of Morality"?

Ah, 2 March 1899
". . . . the realization of a secret wish . . . might *mature* at same time as Rome.
This secret wish—is it that he *matures* in Rome? But how?

FREUD
The letters! I've got to burn them!

MISS PORTERO (Turning pages in a pad.)
Yes, The money I handed Flora, a rather large sum, was well worth it. From your own hand I also learned about your having played Cain to your infant brother Julius, and, of course, the related fratricidal sense of guilt—a torment which is always with you. And earlier in this very same letter, that of 3 October 1897, I learn about your nanny and her very careful instruction.

FREUD
Sinners burning in Hell—

MISS PORTERO
Doomsday, Judgment Day—
FREUD
Nothing can erase that wonderful instruction either . . . The seductive promise of Salvation through Christ —
(Looking at the fireplace cross)

MISS PORTERO
What?! You have considered converting to Roman Catholicism? No!

FREUD
I had a Catholic mama, didn't I? Imagine a precocious two year-old from a Hasidic background surrounded by all those vespers candles and that music—

MISS PORTERO
"Give us a child."
FREUD
If this tormented Cain can consider a pact with Lucifer, then why not one with Jesus, whose blood, after all, cleanseth us from all sin, brother-murder included? . . . From Vienna, Rome promised me redemption—If not one way, then another.
MISS PORTERO
On the one hand, the promise of redemption by becoming the Deliverer of your people; on the other hand, the promise of redemption by—

FREUD
The simple act of bending the knee,
(Facing the Crucifix, he starts to kneel—)
and this Cain's inner torment would be behind him . . . forever.

(HE looks up at the Crucifix... his eyeballs roll back as his eyes close; his mouth is about to welcome the Communion Wafer—)
(This isn't an act: HE's in a trance-like state.)

MISS PORTERO (Oblivious)
The steep steps off the Corso Cavour leading to that gloomy church, they may be your road to Damasc—
(SHE now realizes HE is in another state.)

FREUD
(Catching self, HE brushes host from his face, begins to rise, and turns to Miss Portero)

Almost twenty years ago, five days before Christmas, 1883, I visited Dresden's Zwinger Museum, where for the first time I viewed Titian's *The Tribute Money*—and was captivated by the head of Christ—

MISS PORTERO
It remains a mystery: How Titian conveys directly the very souls of his subjects.

FREUD
Far from beautiful, Christ's noble human countenance is filled with seriousness, intensity, profound thought, and deep inner passion. . . . Lost in wonder, I found myself saying, "This is Christ." . . .
(Titian's head of Christ is now projected on FREUD's head.)

Where that sensation came from, I didn't then know. I would loved to have walked out with the painting. But there were too many people. I left with a heavy heart.

MISS PORTERO
Tell me, your Catholic mama, you think she had you secretly baptized?!. If she loved you, which I am sure she did, she would have been concerned about your soul. More so, since that of baby Julius, in all likelihood, was already lost.

FREUD
Hm! I remember her bathing me in reddish water. Looking back, I had assumed it was her period.

MISS PORTERO
"The blood of Jesus Christ His Son cleanseth us from *all* sin."
(FREUD almost gags.)
(With a wet napkin, SHE starts wiping his forehead—
FREUD resists.)

How you react! You may be already a Christia—

FREUD
Don't! . . . Please, don't say it.
(SHE doesn't complete "Christian.")

(FREUD is now looking at the Crucifix, an uneasy searching in his glance.)
(CHURCH BELLS peal twelve times.)

THE UNKNOWN FREUD: FIVE PLAYS . . .

Just a few more hours.

MISS PORTERO
Your hand, please. The right one.
> (Troubled, FREUD gives her his hand, expecting a 'reading'.)
> (Before HE knows it, SHE puts her green stone ring on his right ring finger.)

FREUD
What's this?!

MISS PORTERO
The head is of Jupiter. Today, Thursday, is his day . . .
> (FREUD's about to remove the ring —)
> (SHE stops him.)

Let me share this moment! . . . And who knows? The stone even may be a potent charm.—

FREUD
Well, what's one more superstition?
> (HE kisses it. He then puts the Garibaldi hat back on.)
> (MISS PORTERO gets a wooden cane from the armoire; places it in a large planter by the terrace, as a stake.)
> (Plucking it free easily, FREUD admires it.)

Oak?

MISS PORTERO
Oak, evergreen oak. Solid, no? Could pass for Aeneas' bough.
> (FREUD holds it as a Pope's staff and extends his ring hand towards the terrace, making out he is Pope.)

The Pope is dead, long live the pissing pope, the new papa of the world!
> (HER right hand above her, and moving from right to left, SHE "mocks" holding aloft a printed announcement to this effect.)

FREUD (Laughs.)
When I gather my inner circle, I may just give each a stone like this to mount into a gold ring.

MISS PORTERO
For your community of elect? . . . Now, that I would like.

FREUD (Examining at the stone.)
Was I hypnotized?

FREUD IN ROME: It Takes a Little Courage

MISS PORTERO
Perhaps this is a dream . . . A big dream.
  (FREUD is momentarily shaken.)
  (MISS PORTERO takes his hand.)

FREUD
One day you'll show me how you interpret dreams?

MISS PORTERO (Studying his palm.)
And, if you like, how to read posted letters, the inner text—

FREUD
You made sure I'd get room 51, didn't you?

MISS PORTERO
It affords a glorious view of Rome, don't you agree?

FREUD
Taking advantage of my superstitions. That's not playing fair.

MISS PORTERO (Still examining his hand.)
Shush! . . . . You must understand, here, I am a novice. But if I divine correctly, the day of your death will be one of deep remembrance.

FREUD
All over the world?

MISS PORTERO
Over all the world and for ages to come.

FREUD
  (HE eyes the large hourglass. Then, HE 'studies' the two rings on his finger—his wedding band and Jupiter ring—slowly spreading his fingers. Looking at her, HE decides to tell:)
Today is Julius's birthday. He would have been forty-four.—

MISS PORTERO
  (Off-guard, but collects self.)
I should have known! What better day for a new beginning?!

FREUD
Time for casting my final lot! . . .

(Handing her the oak cane, he picks up *The Aeneid.*)
(HE closes his eyes and extends his hand, palm up, for the golden bough; SHE places it in his palm.)

Let it fall where it will!

(Arriving at a lot, HE can't believe his eyes. He nods head to self. He sits down. He reads it aloud but to himself and with pleasure, savoring the words. As he recites, he seems to be praying, *davening,* as Jews in the synagogue do, moving the upper body.)

revocate animos, maestumque timorem mittite:
forsan et haec olim meminisse iuvabit.

MISS PORTERO

(While HE 'prays,' SHE retrieves *The Aeneid* from him.)
Now call back your courage, and have done with fear and sorrow. Someday, perhaps, remembering even this time of struggle will be a pleasure.

See! No crack in the spine!

FREUD

I know!

(HE looks at Jupiter ring, slowly spreading and closing his fingers.)

MISS PORTERO

(Searching in the oblong table drawer.)
The warriors of Aeneas' day had one especial supersti, er, tradition. Before battle they were washed and rubbed down with oil, a very special oil . . . . Ah!

(Removing a small dark blue vial, SHE savors the fragrance.)

FREUD

When in Rome—

(As HE starts to take off his shirt, SHE helps him from bottom up; touches his arms; very sensual.)

MISS PORTERO

Lucina! Ready the bath . . . "Of arms and the Jew I sing." (Singing.)

(SHE starts removing earrings, bracelet, blouse.)
[There is thunder and lightning.
Also a long SHOFAR BLAST. In the background there is *MOSES* with his shining visage; (if possible a huge statue

of *MOSES.*) Beside him is Botticelli's *VENUS* (model or picture?).

The Crucifix and the clay bust of MOSES light up, as do the paintings of Garibaldi, Aeneas, Virgin nursing Child, and the Sybyl.
The armoire re-opens revealing the Garibaldi outfit.]

(We hear LUCINA's laughter.)

END OF ACT II
CURTAIN

EPILOGUE (optional)

(The actor who had played PROSECUTOR alternates as NARRATOR and as 'FREUD'. The Strobe-lights segment the activities of MISS PORTERO and FREUD.)

(A CANTOR and CHOIR sing *Kol Nidre.*)

NARRATOR/'FREUD'
(A cigar in his mouth, HE is looking at the bust of Janus in his hands.
Spotting the audience, HE places the bust on a shelf.)

Several months after his pilgrimage to Rome, Freud gathers his first disciples,
(HE looks at his Jupiter head ring, slowly
spreading and closing his fingers.)
and he is on his way.
(HE heads for the Aeneas painting.)
On April 15, 1908, the fiftieth anniversary of Julius's death, the Psychological Wednesday Society is—on Freud's carried motion—re-named the Vienna Psychoanalytic Society. Freud, thereby, secretly dedicates the psychoanalytic movement to the memory of Julius, a movement which would establish his —and Julius's—Promised Land, a boundless peaceable brotherly world where *der Kinder,* the seed of Abraham, at long last are free to develop their talents and satisfy their needs.

Five years later, at Berggasse 19, Freud, on the afternoon of Sunday, the 25th of May 1913, hands each of his five favorite adherents an ancient stone engraved with a scene from classical antiquity to be mounted into a gold ring like his. In the Jewish calendar this date is the eighteenth of Iyar or *Lag B'Omer,* the feast day marking the end of a plague which was killing students of Rabbi Akiba Ben Joseph. It was Rabbi Akiba who gave Bar Kochba—famous for his near-successful Second Century revolt against the Romans—his name, which means "Son of a Star"—as in "There shall come a Star out of Jacob . . ." Calling itself the Committee, this community of elect, under Freud's leadership, works behind the scenes, directing and protecting the psychoanalytic movement. Gracing Freud's ancient stone is the head of Jupiter, who had ordered Aeneas into the underworld.

Up until the First World War, Freud visits *Moses* regularly. And, at some point, he appropriates the manner of his stoned-faced therapist:

('FREUD' sits in a chair behind a couch 'listening' to a patient. It could be the Jewish stone-thrower . . . A clock chimes. The patient gets up; nods to 'FREUD'. 'FREUD' takes a puff of his cigar; nods matter-of-factly to the patient. Patient leaves. 'FREUD' picks up a journal beside him and reads:

The [psychoanalyst] should be opaque to the patient . . .
(Closing the journal.)

Which is to say, an impenetrable, shadowy figure . . . a statue.
(HE responds to a "question":)
No, Freud and Herzl never did meet. Herzl died in 1904 at the age of 44 . . . Yes, Freud did write about the statue, an essay, "The Moses of Michelangelo." It was published anonymously . . . Why take chances? He began working on it Christmas Day, 1913,
(Turning pages of calendar on desk.)
and completed it *New Year's Day,* 1914 . . . Chance coincidence? . . .
(Puts journal down.)
(We hear Jewish glass fronts shattering, along with menacing music, or, perhaps, Wagner; followed by Nazi troops marching into Austria, with hearty *"Seig Heils"* from the populace.)
(A stone comes through a window.)

('FREUD', in the manner of a frail old man, lifts the stone; looks at it; nods head in recognition.)

It's come!

(Hate in his eyes, HE tightens his hand around the stone, and puts it in his jacket pocket. With dignity, HE gathers both Dream Book and *The Aeneid.* There's an upsurge of fire-place flame. He turns to it.)

In addition to Freud and Herzl, a third Austrian, an ardent admirer of Herr Dr. Karl Lueger, has his own solution to the Jewish problem.

[Turning from the fireplace, HE picks up Janus and MISS PORTERO'S Grecian urn, cradling the four objects the way Aeneas' father, Anchises, cradles the family gods.
Putting the urn on a column, HE places the two books and Janus on an antiquities-covered (formerly Miss Portero's) desk. HE sits down and begins to write with a pen. A cigar is in his left hand. HE's old, bent.]

In 1938, in exile in his temporary London home, 39 Elsworthy Road, N.W. 3, Freud pens   (HE mimes this:)
the final sentence of his last major attack on religion, *Moses and Monotheism* on Sunday, 17 July 1938—or the civil date of the Fast of Tammuz, the day of mourning commemorating both the Chaldean breach (586 B.C.E.) and the Roman breach (70 C.E.) of the walls of Jerusalem, which led to the destruction of the First and Second Temples. And this is fitting, for universal acceptance of the book's essential premise that Judaism stems from a patricide—that is, from the murder of Moses by the Israelites—would result in the destruction of the Jews' 'stone' fortress, the Torah. . . . Or, more to the point,
        (Patting each head of Janus:)
Moses; Jesus. . . . Caught together, hanged together!
        (He turns ear to audience member.)
Exactly! 'Root and Branch'! . . .

One year later, on Thursday, September 21st, 1939, Freud, 83, and wasting away from cancer of the mouth and jaw . . .
        ('FREUD' wearily takes off his jacket.)
and which he has borne stoically for 16 years, . . . 33 surgical procedures in all . . .
        ('FREUD' lies down on the couch.)
tells his friend and physician, Dr. Max Schur, the time has come.
        (While unrolling his sleeve, HE says in an old man's voice:)
    Now, it's nothing but torture and makes no sense any more . . .

        (Squints, but HE takes the morphine shot stoically.)
    I thank you . . . Tell Anna about this. (HIS eyes close.)
    (A SHOFAR BLAST!)

        (Startled, frightened, 'FREUD' opens his eyes.)

Freud doesn't die on the anniversary of Virgil's death as he had intended but two days later, Saturday, September 23rd, at 3 A.M.
        (HE puts on a skull cap and a prayer shawl, quietly praying
        as he puts on the latter.)
In the Jewish Calendar,
        (Now, HE is by the Sphinx.)
that fateful *Shabbos* is the Tenth Day of *Tishri,* which is the anniversary of Moses' descent from Mt. Sinai with the Tablets of the Law. That is, the day the Israelites received the Law.
        (The TABLETS of MOSES are lighted up.)
It is known as *Yom Kippur,* the Day of Atonement.

FREUD IN ROME: It Takes a Little Courage

(*Kol Nidre* is plainly heard.)
From Virgil's deathday to the Day of Atonement is a time span which bridges the two worlds of Freud, worlds which had shaped him.... Defiant to the very end, against Jewish tradition, Freud is cremated.
  (HE looks at the urn.)
On the occasion of Freud's death, the poet Auden wrote:
> If often he was wrong and at times absurd,
> to us he is no more a person
> Now but a whole climate of opinion
> Under whom we conduct our differing lives...

My own opinion? Sigmund Freud, the one with the terrible eyes ...
  (Removing the thrown stone from his pocket, HE places it by the urn.)

  (VITTORIO, now wearing a skullcap, and holding on to it to keep it from falling, rushes into the NARRATOR's arms ...)

  [HIS right ARM around VITTORIO, who may be eating a matzoh (although *Yom Kippur* is a day of fasting, youngsters are allowed to eat), the NARRATOR, with his left hand reaches in the urn and grabs a handful of Freud's ashes. HE looks at the ashes in his hand.... HE tosses the ashes in the air, in the direction of MISS PORTERO and FREUD.]

There was a *mensch!*

  [Unfolding like a Torah scroll are three large photos of Freud; the middle one is preeminent. This 'triptych' tells a story: on the left side, Freud as a boy, beside his father who has *The Philippson Bible* in his lap; in the center, a vigorous Freud with penetrating eyes, wearing the Jupiter ring; on the right side, Freud, in old age, still at work, pen in hand: "Die in harness!"

  The left and right photos fade. Superimposed on the center photo is the divine radiance. And *Kol Nidre* is cut short, as is the Shofar note. There is the beginning of a crack in the Dome; a boys' choir singing a Gregorian Chant stops in midair. And the Four Passover Questions are also cut short.

All the while, Freud's photo **glows and glows:** violet, purple, scarlet and gold. And outside the glorious dawn of a New Day.

> (If there is a good photo of Freud in his prime with pen in hand, we should use it. Perhaps this photo could slowly begin to multiply on the stage so that like a hundred TV monitors, all of these Freuds fill up the stage.)]

> (We hear LUCINA's laugh.)

END of EPILOGUE

Note: In the play, Freud states that his brother Julius was born on September 5th [1857]. The actual date, however, seems to be unknown.

Ann and Aaron Look on as Freud on his Deathbed Turns the Pages of Balzac's **La Peau de Chagrin**

Honore de Balzac in 1842; daguerreotype
by Louis-Auguste Bisson

Ann and Aaron Look on as Freud on his Deathbed Turns the Pages of Balzac's *La Peau de Chagrin*

A Play in Two Scenes

If you are to judge a man, you must know his secret thoughts, sorrows, and feelings; to know merely the outward events of a man's life would only serve to make a chronological table—a fool's notion of history.
—Honore De Balzac

CAST of CHARACTERS

Rabbi Aaron Handel — Sixty, looks like Sigmund Freud, beard and all.

Ann Handel — Rabbi Handel's wife, about the same age, attractive.

SETTING

The book-lined library-study of Rabbi Handel in Louisville, KY. On the mantle above the fireplace there is a large Menorah and also a 14-inch or so bronze-colored figurine of Michelangelo's *Moses*.

TIME

About 8:30 P.M., Wednesday, April 15, 2014—the 3rd day of Passover.

SCENE I

ANN
"Convinced"? Then you have no actual evidence that he had read the book before?
(Raising the translation, *The Wild Ass's Skin*.)

AARON
Right! Just the correspondences.

ANN
"Correspondences"?

AARON
Ann, he chose the book to relive his life.

ANN
To call up memories?

THE UNKNOWN FREUD: FIVE PLAYS . . .

AARON

Right! To stimulate or arouse recollections. Significant ones, as you'll see. ... Several pages into the book the main character, Raphael, a profoundly depressed 26-year-old intending to throw himself in the Seine that evening, enters a dusty antique shop where "statues seemed alive," and whose mysterious elderly owner has "the look of one of those Jewish types who serve artists as models for Moses." Ann, anything about Freud—his biography—come to you?

ANN

I draw a blank.

AARON

This ought to help. Among the shop's works of art there was an unspecified "magnificent" statue by Michelangelo—

ANN

Michelangelo's *Moses?*

AARON

Right! Freud's trials before the statue.

ANN

"Trials"?

AARON

Trials, ordeals. . . . Ann, now please read. Just my underlining.
(Hands her *The New York Review of Books*.)

ANN

The New York Review of Books?

AARON

It just came. The quote is from a memoir by Diane Johnson, who co-wrote *The Shining* with Stanley Kubrick. Please read, you'll understand.

ANN (SHE Reads)

Kubrick was concerned that the movie be scary, but what makes something scary? We sought the answer in the works of Freud, especially in his essay on the uncanny . . . for why things frighten us, and about what things are frightening, for instance the sudden animation of an inanimate figure. Dark is scary. Eyes can be scary.

Aaron, where is this heading?

AARON

For now, to this from Freud's 1914 essay "The Moses of Michelangelo," which he insisted be published anonymously. As I read, please keep in mind that the setting for *The Shining* is a deserted hotel . . .
    (HE reads with emphases:)
    . . . No piece of statuary has ever made a stronger impression on me . . . How often have I mounted the steep steps from the unlovely Corso Cavour to the *lonely* piazza where the *deserted* church stands, and have tried to support the *angry scorn of the hero's glance!* Sometimes I have crept cautiously out of the half-*gloom* of the interior as though I myself belonged to the mob *upon whom his eye is turned* . . .

ANN (Re-reads *NYR:*)

Dark is scary. Eyes can be scary—
For his paper on the uncanny Freud drew on his experience before Michelangelo's *Moses?*—

AARON

Right! The gloomy, deserted Church of St. Peter in Chains was a fitting setting for that glowering stone image to become Moses. Now, for six months starting in October 1885, when he was 29, just three years older than Raphael who is Balzac's main character, Freud was in Paris, the setting of the novel. He's there on a grant to study with the renowned neurologist, Charcot.

ANN

The book brought back his stay in Paris? Okay.

AARON

Now Raphael had fallen hard for a young courtesan, a certain Foedora, the belle of Paris. In time, however, he realizes that instead of that "unapproachable" narcissist that he actually loves another, his landlady's beautiful young daughter. Pauline worshipped him, voluntarily did all sorts of chores for this impoverished scholar then existing on practically nothing—and who, while boarding there, to quote Raphael, "had laid commands upon myself to see only a sister in Pauline . . ." "See only a *sister* in Pauline . . ." Ann, sound familiar?

ANN

Freud and Martha's younger sister, Minna?—

AARON

Whom Freud called *"Schwester."*

ANN

Another apparent correspondence? Okay.

AARON

As he is about to leave the dusty, dimly lit shop to head for the Seine, Raphael cries, "And now for death!" Spotting an opening, the ancient shop owner clasps Raphael's "wrists in a grip like a vice," directing Raphael's attention to an ass's skin, claiming that this magic skin marked with the "Seal of Solomon" grants its possessor any wish, but there is a catch, a big one—with each fulfilled wish not only does this magic skin shrink but so does one's life. And, Ann, what has Raphael to lose? He's penniless and his dream of becoming renowned by "opening up new paths in science," it is clear, would never be realized—

ANN

"Opening up new paths in science."—Another identification with Raphael. Okay.

AARON

The year before leaving for Paris, Freud writes Martha, then his fiancee, that he has destroyed his "notes, letters, treatises," etc. And his reason? To elude his biographers! Quote: " Each one of them will be right in his opinion of 'The Development of the Hero,' and I am already looking forward to seeing them go astray."

ANN

Freud's early dreams of glory returned. I already got that!

AARON

Dreams of glory which persisted. Now, having plugged along, denied himself for three years, with nothing to show for it, and about to commit suicide anyway, Raphael enters into a compact with that thin old "specter with green eyes—eyes with quiet malevolence." And thanks to that "oriental leather talisman with terrible powers" he becomes wealthy, obscenely so—and in short order, he and Pauline marry. And in no time, this otherwise indestructible skin is, as you can imagine, reduced considerably. Raphael, now fearful for his life, not only banishes Pauline from their bed but also from their magnificent house—even orders his servant, Jonathan, to make sure she never enters.

ANN

To keep from being aroused?

AARON

No Pauline; no lusting her—

ANN

Just a living death. Some choice! . . . Wait! Aaron, after finishing it, Freud, you say, told Dr. Shur that the novel, because it deals with "shrinking and starvation," was an appropriate book for him to have read.

AARON

Right!

ANN

So, supposing Freud's relationship with Minna was, as you claim, actually evoked—then "starvation" pertains more to his yearning for—his hungering after—his "*Schwester*" Minna than to his difficulty eating due to his oral cancer—

AARON

For which he had undergone 33 operations since 1923. That, Ann, is exactly how I see it.

ANN

There's a new novel about Minna being his mistress—

AARON

I know. That's garbage!—

ANN

"Garbage"? Maybe you don't wish to believe it.

AARON

Ann, I'll say it again, garbage . . . Still, somewhere along the way, Freud's passion for Martha was transferred on to Minna, who was four years younger, and more intellectual—

ANN

At least it stayed in the family.

AARON (Shakes his head.)

Around 1895 or 1896, Minna, whose former fiancé died of tuberculosis about ten years earlier, moved in with Freud and Martha, and became a permanent member of the household, that is to say, not only at Berggasse 19, but, also, after the family emigrated to London—that was in June 1938, after the invasion of Austria. . . . By giving him courage to persevere during "the years of struggle," as Freud called them—well before he became FREUD—when he desperately needed it, Minna, without her knowing it, had helped him prepare the ground—

ANN

For his Promised Land?

AARON

You remembered?

ANN

A secular world where anti-Semitism is unknown.

AARON

Right! An enlightened world in which the seed of Abraham can move freely across frontiers.

ANN

And he actually believed he could pull it off?

AARON

Let's say that he hoped against hope. Now, unlike Theodor Herzl, Freud doesn't broadcast his Promised Land. You see, Ann, secrecy is essential. His creation, psychoanalysis, must not be seen, like Herzl's Zionist movement, as a Jewish National Affair. And, Ann, a sexual scandal—especially with his wife's sister—would jeopardize the realization of his Promised Land, wouldn't it?—

ANN

Let alone what it would do to Martha and their six little ones...

AARON

Freud had firsthand knowledge of contraceptive failure—the birth of his last child, Anna. Regardless, he couldn't have lived with himself.

ANN

So, to be clear, according to you, Freud, like Raphael, was torn—but in his case, it was between his love, his passionate love, for Minna and his mission, his redemptive mission?

AARON

Right!

ANN

What a cruel predicament.

AARON

In the movie about Freud and Jung, you remember Jung's lover, his patient Sabina Spielrein?

ANN

Who stabbed him with a letter opener? How can I forget?!

AARON

In 1914, Freud penned this to Spielrein, then twenty-eight, who was still longing for Jung.   (HE reads:)
> . . . Warm your life's intentions with your inner fire instead of burning yourself up with it. Nothing is stronger than controlled and sublimated passion. You can achieve nothing while you are at loggerheads with yourself.

ANN

And Freud, you believe, took his own advice?

AARON

To the letter. Ann, all his energies went into making his Promised Land a reality. Whatever passion he might have had for Minna went there.

ANN

Aaron, assuming you have pegged Freud correctly, why did it fall to him to deliver us from anti-Semitism? To avenge the thug's knocking Jakob's new *shtreimel* into the mud and ordering him off the pavement?

AARON

Hearing his grey-haired papa on one of their Sunday walks around the Ringstrasse relate that horror when Jakob was a young man—well, it was nothing if not traumatic, especially Jakob's not taking up for himself, but meekly going into the gutter and picking up his muddy *Shabbat* hat—

ANN

It's as though God Himself had died.

AARON

You could say that. Still, that fateful walk when Sigismund was ten or twelve wasn't determinative. Nor was the miserable Dreyfus Affair or his having grown up in Vienna, Europe's most anti-Semitic city.

ANN

Well, what then?

AARON

A dreadful return of the repressed. Let me explain. After Jakob passed away—that was in October, 1896—Freud, feeling uprooted—began his systematic self-analysis, mainly by studying his dreams. Soon after, some time in 1897, he discovers that he is a Cain—

ANN

"A Cain"?

AARON

A brother-killer. This is from Freud's letter to Wilhelm Fliess, a nose and throat specialist in Berlin, then his best friend—it was written on October 3rd.
 (HE reads:)
> ... I welcomed my one-year-younger brother (who died within a few months) with ill wishes and real infantile jealousy, and ... his death left the germ of guilt in me.

Ann, Freud couldn't shake his belief that he had killed his baby brother, Julius—

ANN

With his hateful wishes? As brilliant as he was, and whose god was reason, he actually believed this?

AARON

Yes, against his better judgment.

ANN

How old was he?

AARON

At the time? Sigismund was twenty-three months old.

ANN

One more apparent correspondence, a dreadful correspondence. Death follows desire.

AARON

Throughout his life Freud had migraines and suffered from periodic depressions. His unconscious guilt had to have played a role.

ANN

"Unconscious guilt"?

AARON

An oppressive sense of guilt below the threshold of consciousness. Take, for instance, Freud's and Martha's first home, an apartment in a building commissioned by Emperor Franz Joseph. It was built on the site where a theatre had burned down. Over 400 died. The rent went to support the orphans, most, if not all, Jewish—

ANN

Freud's rent, an atonement for killing Julius—this is what you believe?

AARON

Right! An unconscious atonement. Well, after the return or surfacing of his having played Cain to Julius's Abel, Freud, oppressed by his sense of guilt, secretly resolves to redeem himself by delivering other Juliuses, and Sarahs, from anti-Semitism.—

ANN

This is your reading?

AARON

Right! And that very year, 1897, this haunted Cain not only comes up with the Oedipus complex but also a dazzling derivative: the God-idea stems from the Father complex. That is to say, God the Father is a mere projection out on to the universe of the oedipal boy's idealized perception of his own father. With this godsend—or God-send—Freud would cut the ground out from under religion, and, thereby, deliver, for once and for all, the seed of Abraham: no God; no Law, no Judaism, no Christianity, no miserable anti-Semitism.

ANN

Root and branch. Okay.

AARON

Now, Freud keeps God's humble beginnings under wraps, that is, until he'd gain major recognition. You see, first he must be seen as a scientist of the first order.

ANN

An essential precondition. Okay.

AARON

Ann, in his last major assault on religion, *Moses and Monotheism*—it was completed in late 1938—Freud, at long last, reveals his explanation for anti-Semitism.

ANN

Which is?

AARON

In essence, here it is ...The good Christian, not having the moral courage to acknowledge his hatred for his religion which obliges him to renounce his aggressive tendencies and illicit sexual desires, displaces this unconscious hatred onto the ones responsible for his misery, the ones who handed him his chains, the Jews. That is to say, the Apostles—all Jews—had enchained him.

ANN

And because Christianity and that scourge go hand in hand—are inextricable—Judaism must be sacrificed?

AARON

To Freud, there is no alternative. Now, before setting others free from their religious chains, he intends to set himself free from the Law. But how?...

Well, Ann? ...

(As HE glances at the figurine of *Moses* ...)

ANN

Michelangelo's *Moses?!* Hm! A fitting prop.

AARON

Except a mere prop it isn't. You see, Ann, in the same way that for Roman Catholics the Host is a symbol, that magnificent statue in the gloomy Church of St. Peter in Chains is, for Freud, a symbol.

ANN

The statue is Moses?

AARON

Right! Ann, whenever Freud "crept cautiously out of the half-gloom of the interior," psychical reality was in play—that is to say, the imposing Tablet-bearing Moses stationed in his dark Roman chamber was, for Freud, Yahweh's Messenger. In other words, the world's greatest representation of that great man of our people was Freud's totem.

ANN

His, his "totem"?

AARON

His personal totem, that is to say, Moses himself or his shade.

ANN

Aaron, that's crazy!

AARON

Mortals, according to Freud, are not made to keep secrets, and, Ann, the father of psychoanalysis was he not a mortal? In his personal copy of *The Psychopathology of Everyday Life*—the 1904 edition—Freud, for his eyes only, jotted quote, "My own superstition has its roots in suppressed ambition, immortality." "*Immortality*"! Well, were he to become the new Moses, both as liberator of his besieged nation and as the new moral educator of humanity, would he then not be immortal?

ANN

Moses is dead, long live the new Moses, Sigmund Freud—Such megalo—

AARON

Whose *one* Law would be ...would be?... Hint—an *enlightened* world—

ANN
"Know Thyself!"

AARON
You got it! . . . My mind is slipping. Ann, where were we?

ANN
With Freud on Mt. Sinai—or was it Mt. Olympus?

AARON
(Shakes his head; reads from *The Wild Ass's Skin,* with emphases:)

. . . and [Raphael] beheld Moses and the Hebrews and the desert . . .
(Now quotes the Torah, Exodus 34:30; 33:)

And when Aaron and all the children of Israel saw Moses, behold the skin of his face shone; and they were afraid to come nigh him . . . And *till* Moses had done speaking with them, he put a veil on his face.

Of course, Ann, in his gloomy chamber, Yahweh's Messenger has no veil covering his terrible radiance.

ANN
"No veil covering his terrible radiance." Aaron, you've really lost it!

AARON
For his 35th birthday, May 6, 1891, Jakob gave Freud a re-bound volume of the family Bible as, quote, "a reminder of love from your father, who loves you with everlasting love."—Ann, that's a partial translation of Jakob's Hebrew dedication. Now, the frontispiece of this Bible, *The German-Hebrew Philippson's Bible,* is an illustration of Moses with rays of light shooting up from both sides of his forehead. Imagine that lithograph's effect on Sigismund when he first saw it as a seven-year-old.
(Leafing through *The Wild Ass's Skin.*)
—Ah! Ann, tell me that when Freud came across this that it didn't call up his experience in that dark Church before *Moses*/Moses with his awful radiance.
(HE reads:)

. . . only about the size of a fox's skin, the wild ass's skin seemed to fill the *deep shadows of the place with such brilliant rays* that it looked like a small comet.

ANN
Aaron, you seek, you find. A real Kabbalist—

AARON
Ann, at the seminary this "Kabbalist" was exhorted to return to the texts. Well, Ann, in that famous paragraph from his essay on Michelangelo's *Moses,* the German word "*Blick*" denotes the glance of Moses—as in, "I tried to support the angry scorn of the hero's glance!"

ANN
Okay?

AARON
Now in this German-English dictionary, please look up *Blick* with "ck."

ANN (Looking at the worn book.)
Cassell's, 1906?

AARON
Goodwill.

ANN (Shakes her head.)
Blick—"Touches of Light."

AARON
Now how about the verb form?

ANN
Blicken—"to glance, to look; to appear shining; to shine."
(SHE looks at Aaron.)

AARON (Retrieving *Cassell's*)
Chance coincidence that for the statue's glance Freud chooses a word that can allude to the *mana,* that shining or terrible supernatural power, the radiance of Moses? Now, Ann, look at *anblitzen* (Pointing at word) which stems from the same root—

ANN
Aaron, you already made your point.

AARON
Humor me.

ANN (Reluctantly takes *Cassell's*)
Anblitzen—"to cast a furious look upon, to dart a look upon; to throw a ray on."

Impressive.   (SHE is about to hand him *Cassell's*)

AARON (Refusing *Cassell's*)
From *Blick*, Ann, let's now turn to the word that's translated as "support," as in Freud's trying "to support *the angry scorn of the hero's glance.*"—

ANN

Aaron!

AARON

After this we're through with *Cassell's*. Ann, I promise.
> (Writes on a yellow legal page "*Standhalte*n: support"; hands it to Ann.)

ANN (Reads *Cassell's*)
> *Standhalten*—'To withstand; to resist; to hold one's own; to stand firm"

AARON

Just so! Freud aims to *Halt!* (mimes a soldier halting!), *stand* defiantly before *Moses*/Moses and not be budged; he'd take anything that he throws his way, the potentially fatal radiance included.

ANN (Returning *Cassell's* to Aaron)
Aaron, I shouldn't encourage you, but there seems to be one other, er, correspondence.

AARON

And that is?

ANN

Freud's mother believed that he was destined to become a great man.

AARON

And never let him forget it.

ANN

And, Aaron, just what made Amalia believe in her *goldener* Sigi's great destiny?

AARON

The caul—his having been born in a caul on his head.
> (AARON leafs through *The Interpretation of Dreams*.)

Ah!
> At the time of my birth an old peasant-woman had prophesied to my proud mother that with her firstborn child she had brought a great man into the world . . .

ANN

On the one hand, Raphael's magic hide, and, on the other, Freud's prophetic caul. A kind of a symmetry, wouldn't you say?

AARON

Not bad. Not bad at all. Hm! The ass's skin was engraved with the "Seal of Solomon." Ann, Freud was born Sigismund Schlomo after Jakob's father—Which raises the question, Did this Solomon then see the caul—?

ANN

As his seal of authority? Aaron, that's a stretch.

AARON

Is it? After all, this Schlomo or Solomon was name-sensitive.

ANN

Aaron, how hard would it be to get permission to look at the book?

AARON

For Freud's jottings or underlinings?

ANN

Worth a try.

AARON

Klein would vouch for us. Even so, I doubt that The Sigmund Freud Archives would give us permission.... Now, as for the totem business, it can be traced back to *goldener* Sigi's other mother, that is to say, if bread can be Jesus, what's to keep stone, marble, from being Moses? Ann, bear with me. Amalia was just 22 when Julius died, and the month before his death, her brother, also named Julius, had died. And with Jakob, a struggling textile merchant trying to keep the family afloat financially and with Amalia, again pregnant, and suffering a double grief, his faithful nanny—in all but name—became his mother—

ANN

Filling the maternal void—

AARON

Giving her the opportunity to instill a Catholic sensibility. Accordingly, she took him to Mass regularly, transforming her lost, precocious Jewish charge into a good little Catholic—or tried to.

ANN

"Give us a child."

AARON

Right. Even though dismissed when Freud was two-and-a-half—for stealing, even his toys—it was long enough for her to have left, ever so lovingly, her mark. Not that his instructress in the faith had him baptized—though come to think of it, since she had a free hand, she very well may have. At any rate, in addition to his Jewish sensibility, Freud possessed a Roman Catholic sensibility, of which he was fully aware by the time he resolves to eradicate anti-Semitism. That he eventually summoned courage to enter the Eternal City is a wonder. You see, Ann—

ANN

Again, this all-important visit, when was this?

AARON

In September, 1901. He was 45 and believed that he had just six years left to live—

ANN

That he'd die at 51?

AARON

In his eyes, he was in a race against time. It's in his Dream Book, quote: "... my fear of 51 years being the limit of my life". . . . Now, during those four years, not only was Freud readying himself for his dreaded face-off with *Moses*/Moses—and who really can be prepared for Moses?—he also was readying himself for—

ANN

The awakening or re-awakening in the Seat of Catholicism of his 'Catholic head'.

AARON

"Catholic head." That's one way of describing it. And the anticipated stirring up of his suppressed Roman Catholic sensibility, why should that prospect trouble him? Ann? . . . Hint. What was he all about?

ANN

Ultimately? Redemption . . . *Self*-redemption!

AARON

And, were his broken through Roman Catholic tendencies to prevail, overwhelm his resistance, he'd then—

ANN

Acknowledge Christ—

AARON

Which, Ann, is both a fear and a wish—a suppressed wish.

ANN

Making the Seat of Catholicism potentially his road to Damascus—

AARON
More so, since in addition to redemption, conversion to Catholicism holds out for this haunted Cain the promise of reuniting with baby Julius in Paradise. Which brings us back to Raphael and the ancient antiquities dealer whom even his "plump-faced young shopman with red hair" claims not to "know what he is." Ann, please—

ANN (Reads;)
"You wish to see Raphael's portrait of Jesus Christ, *monsieur*?"... The sympathy and love, and the gentle serenity in the divine face, exerted an instant sway over the younger spectator—

AARON
Thanks. Now compare this—it's from Freud's letter to Martha dated December 20, 1883. He had just visited Dresden's Zwinger Museum—Incidentally, Dresden plates were in the antique shop.
(HE reads:)
But the picture that really captivated me was the "Maundy Money," by Titian . . .
Ann, this Titian painting, it's actually titled *The Tribute Money*—

ANN
"Maundy Money" is a slip of the pen?

AARON
Right! It's not a simple case of misremembering. Repression was at work, as you'll see. I'm continuing:
(HE resumes reading:)
This head of Christ, my darling, is the only one that enables even people like ourselves to imagine that such a person did exist. Indeed, it seemed that I was compelled to believe in the eminence of this man because the figure is so convincingly presented. And nothing divine about it, just a noble countenance, far from beautiful yet full of seriousness, intensity, profound thought, and deep inner compassion; if these qualities do not exist in this picture, then there is no such thing as physiognomy. I would love to have gone away with it, but there were too many people about. . . . So I went away with a full heart.

ANN
Okay, Freud, like Balzac's protagonist, was moved by an Italian Renaissance master's Christ. But, Aaron, Freud states, quote, there's "nothing divine" about Titian's Christ.

AARON

"I went away with a full"—that is, Ann, a heavy—"heart." Doesn't this suggest that when he misnamed the painting that Freud's suppressed Catholic sensibilities were stirred up but repressed?

ANN

Suggests, yes. Indicates, no.

AARON

Ann, this is from a follow-up letter written four days after his first visit to Notre Dame on a Sunday in November:

(HE reads:)

My first impression on entering was a sensation I have never had before: "This is a church"... I have never seen anything so movingly serious and somber...

"Movingly " Ann, "movingly"! And in a subsequent letter he writes of "coming out of of Notre Dame...with an entirely new idea of *perfection*." No, Ann, that faithful Czech nanny who had taken Sigismund to Mass in the Notre Dame of his Moravian birthplace—Freiberg's the Church of the Nativity of *Our Lady*—had prepared him well, too well—

ANN

For converting?

AARON

For Christianity.

ANN

Aaron, you realize, don't you? that you have yet to make your case.

AARON

Ann, there's a good reason that analysts emphasize the importance of early childhood.

ANN

The plastic stage of development. Okay?

AARON (HE writes on a yellow pad.)

"The plastic stage," when each one of us is essentially shaped.... Now, Ann, please begin again with "The sympathy..."

ANN

Aaron, is this necessary?

AARON

To make my case, yes.

ANN (Reads:)

The sympathy and love, and the gentle serenity in the divine face, exerted an instant sway over the younger spectator. Some influence falling from heaven bade cease the burning torment that consumed the marrow of his bones. The head of the Saviour of mankind seemed to issue from among the shadows. . . . An aureole of light shone out brightly from his hair—

AARON

Thanks. Now, in the Eternal City were Freud—a haunted Cain suffering from "burning torment that consumed the marrow of his bones"—to prevail over the temptation to acknowledge Christ as his savior he'd exorcise his "Catholic head"—or so he believes. And, in this regard, he expects that his greatest test or trial would be in the Sistine Chapel with its powerful works of religious art—especially, Ann, before another masterpiece, this one also by Michelangelo—the huge, over 2,100 square foot incense-blackened *Last Judgment* on the Chapel's altar wall.

ANN

Speculation upon speculation.

AARON

Now, Ann, if there is one quality that Michelangelo's Christ lacks, it is Sympathy; Justice, he has plenty of. It's not for nothing that George Brandes characterizes Michelangelo's depiction of Jesus spurning the damned as, quote, "Christ as Jove, hurling thunderbolts."

ANN

The evidence! Aaron, the evidence!

AARON

I'm getting to it. In September 1897, several weeks after making his resolve, Freud travels to Orvieto—it's about 80 miles north of Rome—where in its Cathedral, the Duomo, he gets to see for the first time, Signorelli's *Last Judgment*.

ANN

To steel himself for Michelangelo's Doomsday?

AARON

Right! Not only is Signorelli's *Last Judgment* the immediate precursor to Michelangelo's *Last Judgment,* but, more importantly, it informed Michelangelo's *Last Judgment.*—Ann, Listen to this from Brandes whom Freud valued. It's from his Michelangelo biography:

(HE finds the passage:)
As for the nudity of the figures, the dead rising from the ground and Charon and his ferry, Luca Signorelli pointed the way.

ANN

All very interesting, But let's just back up. From Balzac's novel Freud's mind travels back in time over forty years to Orvieto in 1897? And just how do you know this?

AARON.

In the dusty showroom where the pact was made there was an Etruscan vase. And on that visit Freud came across, quote, (reads from *The Interpretation of Dreams:*) "an excavated Etruscan grave near Orvieto." You see, Ann, Etruscans had settled in that region well before the Romans or there was even a town named Orvieto—

ANN

Aaron, that's pretty thin.

AARON

Thin or not, the visit was critical! . . .

ANN

And so it simply had to have been called up.

AARON

You be the judge. In September 1898, or twelve months after visiting Orvieto, Freud writes Fliess of his recent failure to, quote, "find the name of the renowned painter who did the *Last Judgment* in Orvieto, the greatest I have seen so far." Ann, "so far"!

ANN

Okay, in Freud's mind there is a connection between the two *Last Judgments*.

AARON

"[T]he greatest I have seen"*so far*"! Don't you see?, Freud intends to take his stand before Michelangelo's *Last Judgment.*

ANN

And this is your mighty evidence?

AARON

Not quite. Continuing, Freud relates that though he recalled Signorelli's first name, Luca, he failed to recall his last name, and that instead the surnames of two other Renaissance painters, Botticelli and Boltraffio, came to him. He goes on to observe: "It is clear why Botticelli had moved into the foreground; only *Signor* was repressed." And " *Signor,*" my dear, means "Lord."

ANN

But, Aaron, just how does Freud, *himself,* account for his failure to recall Signorelli's last name?

AARON

Essentially, it is this. During the lapse he was repressing the recent suicide of a patient, news of which he had learned about on this trip. Or, as Freud writes:
> (HE reads:)
> ... I forgot *the one thing against my will* while I wanted to forget *the other thing intentionally.*

Freud had learned of the tragedy in Trafoi, which, he notes, is similar to "traf-fio"—as in Bol*traffio*. But, Ann, once again, Freud is holding back. You see, Freud is afraid that like his patient who had taken his life that he, too, may be suffering from an "incurable sexual problem"—in his case, his emotional or libidinal ties to Jakob. That is to say, Freud suffers from an unresolved Father complex. But in the Eternal City were he to heal himself, surmount his Father complex—become his own person–then, no longer submissive to Will of the Father—be the Father Jakob Freud, Moses, or Yahweh—he could get on with his messianic mission.

ANN

A potentially *suicidal* mission. Remember the *mana!*

AARON.

Ann, that's terrible.

ANN

So is the fatal *mana.*

AARON

Laugh, but you're right. Recall Yahweh cautioning Moses on Mt. Sinai, "Thou canst not see my face. For there shall no man see me and live." ...

ANN

Like Balzac's Raphael, Freud fears for his life. One more correspondence. Okay.

AARON

Now, let's turn to "Bo," as in Botticellli and Boltraffio. Ann, what comes to you?

ANN

"Bo"? Well, Buddha, he got his illumination under the Bo tree.

AARON
I'm talking about Judaism and I get Buddhism! . . . Ann, how about our Tree of Life?, specifically the Torah portion covering the first Passover, that is, the section Bo which was an integral component of Freud's beloved Hebrew and Scriptures instructor Professor Hammerschlag's curricula at the *Sperlgymnasium*—and which of course begins:

> And the Lord said unto Moses, Go in unto Pharaoh: for I have hardened his heart, and the heart of his servants, that I might show these my signs before him.

With clear "signs," Bo or Exodus 10:1 to 13 reveals both Yahweh's terrible Justice, especially that dreadful last plague, the death of the firstborn son—and His Mercy, our deliverance from Egyptian bondage—

ANN
Setting the stage for the revelation of the Law at Mt. Sinai. Okay.

AARON
Ann, in "Bo," as Freud knows only too well, Yahweh commands the Israelites:
> . . . all the firstborn of man among thy children shalt thou redeem.

ANN
Let's see! Having spared the firstborn of the Israelites when He killed the firstborn of the Egyptians, Yahweh makes a claim on Freud's firstborn son. And only by being pious—by not transgressing—could this Israelite redeem his firstborn son.

AARON
Right! Yahweh must be obeyed—or else!

ANN
During the Signorelli lapse, the Torah portion Bo, then, was called up?

AARON
Right! Evoked, but repressed.

ANN
Repressed? Because Bo is so threatening?

AARON
Right—too threatening for him to become conscious of

ANN

Aaron, again, this is what *you* infer. But, how does Freud, himself, *actually* account for the substitute names beginning with Bo?"

AARON

He doesn't.

ANN

He doesn't?! His words, please.

AARON

All right, give me a second. (looks it up; reads:)
> The repetition of the sound 'Bo' in the two substitutive names might have led a novice to suppose that it belonged to the missing name as well, but I took great care to steer clear of that expectation.

Ha! You better believe he steered "clear of that expectation"!—The expectation of trouble!... Ann, you've just cued me in.... Please read this. It's from the first edition of *The Interpretation of Dreams*. Freud has yet to enter the city of his dreams.

ANN (Reads:)
> For a long time to come, no doubt, I shall have to continue to satisfy that longing in my dreams; for at the season of the year when it is possible for me to travel, residence in Rome must be avoided for reasons of health.

Okay?

AARON

Ostensibly, Freud, here, is alluding to his fear of contracting malaria in Rome, but, Ann, "reasons of health" may it not be, in addition, and more importantly, a veiled allusion to Freud's fear of the last and most horrific of the Bo plagues, the death the firstborn son?

ANN

Already Freud is responsible, he feels, for the death of one child, baby Julius. And yet he would stay on this potentially catastrophic path, one for which not only Martin but all his other little ones "unto the third and fourth generation" would pay for their papa's rebellion?

AARON

That's the question isn't it?!—But, Ann, for Freud, not for us... Now, the day after arriving in Orvieto, he makes a twelve mile side-trip to the little town of Bolsena where, during one particular mass, drops of blood seeped from the Communion Wafer.

ANN
This alleged bloody miracle, when was this?

AARON (Looks it up)
In 1263, The Orvieto Cathedral was built in memory of the Miracle. For the faithful, the blood-stained chalice-cloth is *the* treasure of the Duomo. Today, *the Santo Corporale* is on open display daily but wasn't so when Freud visited Orvieto. The chalice-cloth was then stored—as it had been for centuries—in a silver-gilt and enamel reliquary depicting the miracle. And, Ann, here is where Raphael, the Renaissance master, again enters the picture. You see, about 250 years after the alleged incident, Raphael—he was a favorite of Freud's—portrays the miracle in *The Mass of Bolsena*. Commenting on this mural in the Papal Palace, Vasari, a contemporary of Raphael, makes the following observation in his *Lives of the Painters,* which, as part of his preparation, Freud may very well have read. At any rate, Ann, according to Ernest Jones, in the 1890's Freud in his correspondence referred to Vasari's *Lives*.
(Reads with emphases:)
> One sees the priest, as he says Mass, flushing with shame as he realizes that through his disbelief in the doctrine of transubstantiation he has made the Host on the corporale turn to blood. *With terror in his eyes, distraught and dumbfounded* in the presence of the congregation, *he hardly knows what to do;* and in the movements of his hands *one can almost see the fear and trembling* to be expected in such circumstances.

Ann, on the fresco's right side, anachronistically taking in this extraordinary 13th century scene, is the figure of Pope Julius the Second, but for whom, since he had commissioned Michelangelo to create the statue, there would have been no *Moses*/Moses for Freud, with "fear and trembling," to stand defiantly before. . . . As for the Miracle's blood-stained relic, Freud, more than likely, did not get to see it—

ANN
Wait just one minute! Wouldn't he have made it a point to visit Orvieto when this evidence for transubstantiation is actually displayed?

AARON
Right! For no other reason than to test himself: "Like that young doubting Bohemian priest would I become a believer, that is, in my case would I, overwhelmed by the sight of the chalice-cloth, acknowledge, on the spot, that God is not a mere wish-fulfillment stemming from a longing for the father but that He actually exists—and that He is Jesus Christ 'whose blood . . . cleanseth us

from all sin'?" "*All sin,*" Ann, even brother-murder—In one of the galleries there was quote, "a sleeping child modeled in wax—"

ANN

Mingled among how many other depicted specimens, hundreds? Aaron, you realize, don't you, that just now you've all but confessed that you've erected a house of cards?

AARON

I believe that he was misled by his guidebook.

ANN

Freud "misled by his guide book"?

AARON

Baedeker's Italy From The Alps To Naples.
         (Hands Ann the 1909 English translation)

ANN

"Louis Ochs, Louisville, KY." Goodwill?

AARON

Locust Grove book sale. Freud consulted it the year before, when he visited Florence in 1896. Just the underlining, please.

ANN (Reads:)
    behind the altar is a reliquary of 1337 containing the blood-stained chalice-cloth or *corporale* connected with the Miracle of Bolsena, shown on great festivals only.

AARON

Thanks. Freud arrived in Orvieto on September 8 or the Feast Day of The Birth of Mary—

ANN

A festival in honor of the birth of Jesus' mother.—An apparently suitable Holy Day for the *corporale* to be on open display. Okay?

AARON

That's what one would have thought—including, I suspect, Freud. Well, he got to Orvieto that evening, but even if he had arrived there earlier that day he still wouldn't have had a chance to view it, that is, unless he bribed the sacristan. You see, the *Corporale* was then shown on two Holy Days only: Easter Sunday and the Holy Day instituted in memory of the miracle, namely, Corpus Christi, aka The Feast of the Real Presence of Jesus Christ in the Blessed Sacrament –

ANN

"This is my body . . . this is my blood . . ."

AARON

And, here is where—no pun intended—Freud's "Maundy Money" slip enters the picture. You see, Ann, Maundy pertains to Jesus washing the feet of his disciples on the occasion of the Last Supper, which, of course, is when Christ established the Eucharistic ceremony.

ANN

So much, then, for there being "nothing divine" about Titian's Christ!—

AARON

In the Zwinger museum, right! . . . Well, Ann, have I made my case that Freud, well before the surfacing in 1897 of his having 'murdered' baby Julius, had viewed, albeit unconsciously, conversion—being cleansed by the blood of Christ—as his possible ticket to redemption?

ANN

I don't know about psychonalysts, but to me you've made your case. Still, Aaron, you seem to have blinded yourself.

AARON

Blinded myself?

ANN

To the elfin in the gloomy showroom.

AARON

Elphin?

ANN

The malevolent green-eyed elfin . . . If Freud's 'Roman Catholic head' believes in the Last Judgment, then it must also believe that Lucifer—as in Luca—exists. And, Aaron, what's to keep Freud from entering, like Raphael, into a Faustian pact with that tempter? What's he to lose? His inner torment?

AARON

But sell his soul for what?

ANN

Freud, as you say, is in a race against time. Well, how about—?

AARON

Time to prepare the ground! . . .
    (Leafing through Freud's 1898 essay on the Signorelli lapse.)
Ann, listen to this:
> . . . I was able to conjure up the pictures with greater sensory vividness than is usual with me. I saw before my eyes with especial sharpness [Signorelli's] self-portrait—with a serious face and folded hands—which he has put in a corner of one of the pictures, next to the portrait of his predecessor in the work, Fra Angelico . . .

ANN

Okay?

AARON

Well, in this particular fresco of Signrorelli's *Last Judgment* cycle in Orvieto, the Devil counsels the Antichrist, whispering in his left ear. According to Paul Vitz, Signorelli's bearded Antichrist resembles Freud, but I don't see it.

ANN

What do you think, did he or didn't he?—

AARON

Make a Faustian pact? Though he may have been tempted, I doubt it.

ANN

Or, you'd like not to think so. To tell the truth, Aaron, neither would I, neither would I.
    (Heads for computer; types "Signorelli Antichrist.")

AARON

Ann, e-mail can wait!

ANN (Finds the fresco)

I also don't see a resemblance between Freud and Signorelli's Antichrist.

AARON

The question, though, is, Did Freud?

ANN

So, Aaron, are we now ready to head for the Eternal City, circa September 1901?

AARON

But first one more preparation. On August 8th, three weeks before boarding the train for Rome, Freud, who doesn't particularly care for music, sets out for Salzburg to attend a performance of Mozart's *Don Giovanni*, which he had seen before—

ANN

Ah! The banquet scene!

AARON

Right! The fateful encounter between Don Juan and the marble statue of the *Commandatore,* the father-figure he had killed—

ANN

One more stone come to life.

AARON

Because he had shaped us by giving us the Law, Moses, according to Freud, is *the* ancestor—the father—of each and every Jew. And since he intends, by destroying the Law, to kill Moses, it is reasonable to assume that Freud identifies with that father-killer, Don Juan.

ANN

Okay, I get the picture—On the one hand, Freud and *Moses* /Moses, and, on the other, Don Juan and the *Commandatore*/Commandatore –

AARON

Right! ... Refusing to repent of his sins, Don Juan wrests his hand free from the *Commandatore*'s "icy clasp," thereby sealing his fate—

ANN

The "icy clasp"—much like the antiquarian's clasping Raphael's "wrists in a grip like a vice"—

AARON

Right!   (Making liberal use of a libretto translation:)
 Smoke and flames rise and begin to envelop the sinner, while the *Commandatore,* moving away, announces, "Ah! there is no more time." Then from below a chorus of demons summons Don Juan to Hell where "worse is in store for you ." Terrified, he cries, "*Ah! che inferno, che terror!*—and sinks to Hell, uttering one final scream, "Ah!."

ANN

What comes to me is that solitary anguished soul in *The Scream* covering his ears.

AARON
Ann, picture, if you can, Freud as he tries to contain himself.

ANN
It may be a dress rehearsal—but what a rehearsal!

AARON
Ann, you'll agree, to steel Freud for both Michelangelo's *Moses* and his *Last Judgment* a more fitting scene than this gripping climax would be difficult, if not impossible, to find.

ANN
Aaron, the punishment of Korah and his cohorts is structurally similar—uncannily so.

AARON (Reads from Numbers 16:31–35:)
And it came to pass, as [Moses] had made an end of speaking all these words, that the ground clave asunder that *was* under them. And the earth opened her mouth, and swallowed them up, and their houses, and all the men that *appertained* unto Korah, and all *their* goods. They, and all that *appertained* to them, went down alive into the pit; and the earth closed upon them and they perished from among the congregation...And all Israel that *were* round about them fled at the cry of them . . . And there came out a fire from the LORD . . .

ANN
Conceivably, then, during the Signorelli lapse, Korah's revolt against Moses in Sinai was called up.

AARON
"Conceivably"?! How could it not have been? Especially since in *The Punishment of Korah, Dathan, and Abiram*—it's in the Sistine Chapel—the substitute painter Botticelli clearly depicts rays of light shooting up from both sides of Moses' forehead.

ANN (Googling "Botticelli Korah")
But, Aaron, Freud hadn't yet been to the Sistine Chapel.

AARON
And, Freud, with his self-aknowledged obsessive personality, he wouldn't have pored over images of the murals surrounding *The Last Judgment*?!

ANN (Studying the computer image)
Especially, Aaron, (Gestures for him to look at the image; HE does.)

the bottom left corner of *The Punishment of Korah, Dathan, and Abiram* where Moses raises his right arm in judgment, tilts his head with its destructive radiance in the direction of Korah *et al*—

AARON

And the ground gives way, and Korah and his band of rebellious Israelites sink into the fiery pit—

ANN

Alive, just like Don Juan.

AARON

As you say, "structurally similar—uncannily so."

ANN

Nu, Aaron, on to Rome already?!

AARON

Right! Next station, the Eternal City.

END of SCENE 1

THE UNKNOWN FREUD: FIVE PLAYS . . .

SCENE 2

AARON

Summoning courage, Freud finally enters Rome on September 2nd—bringing Alexander along, just in case.—

ANN

Just in case?

AARON

Freud has a train phobia, but I think he is afraid he'd come unglued, possibly have a psychotic break, or even a fatal heart attack. Remember, he already had signs of a heart condition.

ANN

But, Alexander, he doesn't know what his ambitious older brother was about?

AARON

Right! He is in the dark. Well, on the fourth day, Thursday, September 5th, Freud stands before *Moses*/Moses. At the time he still holds to the cathartic method of therapy. Ann, please read—it's from an 1896 paper, "The Aetiology of Hysteria." (Hands it to her)

ANN (Reads:)

... [we] lead the patient's attention back from his symptom to the scene in which and through which that symptom arose; and having thus located the scene, we remove the symptom by bringing about, during the reproduction of the traumatic scene, a subsequent correction of the psychical course of events which took placeat the time.

Okay?

AARON

In other words, when a patient in the relative safety of his analyst's office relives a traumatic experience, there is a purging of the emotions that sustain the neurotic symptom which arose from that event.

ANN

The symptom is then purged, washed away? Okay.

AARON

At any rate, that's what's supposed to happen. Now, Freud's major neurotic symptom, as he sees it, is submission to the Will of the Father, right!?

ANN
Ah! So, in addition to being the biblical Moses or his ghost, the statue is also a stand-in for Jakob.

AARON
Exactly. There'd be uprushes of his feelings and attiitudes pertaining to Jakob—especially the patricidal rage and the terror while awaiting the dreaded retribution, Jakob's castrating him—

ANN
Just as Freud dreads Yahweh's retribution—

AARON
Right! His Visitations. But for now let's just stay with Freud and Jakob.

ANN
Okay?

AARON
As his oedipal emotions and feelings get stirred up and surface, Freud's got to recognize them for what they are, especially the return of his castration anxiety, which, Ann, caused little Sigi to abandon his impious ambition to kill Jakob in order to bed Amalia.

ANN
Aaron, let's see if I have it. If succesful, that is, if he is able to withstand, not get overwhelmed by, by this dreaded "return of the repressed," Freud then resolves his, his Father complex—

AARON
That's the premise.—He'd have set himself free from the Father, again, whether he be Jakob Freud, Moses, or Jehovah—

ANN
And he could then get on with his ambition–

AARON
Now, Ann, when the Torah was translated into Greek, the Hebrew for "rays of light" was mistranslated as horns, and in the fourth century, St. Jerome carried this error over to the Latin version of the Scriptures, the Vulgate—

ANN
So that's why Michelangelo gave *Moses* horns. Okay—

AARON

That crown of horns, it had to have called up both the *mana* and the dreaded castration.

ANN

And Freud wasn't overwhelmed? He didn't lose it?

AARON

Not only did Freud not 'lose it,' but because he didn't, he was transformed into an exceptional being with all the qualities of Moses, his *mana* included—

ANN

Aaron, you expect me to believe that?

AARON

Ann, Freud believed it—his superstitious side did. Returning to Vienna, Freud writes Fliess that Rome was, quote, a "high point." Ann, actually, it was a turning point—for both Freud and pychoanalysis. You see, in no time not only do disciples gather round this former forty-five-year-old Jew boy from the miserable streets of Vienna, but, transference, which Freud had seen as a nuisance—as something to be gotten out of the way—becomes the key instrument of analysis. The first mention of its crucial significance is here in Freud's 1905 Postscript to *Fragments of a Case of Hysteria*....
(HE reads:)
. . . it is only after the transference has been resolved that a patient arrives at a sense of conviction of the validity of the connections which have been constructed during the analysis.

ANN

Does he say what alerted him?—

AARON

To transference's great significance? Never. Not in this Postscript, not ever. Nor for that matter does the father of psychoanalysis reveal when, in order to isolate the transference, and, thereby, make the analysand aware of just what is repressed, he had come up with the so-called analytic incognito.
(Reads from Freud's 1912 paper on technique, "Recommendations to Physicians Practising Psycho-Analysis")
The doctor should be opaque to his patients and, like a mirror, show them nothing but what is shown to him.

THE UNKNOWN FREUD: FIVE PLAYS ...

ANN

In other words, the analyst is to be like a statue—

AARON

You got it! Freud modeled himself after his mute, stone-faced co-therapist.

ANN

So, had Freud not gathered courage and faced *Moses*, analysis wouldn't have moved beyond catharsis?—

AARON

To transference? I doubt it. Which raises a related question: But for its 5-foot, seven-inch autocratic leader "who," to quote Jones, "could on occasion create a formidable impression with a stern and somewhat scowling glance,"

(Pointing to scowling glance of the *Moses* figurine.)

would there today be a psychoanalytic movement, let alone one that's international in scope? Well?!

ANN

Aaron, you realize, we haven't covered Michelangelo's *Last Judgment*.

AARON

As far as I know, Freud never gave an account of his experience. But from this, which he had written Fliess upon his return, it's clear that Freud had resisted, prevailed over, his aroused or 'broken through' Roman Catholic tendencies.

(AARON hands Ann *The Complete Letters of Sigmund Freud to Wilhelm Fliess*.)

Please, just the underlining.

ANN

(Reads from letter of September 19, 1901:)

Dear Wilhelm;

I should write to you about Rome now....I found it dificult to tolerate the lie concerning man's redemption, which raises its head to high heaven—for I could not cast off the thought of my own misery and all the other misery that I know of.

"[A]ll the other misery...." Anti-Semitism?

AARON

Right! The "misery of the Jews" or *Judennot*, as Herzl called that scourge in *The Jewish State*. Ann, now let's move ahead six years, to September 1907. At the fatal age of 51, Freud re-enters Rome, having the day before detrained at Orvieto, where on this, his third visit, he's alone—.

ANN

Where are you head—? . . .

AARON

Alone with Signorelli's *Last Judgment*.—

ANN

Ah! His "Catholic head," it, then, hadn't been rooted out, extirpated?

AARON

Think about it! Try as we may, could we at our very core, really turn into unbelievers, atheists?! It's an impossibility, isn't it? Well, this self-professed "out and out unbeliever" remains stuck with both of his religious heads, one of which promises this haunted Cain not only redemption, but also Julius reuniting with him.

ANN

But Julius, he died unbaptized. And, as I understand—

AARON

Who knows? To comfort him, his instructress in the faith may have told her sad Jewish charge that baby Julius would welcome him to Paradise, that they'd be reunited ...

    (Getting *Letters of Sigmund Freud*, he opens it to Freud's Sept 21, 1907 letter to his wife, Martha, from Rome; *Yom Kippur* fell three days earlier, on the 18[th.])

But back to Rome. It's a day or so after *Yom Kippur*. Freud visits, descends into Christian and Jewish catacombs. His guide, however, forgets to bring her exit key—and, Freud, "the only visitor," can't get out.

ANN

He's locked in?

AARON

Until nightfall.

ANN

That's unreal!

AARON (Now Recites from memory:)
    And the earth opened her mouth...they went down alive
    into the pit, and the earth closed upon them.

To quote Freud: "It is cold, dark, and not very pleasant down there."

THE UNKNOWN FREUD: FIVE PLAYS . . .

(Handing the book to ANN, HE points:)
Here, where he writes about the Menorah.

ANN (Reads:)
In the Jewish catacombs the inscriptions are Greek, the candelabrum—I think it's called Menorah—can be seen on many tablets. "I think it's called Menorah."?! (Disbelief!)

AARON
Don't you see?! Freud knew that somewhere down the line his letters to Martha will be pored over—

ANN
But why conceal his knowledge of Judaism?

AARON
His creation, psychoanalysis, must be recognized as a science, an objective discipline, one that anyone, Jew or Gentile, could have created.

ANN
It was dismissed as a Jewish science, wasn't it?

AARON
Which would mean, of course, that it's not a science at all. That's why, before their final break in 1913, Freud had pinned his hopes on Carl Jung, the magnetic son of a Swiss pastor. . . . But let's move on from 1907 to 1908—

ANN
A year–by-year account? Aaron, I've still papers to grade.

AARON
Ann, this is too important to pass over. On the night of April 15, 1908, that is, on the fiftieth anniversary of Julius' death, the six-year-old Psychological Wednesday Society—on Freud's carried motion—is re-named the Vienna Psychoanalytic Society—

ANN
In this way, he dedicates to the memory of baby Julius the psychoanalytic movement?

AARON
Secretly so—a movement which, if all goes according to plan, would purchase this Cain's redemption. But, again, first he must receive a major recognition. And that won't come until—

ANN

But he already had gotten it with his masterpiece, *The Interpretation of Dreams*.

AARON

In the first six years less than four hundred were sold. No, Ann, his first actual significant recognition comes in September 1909, with his series of five lectures on psychoanalysis at Clark University on the 20th anniversary of its founding. . . . Well, according to Jung, while sailing on the *George Washington* to America, he and Freud analyzed one another's dreams, and when Jung asked Freud for "personal associations" to a particular dream of a series of dreams, all involving him, Martha, and Minna, Freud, quote, "looked at me with bitterness and said, 'I could tell you more, but I cannot risk my authority.'" According to Jung, Freud's "placing personal authority over truth" foreshadowed their eventual breakup.

ANN

And the dream?

AARON

It seems to be lost. Jung never revealed it, as far as I know. But consider—At long last, Freud is receiving a major recognition, and so—.

ANN

Okay?

AARON

Don't you see? It's on the horizon.

ANN

What is?

AARON

Freud's Promised Land.

ANN

I can't follow—

AARON

Were Freud to open up to Jung, give him his "personal associations" he'd place at risk his, his becoming the new moral authority—

ANN

As in, "I cannot risk my authority! ?!

AARON

You got it.

ANN

Not really.

AARON
Ann, they're on the *George Washington*, and our first President, wasn't he the liberator of his besieged people? And who but Freud's beloved, his "*Schweste*r" Minna, by lending him courage, has been preparing the ground with him? Moreover, the requisite recognition, isn't he, at long last, receiving it?

ANN
And these aren't *your* "personal associations"?

AARON
(Handing Ann *The Freud/Jung Letters.*)
Ann, Freud had written this to Jung eight months earlier on January 17, 1909. Earlier in the letter Freud referred to that upcoming Clark University conference. It's relevant—
(HE points:)

ANN (Reads:)
We are certainly getting ahead: if I am Moses, then you are Joshua. And will take possession of the promised land of psychiatry, which I shall only be able to glimpse from afar—

AARON
Thanks. "Promised Land *of psychiatry*." Nice touch . . .

ANN
If you say so.

AARON
Now, Ann, please visualize Freud, cigar in hand, beside his Joshua who would break down the Gentiles' walls of resistance to psychoanalysis, looking out over the Atlantic—

ANN
At the horizon.

AARON
The promising blue horizon; more so, since, having survived the fatal age of 51, he has more time to prepare the soil with Minna, who, four years later, in September 1913, will accompany him to the city of his dreams, the thirteenth day of which Freud'll write Karl Abraham, "it is pleasant to watch her feeling more at home and growing more enthusiastic about Rome every day." That was penned from Rome's Eden Hotel.

ANN & AARON LOOK ON AS FREUD ON HIS DEATHBED ...

ANN

"Eden"? An apt name?

AARON

He'll write Jones that those seventeen days were "delicious."

ANN

"Delicious"? And, at the Eden, he didn't sample forbidden fruit?

AARON

Ah! Here it is. Freud's take on Michelangelo's portrayal of Moses. Ann, it, too, is relevant.

(Reads from *Moses and Monotheism*, begun on Christmas 1913 and completed on New Year's Day, 1914.)

... [Michelangelo] has modified the theme of the broken Tables; he does not let Moses break them in his wrath, but makes him be influenced by the danger that they will be broken and makes him calm that wrath, or at any rate prevent it from becoming an act.—

ANN

Aaron, what's this to do with—?

AARON

You'll see. (HE continues reading, with emphases:.)

In this way [Michelangelo] has added something new and more than human to the figure of Moses so that the giant frame with its tremendous physical power becomes only a concrete expression of *the highest mental achievement* that is *possible in a man,* that of *struggling successfully against an inward passion for the sake of a cause to which he has devoted himself.*

Now, according to Jones and other analysts, this observation of Freud's pertains to his red-hot anger towards his then rebellious 'sons,' Jung especially; that is to say, for the sake of his cause, psychoanalysis, Freud, by heroic self-possession, would contain his wrath. But, Ann, Freud's observation, may it not also pertain to—?

ANN

His intense desire for Minna?

AARON

Right! For his cause, his Promised Land, Freud would heroically restrain himself, keep from following through on his red-hot desire. Even if that meant sacrificing the personal happiness of Minna as well as himself. You see, according to my reading, Freud believed, correctly or not, that she was passionately in love with him.

ANN

And you're not projecting?

AARON (Handling the figurine of *Moses*)
I guess anything's possible. But this I am sure of: Michelangelo's rendering of *Moses*—that is, as Freud perceived that masterpiece—was internalized, taken into Freud's very being.

ANN

Making this latest comer a Moses, who, for *his* cause—*his secret* cause—restrains himself.

AARON

I couldn't have said it any better. Ann, this initimately related paper
(HE raises "A Disturbance of Memory on the Acropolis")
was probably written in January, 1936, four months shy of his 80th birthday.

ANN

He's nearing the end. Okay.

AARON

It deals with Freud's odd experience on the Acropolis in Athens in 1904—

ANN

1904? Aaron! Remember, I've still papers to grade.

AARON

I'll try to be quick. According to Jones, this incident took place on the morning of September 4, 1904, which was just one day shy of the third anniversary of the first time he *"mounted the steep steps"* leading to the gloomy Church of St. Peter in Chains. And, Ann, given that Freud was date-sensitive, it's not a great leap to suppose that Balzac's novel also called up this strange experience on top of the Acropolis.

ANN

Okay, but what's this to do—?

AARON

Only this. It shows, as you'll see, that to the very end, Freud continued to fear Yahweh. Here's Freud:
(HE reads from "A Disturbance of Memory on the Acropolis":)
When, finally, on the afternoon of our arrival I stood on the Acropolis and cast my eyes upon the landscape, a surprising thought suddenly entered my mind: "So all this really *does* exist, just as we learnt it at school!"

ANN

And his explanation?—

AARON

Essentially it is this. His standing on the Acropolis signified the fulfillment of a forbidden wish, the wish to excel one's father, and the derealization or his fleeting disbelief in the Acropolis kept him from acknowledging that this impious wish had been realized—

ANN

I don't under—Wait! Guilt, then, took away from his pleasure at having risen higher in the world than Jakob.

AARON

Right! Guilt. Or, as Freud writes, "what interfered with our enjoyment was a feeling of *filial piety*." But Freud is holding back. You see, the "feeling of filial piety" sabotaging his enjoyment pertained not only to Jakob, whom he has excelled, but also to Moses whom he is bent on surpassing.

ANN

Aaron, that's too pat.

AARON

Is it? Can you think of a better scenario than Freud, for the first time standing on the heights of the Acropolis in Athens—the fountainhead of Western Civilization—to call up his enlightened Promised Land, a socially just world grounded in Reason where all freely abide his one commandment, the Delphic precept, "Know thyself."? Well, Ann, can you?! . . . Now, consider this from *The Future of An Illusion*, the illusion, Ann, being religion.

ANN

Why am I not surprised?

AARON (HE reads with emphases:)
I was already a man of mature years when *I stood* for the first time on the hill of the Acropolis of Athens, *between the temple ruins, looking out over the blue sea.* . . .

ANN

"The temple ruins," The Torah?—

AARON

Judaism and Christianity.

ANN

Again, 'Root and Branch.' Okay.

AARON

And his enlightened secular Promised Land is now within range or on the horizon.

ANN

"Looking out over the *blue* sea."

AARON

You got it! Accordingly, while in his brief confusional state, Freud is in a state of exaltation.

ANN

His "enjoyment."

AARON

Right, His joy. Needless to say, this fleeting delusion on the Acropolis is subconscious, below the threshold of consciousness—

ANN

Okay, but where in all this do you see Freud fearing Yahweh?

AARON

Fair enough. Please read; for now, skipping the German. (Hands her a typed sheet.)

ANN (Reads:)

... what interfered with our enjoyment was a feeling of *filial piety*. And now you will no longer wonder that the recollection of this incident [*erlebnis*, experience] on the Acropolis would have troubled me so often [*mich . . . so oft heimsucht*] since I myself have grown old and stand in need of forbearance [*nachsicht*] and can travel no more.

AARON

Ann, please hang on to the sheet. This is S.S. Prawer, a distinguished Oxford professor of German. He's commenting favorably on Strachey's translating "*heimsucht*" as "troubled."

ANN

"[T]he recollection of this incident . . . on the Acropolis . . . troubled me so often."?

AARON

Right!   (HE reads:)

... "Heimsuchen" is the verb Luther's Bible uses as its equivalent for God's "visiting" the sins of the fathers on future generations, and any appropriate German dictionary will furnish plenty of examples in which "heimsuchen" has to do with "smiting", "afflicting", "being stricken", and "suffering", as well as "being favored with benefits." . . .There is something troubling about the sudden irruption, the "Auftauchen", of the memory image. . . .

Ann, when writing the essay, Freud in all lilkelihood suspects that Yahweh's visitations have already begun. And with a vengeance! On January 25, 1920, Freud's middle daughter, his beautiful "Sunday child," Sophie Halberstadt, died at the age of twenty-six from influenza. Two and one-half years later, and just two months after undergoing the first of thirty-three surgical procedures for his mouth and jaw cancer, Freud's favorite grandson, Sophie's four-and-a-half-year-old son Heinele, died from a type of tuberculosis. That was on June 19, 1923.

ANN

And all in less than three years—

AARON

In March 1928, almost five years after his beloved Heinele's death, Freud will write the following to Jones, who had just lost his daughter, an exceptionally brilliant little girl.

ANN (Reads letter of March 11, 1918:)
... Only when ... little Heinele died did I become weary of life for good. He ... was of superior intelligence and indescribable spiritual grace, and repeatedly said that he would die soon! How do these children come to know those things?

"How do these children *come to know* those things?"!

AARON

On the *Shabbos* three days before Heinele's death, Jews all over the world recited the designated *parashah* or weekly Torah portion, verses from Numbers 16—

ANN

The dreadful Korah episode! Did Freud know?

AARON

Given his obsessional nature, it's a good bet that he did.

ANN

And yet he stays on his potentially calamitous path?

AARON

Ann, he *must* deliver *der Kinder*!

ANN

He's, then, trapped.

AARON

Right! Trapped, imprisoned in a sealed-off world of his own... Now, according to Freud, the Acropolis incident has been returning to him, quote, "During the last few years," He doesn't mention it, but during those years, Ann, he had been laboring over *Moses and Monotheism*, about which he'll write Charles Singer, a professor of the history of science. Ann, Please read—at the time it's at the printer's. We're about through.

> (Hands her *The Letters of Sigmund Freud,* edited by his son Ernst.)

The third paragraph, "It can be . . ." To the very end, please.

ANN

> (Reads from letter of October 31, 1938.)

It can be called an attack on religion only in so far as any scientific investigation of religious belief presupposes disbelief. Neither in my private life nor in my writings have I ever made a secret of my being an out-and-out unbeliever—

> (ANN and AARON give each other a knowing look: "an out-and-out unbeliever"—Right!)
> (ANN resumes reading:)

Anyone considering the book from this point of view will have to admit it is only Jewry and not Christianity which has reason to feel offended by its conclusions. For only a few incidental remarks which say nothing that hasn't been said before, allude to Christianity. At most one can quote the old adage "Caught together, hanged together!"

"Caught together, hanged together!" An unguarded moment?

AARON

An uncharacteristically unguarded moment . . . Well, we now come full circle to Freud on his deathbed as he reads the final scene of this, Balzac's novel dealing with "death and starvation."

> (Raising the book.)

First, the context. Having "cajoled Jonathan," Pauline surprises Raphael in their bedroom, where he opens up about the magic skin, and she takes what remains of the accursed talisman; as Raphael's desire for her intensified, she, quote, "felt a light movement in her hand, and the skin contracted. She did not stop to think; she fled into the next room, and locked the door."

> (HE reads:)
> "Pauline!, Pauline!," cried the dying man, as he rushed after her: "I love you, adore you. I want you. Pauline! I must curse you if

you will not open the door for me. I wish to die in your arms!"—
Ann, at the time Minna may have been confined to her room, as she was in ill-health and, suffering from glaucoma, her eyesight was failing.
(Resumes reading:)
With unnatural strength, the last effort of ebbing life, he broke down the door, and saw her writhing upon a sofa. She had vainly tried to pierce her heart, and now thought to find a rapid death by then strangling herself with her shawl. "If I die, he will live," she said, trying to tighten the knot she had made. . . . [A]s her exceeding beauty met Raphael's intoxicating eyes, his delirium grew. He sprang towards her like a bird of prey, tore away the shawl, and tried to take her in his arms. The dying man sought for words to express the wish that was consuming his strength; but no sounds would come except the choking death-rattle in his chest. Each breath he drew sounded hollower than the last, and seemed to come from his very entrails. At the last moment, no longer able to utter a sound, he set his teeth into Pauline's breast.—

ANN

What must have passed through Freud, I can't imagine.

AARON

I'm coming to the very end. Okay?
(ANN nods.)

(AARON resumes reading:)
Jonathan appeared, terrified by the cries he had heard, and tried to tear away the dead body from the grasp of the girl who was couching in a corner. "What do you want?" she asked, "He is mine. I have killed him. Did I not foresee how it would be?"

ANN

How sad, how very sad.

AARON

The day after finishing the novel, Freud, wasting away, tells Dr. Schur that the time had come, quote : "You promised... not to forsake me when my time comes. Now, it's nothing but torture and makes no sense any more."

ANN

"Makes no sense any more"? Does he feel, then, that it had been all in vain?"

AARON
I suspect that deep down he was still hoping against hope. Well, that day, Thursday, September 21st, Schur begins to administer the first of three injections of the fatal morphine, hours apart, and Freud passes away two days later, Saturday the 23rd, at 3 A.M. That fateful *Shabbos*, Ann, was the Tenth of Tishri.

ANN
Yom Kippur?! The Day of Atonement?

AARON
Right! The day we received the Law—

ANN
And which your hero had resolved to destroy.

AARON
Ann, Freud's Promised Land where all can move freely across frontiers, develop their talents, and satisfy their needs, is that not more humane than that increasingly bitter reality, the Promised Land of that other would-be Moses of the Berggasse, Herzl?

ANN
Correction: Freud's improbable Promised Land.
(The sound of distant thunder.)

AARON
(Turning pages of *Sigmund Freud: His Life in Pictures and Words,* edited by Ernest Freud *et al.*—)
Defiant to the very end, Freud has himself cremated. This is the funerary urn, a gift from Marie Bonaparte.

[ANN and AARON examine the large, double-page photo of the ancient Greek urn. As lights in the room flicker, the two figures gracing the ancient vessel—an elegant woman with a dish of overflowing offerings and a seated garlanded male with a staff in his left hand and a large goblet in his right—begin to move, the woman gliding, her tiara radiant. . . . Neither Ann nor Aaron say a word. Later, they will explain away what they had witnessed that Passover evening: it was just an uncanny effect due to the darkness, the isolation, and the silence . . . Still, the experience continues to haunt them. Do they share this with one another? You'll have to ask them.]

END of PLAY

Freud at the Crossroads in Rome

A Monologue

Michelangelo's *Moses* (c. 1513–1515),
The Church of St. Peter in Chains, Rome

FREUD AT THE CROSSROADS IN ROME

Freud at the Crossroads in Rome
A Monologue

... *I, Levi Yitzhak, son of Sarah, am come before you with pleas and prayers. What have you to do with Israel? To whom do you speak? To the children of Israel! To whom do you give commandments? To the children of Israel! Whom do you bid say the benedictions? To the children of Israel! And so I ask you: What have you to do with the children of Israel? Are there not plenty of Chaldeans, and Medes, and Persians? It must be that they are dear to you, the children of Israel—children of God they are called. Blessed art thou, O Lord our God, King of the World!*

—The revered Hasidic Master, Rebbe Levi-Yitzhak (1740–1809), delivering his Kiddush one Rosh Hashana before reciting the Prayer of Benediction; in Buber, M. (1947), *Tales of Hasidim: The Early Masters.*

When [Freud's taller stories] were concerned with clairvoyant visions or episodes at a distance, and visitations from departed spirits, I ventured to reprove him for his inclination to accept occult beliefs on flimsy evidence ... I then asked him where such beliefs could come to a halt: if one could believe in mental processes floating in the air, one could go on to a belief in angels. He closed the discussion ... with the remark: **"Quite so, even der liebe Gott."** *This was said in a jocular tone ...* **But there was something searching also in his glance,** *and I went away not entirely happy lest there be some more serious undertone as well.*

—Ernest Jones, *The Life and Work of Sigmund Freud*
(1957, p. 381; emphases added).

CAST

SIGMUND FREUD

Impeccably groomed, the 5 ft. 7-inch, 126 pound, forty-five-year-old bearded father of psychoanalysis has penetrating brown eyes. Wearing a 3-piece gray suit, he has a skull cap on his head and prayer shawl or Tallith over his shoulders; in his right hand, he carries the Torah or Pentateuch (the Five Books of Moses).

SETTING

Rome: The Church of St. Peter in Chains, the home of Michelangelo's *Moses*. The statue need not be visible. A slide projection of *Moses* can be used.

TIME

Thursday, September 5, 1901, 3 P. M.

FREUD
(Moving tentatively towards Michelangelo's 8ft-4-inch horned *MOSES.*)

With each step I experience increasing dread and creeping horror. Another heart attack could do me in. And after I am wheeled out of this gloomy Roman church who would look after Martha and the children?
(From pocket removes train schedule.)

Besides the whole thing is crazy . . . I can catch the 5:30 train back to Vienna.
('Other' FREUD Self:)

Turning tail? Some hero!!! Remember, you are of the line of Jesse, of David! Your necessary task, now get on with it!
(FREUD resumes moving; halts before *Moses,* looks up at the statue.)

Moses, you have shaped me, just as you have every other Jew . . . By assuring us that we are God's Chosen People, you have made us confident, optimistic, even proud. . . . To you, Moses, we Jews owe our tenacity of life. But, Moses, if Yahweh exists, where is His strong hand? His Chosen People, they haven't suffered enough? Why doesn't HE put an end, once and for all, to the perpetual persecution? . . . Moses, Judaism has a poisonous shoot, the Christian religion. Its faithful, they detest your people, the people of the Book.
(Raising the Torah high.)

This undying hostility is rooted in the psychology of the Christian. Not possessing the courage, the moral courage, to acknowledge that he hates his religion which obliges him to renounce and deny his aggressive tendencies and illicit sexual impulses, the good Christian displaces this hatred on to the ones who had enchained him, had shackled him with his demanding religion. Moses, so long as there is such a thing as Christianity, Jews will continue to pay dearly for their gift to the good Christians. This summer while vacationing near Salzburg, in my so-called 'fatherland,' Austria, my two older boys were on the lake fishing, when grown men jeered at them. Calling them "dirty little *Yid* Jew boys," they accused Oliver and Martin of stealing fish. With such abuse, and worse, can one live?! My little ones are only ten and eleven. Well, later that afternoon, Martin and I chanced on those good Christians! (Furious!).

The human trash made way, let me tell you! . . . Moses, it is with a heavy heart that I say this: The Law, the Torah, it must be sacrificed.
(Emphasizing with fingers, one at a time):

No Law, no Judaism, no Christianity, no miserable anti-Semitism. You look down on me with scorn. But I will not, must not cower before your wrathful glance! The time for Jewish martyrdom, it is over!

(FREUD starts removing both the tallith and yarmulke,
when a thunder-clap occurs, followed by brilliant lightning.)
Moses' terrible radiance!—I am doomed!—
(Clutching his heart, he shields his face with the Torah.)

I held my ground. Then I, I, prevailed. (Disbelief!)
(Noticing in his hand what had been the Torah . . .)
My book, *The Interpretation of Dreams*? But I was holding the Torah.
My theoretical knowledge, then, really *did* support me.
(Raising high *The Interpretation of Dreams*)
did keep me from creeping away or fainting— . . . God the Father once strode on earth in bodily form,
(Walking with authority)
in the form of the young boy's all-powerful, all-knowing papa, the oedipal papa . . . Religion is but a wishful illusion that stems from a longing for the father—My Dream Book, you've become heavy . . . like stone.
(Looking at his Dream Book, now a 'Tablet'.)
What's this?! By some mysterious alchemy you've become a marble tablet—
(Seeing his 'radiant' face reflected in the 'Tablet,' he reacts
initially as though terrified, turning away.)
Uncanny! The terrible radiance of Moses which had so terrified the Israelites at the foot of Mt. Sinai—it has been transferred on to me.
(FREUD'S face can be bathed in light.)
But this radiance business, it's just a Bible story that I had learned on my papa Jakob's knee—What's this? I'm limping. Well, to limp is no sin, especially for one who now is in possession of the field as the new Lawgiver, with but one Command,
(Raising over his head for all to see his one Law, gilt
lettered: 'Know Thyself!')
One moment I'm a Jew boy from the miserable streets of Vienna, and the next the new Lawgiver, the new Moses whose Law, 'Know Thyself!,' is *the* Law of the Land, . . . of Mother Earth!
('Coming down' from this manic excitement, FREUD, now
flooded with guilt, cries:)
For destroying the Torah—our people's Tree of Life—father would have disowned me. To that dear man I'd be dead. Guilt now floods me—
(The floor shakes, smoke rises as if from a fiery pit.)
The punishment of Korah and the other Israelites who rebelled against the authority of Moses! Yahweh's terrible desert visitation, it now returns!! 'They, and all that *appertained* to them went down alive into the pit.'—The fiery pit. The Bible Story, then it *is* true! No! (Horrified!) Martha and the

children! What have I done?! My little ones, Mathilde, Martin, Oliver, Sophie, Ernst, Anna, your papa, he has doomed your sweet, precious mama—he has doomed you all! . . .This must not happen! I will undo this! . . .
>(About to fling his 'Tablet' to the ground—)

Collect yourself! It is still miserable outside. And much worse is to come! Daily, the noose round the necks of *der Kinder*, it is being tightened—
>(Restraining himself from dashing the 'Tablet,' a mighty effort, he clutches it to his breast.)

>(We hear *Kaddish*.)

Kaddish, the prayer for the dead?! Now, I hear a voice. It's a child, an infant, crying—is that you, Julius? Julius, all I wanted was for you to just go away.—Well, when you were eight months old I got my hateful wish . . . Julius, if there really *is* a *liebe Gott in Himmel,* would He have allowed you to die? Cause me to suffer so?
>(Checking torrent of tears.)

You would be forty-four. Your death and my guilt—the guilt of a guilt-ridden Cain—surfaced, returned, four years ago. Then and there, to you, I made a secret vow, a silent promise:

>An enlightened world I will institute—a brotherly world, where, my dear Julius, children like you, children of our detested and homeless race, can move freely across frontiers—a world in which the seed of Abraham are free to develop their talents and satisfy their needs. A peaceable, secular world where that miserable scourge, anti-Semitism, is unknown.

And at long last your tormented Cain of a brother purchases his redemption . . .

But before setting others free from their religious chains, I must set myself free from the Law. And it is for this purpose that I have come to this gloomy church. You see, Julius, our devout Czech nanny, Resi, instructed her two-year-old Jewish charge well. She left her stamp—If bread can be Jesus,
>(Mimes swallowing a Communion Wafer.)

then stone, marble, can be Moses, no?

After four years of detailed preparation, especially by studying my dreams, I at last summoned courage for this dreaded meeting with that Great Man of our people. Tell me, Julius, your ambitious brother, does he need to be put away?—

But wait! The apparition in the half-gloom . . . Like an unlaid ghost, she returns. When Resi disappeared, frantic, I searched for her—even in the kitchen cupboards. Later, our mama, Amalia, told me she was sent away, placed in jail, for stealing from our home, my toy soldiers even. By saying her name, have I called Resi up? Julius, after you went away, our pretty young mama—she was only 22—grieved so. It was then that Resi became my mama. With a grief-stricken young wife, our beloved 42-year-old father, Jakob—he was a struggling textile merchant—had matters more pressing to attend to than my traipsing along with our ugly, elderly but ever so wise nanny to her Church, the Church of The Nativity of Our Lady, in our birthplace, the tiny Catholic town of Freiberg in Moravia. After Mass, this little *pisher* would tell mama and papa about how our Lord Jesus Christ conducts His affairs. Can you imagine?! . . .

Julius, you never knew the joy of the Passover Seder, especially of asking that sweet soul, our gray-haired papa, "Why is this night different. . . ?" His death five years ago left me feeling as though I had been pulled up by the roots. Sh-sh! My Catholic mama, once again she mouths those words, words to comfort me—

Sh-sh! little Sigi, do not cry, baby Julius, he is with Jesus. And when you die as everyone must, Julius will welcome you in Paradise. Together you will be once again, and for all eternity—

> (As though in a trance, positioning his 'Tablet' between his right elbow and side, FREUD kneels; as he begins to cross himself, his 'Tablet' starts to slip, breaking the trance; FREUD grasps the 'Tablet' just in time.)

What's this, bending the knee?! Just as I had anticipated. Here, in the center of Christendom, my long suppressed wish to acknowledge Jesus Christ as my Lord and Savior, it has broken through. By this simple act, Resi, I'd be coming home, wouldn't I?—home to you, home to your, to *our* church, and home to Jesus Christ whose blood cleanseth us from all sin, including brother-murder. Resi, it is so very tempting, this seductive promise of Salvation which I had learned at your breast, but, as you see, (rising) my bloody nun of a mother, I have come through this dreaded test—You and Jesus and his miserable church no longer have a hold on me. You can go now. . . . No, not you, my dear Julius—we have work to do!

> (Removes tallith and skullcap, raises 'Tablet' over his head, looks over the horizon, and cries:)

The ground for our Promised Land, a brotherly world, it must be prepared!

(The bells of St. Stephen's Cathedral begin to chime, awakening FREUD with a start.)

END of MONOLOGUE

(A staged reading was given at the Emerging Artists Theatre in New York City on May 23, 2006.)

FREUD AT THE CROSSROADS IN ROME

EPILOGUE (optional)

The synagogue was ready for Passover, but the dedication was postponed until Lag B'Omer, for that day is considered to be lucky.

—Sholem Asch (1959), Kiddush Ha-Shem.

The following fall (1902) Freud gathers disciples, and he is on his way. Six years later, on the evening of April 15, 1908, or the fiftieth anniversary of Julius's death, on Freud's carried motion the Psychological Wednesday Society is re-named the Vienna Psychoanalytic Society; in this manner, Freud secretly dedicates the psychoanalytic movement to the memory of Julius—a movement which would establish Freud's (and Julius's) Promised Land, a brotherly world in which, anti-Semitism being unknown, future Juliuses (and Sarahs) can at long last live in peace, and move freely across frontiers.

Five years later, on Sunday, May 25th, 1913, a full nine months after writing his disciple Ernest Jones about his enthusiasm for Jones's suggestion of a 'secret council,' Freud who has an easy familiarity with Jewish holidays hands his five favorite adherents an ancient stone engraved with a scene from classical antiquity to be mounted into a gold ring like his. In the Jewish calendar this date was the eighteenth of Iyar or *Lag B'Omer* (5673), the thirty-third day of the Counting of the Omer (Sheaf). This feast day, *Lag B'Omer*, marks the end of a plague that was killing students of Rabbi Akiba Ben Joseph who gave the Jewish warrior Bar Kochba (132–135 C.E. rebellion) his name, which means "Son of a Star," an allusion to the Messiah to come: ". . . there shall come a Star out of Jacob . . ." (Numbers 24:17)—Jacob, as in Jacob Freud. Because Akiba proclaimed that Bar Kochba was their long-awaited Messiah, Jews flocked to Bar Kochba, under whose leadership they recaptured from the Romans all of Judea; after which they minted coins with Hebrew inscriptions: "the redemption of Israel," "the freedom of Israel," and "the freedom of Jerusalem."

The following year, 1914, Freud's essay "The Moses of Michelangelo" is published anonymously. In this paper, which he began on Christmas Day 1913, and completed on New Year's Day 1914, Freud states, understandably, "no other piece of statuary has ever made a stronger effect on me than [Michelangelo's *Moses*]."

Twenty-four years later, the date-sensitive father of psychoanalysis, his Job-like cancerous sores ravaging his mouth and jaw, pens the last sentence of *Moses and Monotheism* on Sunday, July 17, 1938, or the civil date of the fast of the Seventeenth of Tammuz, a day of mourning in memory of both the Babylonian breach (586 B.C.E.) and the Roman breach (70 C.E.) of the walls of Jerusalem, which, three weeks later, on the Ninth of Av (Tisha b'Av), resulted in Nebuchadnezzar destroying the First and Titus the Second Temples, respectively. And with this his last major attack on religion, Freud intends, ultimately, to destroy the 'stone' fortress of the Jews, the Torah—and, thereby, to paraphrase the famous lament of the Babylonian exile, "rase [Christendom] . . . even to the foundation."

The following year, 1939, this weary, relentless, and unknown fighter for the human rights of his people will give up the ghost on Saturday, September 23rd at 3 A.M. To die on the Sabbath, indeed to die on any Jewish Holy Day, is a good sign; it means that one has led a righteous life. In the Jewish Calendar that fateful *Shabbos* was the Tenth of Tishri or Yom Kippur, the Day of Atonement—and the day the Israelites at the foot of Mt. Sinai received the Law from Moses.

Ann and Aaron Pore Over Freud's Fainting Spells in Jung's Presence

THE UNKNOWN FREUD: FIVE PLAYS . . .

Group photo (1909) in front of Clark University in Worcester, MA.
Front row, Sigmund Freud, G. Stanley Hall, Carl Jung.
Back row, Abraham Brill, Ernest Jones, Sandor Ferenczi.

Ann and Aaron Pore Over Freud's Fainting Spells in Jung's Presence

Some day, perhaps, even remembering this
Will be a pleasure.
—Aeneas to his crew. VIRGIL, *The Aeneid*. Book I.
 (Robert Fitzgerald's translation, 1983)

One day you will remember the years of struggle
as the best.
—Sigmund Freud to Carl Jung, in letter dated September 19, 1907,
 one day after Yom Kippur, 5668, posted from Rome.

> *When the empire I founded is orphaned, no one but*
> *Jung must inherit the whole thing. As you see, my*
> *politics incessantly pursues this aim. . .*
> —Letter from Sigmund Freud to Ludwig Binswanger,
> dated March 14, 1911.

CAST of CHARACTERS

Rabbi Aaron Handel   Fifty-five, looks like Sigmund Freud, beard and all.

Ann Handel   Rabbi Handel's wife, about the same age, attractive.

SETTING

The book-lined library-study of the Handel home in Louisville, KY. On the mantle above the fireplace there is a large Menorah, a 14-inch or so bronze-colored figurine of Michelangelo's *Moses* and a photo of Sigmund Freud. Center-stage, in addition to the Rabbi's file and book-cluttered desk which contains several Egyptian, Greek, and Roman antiquities, there is an oblong table between a sofa and a comfortable armchair; a footstool; and a 4-drawer file cabinet, the top of which has a few family photos, a pipe rack, and a Chicago Cubs baseball cap.

TIME

About 9:30 P.M., Friday, the second day of Passover, April 10, 2009.

> AARON is seated on the couch, writing on a legal pad, as ANN enters with a tray containing a teapot, two cups, and a dish of macaroons and tea matzohs.

ANN

Comfort food?

(Laying the legal pad beside him, AARON puts pencil in mouth and clears folders from the coffee table.)
(ANN pours tea as AARON lifts cup, and also for herself. Seating self, SHE lifts the legal pad.)

Another of your hero's dreams?

AARON

No, a fainting spell of his in Carl Jung's presence. (Offering ANN the dish.)

ANN (Choosing a macaroon)

When was this?

AARON

In November 1912, in Munich, just two months before their final break. This wasn't the first time. Freud had fainted before Jung three years earlier. Both times Freud believed that Jung had unconscious death-wishes against him.

ANN

Is this your interpretation, Aaron?

AARON

According to Jung, that's what Freud had told him. But Freud held back.

ANN

You're sure?

AARON

I'm sure. His essay,

(With the legal pad, HE goes to a shelf of Freud's *Collected Works*; gets vol. 21.)

years later, in 1927, on Dostoevsky cued me in. Specifically, Freud's explanation for Dostoevsky's apparent epileptic seizures which Freud claims were actually hysterical fits—fits, Ann, like the two he had before Jung.

(Handing ANN the now open book, HE points to a passage from "Dostoevsky and Parricide.")

Ann, please read.

ANN (Reads:)

... these death-like seizures signify an identification with a dead person, either with someone who is really dead or with someone who is still alive and whom one wishes dead. The latter case is the more significant. The attack then has the value of a punishment.

Ann and Aaron Pore Over Freud's Fainting Spells . . .

One has wished another person dead, and now one is this other person and is dead oneself. For a boy this other person is usually his father and the attack is thus a self-punishment for a death-wish against a hated father.

AARON (Pointing to passage.)

". . . a self-punishment for a death-wish against one's father." This, Ann, is bedrock—

ANN

Are you saying that when he fell away Freud had death wishes against his father, Jakob?

AARON

Not Jakob . . . (From the fireplace mantle HE gets the statuette of Michelangelo's *Moses* with the Tablets of the Law, and lays *Moses* on his back on the floor.)

ANN

Moses? Aaron, haven't you heard? Moses is dead.

AARON

Not so long as the Law exists—
(Pointing to the Tablets.)

ANN (Re-reads, with emphases:)

" . . . the attack is a self-punishment for a death-wish against a *hated* father." Surely, Freud didn't hate Moses?

AARON

Freud admired Moses, even identified with him,
(Lifting *Moses* high, AARON'S eyes stay focused on *Moses*, as if in awe.)
but he held that great man responsible for our people's never-ending misery—

ANN

Anti-Semitism?

AARON

Anti-Semitism.
(Replacing *Moses* on the bookcase, AARON gets the last book on a shelf of Freud's completed psychological works, *Moses and Monotheism*.)

Ann, this is from Freud's last major attack on religion, *Moses and Monotheism*. (HE reads:)

> ... we venture to declare that it was the one man Moses who created the Jews. It is to him that this people owes its tenacity of life and also much of the hostility it has experienced and still experiences.
> (AARON starts flipping pages.)

ANN

Aaron, I don't understand.

AARON

Freud was bent on destroying the Law—

ANN

The Torah? Our Tree of Life? To what end?

AARON

To rid the world of anti-Semitism. (Resumes reading:)
> Christians have not got over a grudge against the new religion which was imposed on them; but they have displaced the grudge on to the source from which Christianity reached them. The fact that the Gospels tell a story which is set among Jews, and in fact deals only with Jews, has made this displacement easy for them. Their hatred of Jews is at bottom a hatred of Christians . . .

In other words, Ann, because of the psychology of the good Christian, anti-Semitism will continue to exist so long as there is such a thing as Christianity.

ANN

"Such a *thing* as Christianity"?

AARON

Just channeling my hero.

ANN

Well, I don't like it! . . . (ANN silently reads the passage.)
Now, let's see if I have it. Not possessing the courage—the moral courage—to acknowledge their own hatred for their exacting religion which obliges them to renounce their aggressive inclinations and their illicit sexual desires or lust, Christians displace their hatred for Christianity on to the ones who had imprisoned them in their moral staight-jacket—
(Mimes being shackled and unable to set herself free.)

AARON

Christians, like the creep who knocked Jakob's new *Shabbos* hat, er, his *Shtreimel,* into the mud as he shouted, "Jew! get off the pavement!"
(Mimes the anti-Semite.)

Ann and Aaron Pore Over Freud's Fainting Spells . . .

ANN

Was Freud there?

AARON

No, it happened before he was born, when Jakob was a young man. Still, just hearing Jakob relate the incident on one of their Sunday walks around Vienna was plenty traumatic. (Gets *The Interpretation of Dreams*.)
This is from his masterpiece, *The Interpretation of Dreams*. Freud is either ten or twelve.

(Miming young Freud or Sigi looking up at Jakob, who is holding his hand:)

—And, papa, what did you do?

—Sigi, I went into the roadway and picked up my hat.

(Mimes humiliated Jakob picking up hat.)

Ann, it was as though God Himself had died.

—This struck me as unheroic conduct on the part of the strong man who was holding the little boy by the hand.

(Miming Sigi, head down, wiping eye.)

ANN

So that's what drove him!—a passionate desire to avenge Jakob.

AARON

Ann, Freud was a good hater, but his thirst for vengeance against Christians wasn't what ultimately drove him.

ANN

What then?

AARON

Guilt.

ANN

Guilt?

AARON

An intolerable sense of guilt from his early childhood. But, for now, let's stay with the spells—

ANN

Aaron, you can't leave me hanging!

AARON

Ann, I'll get to it, I promise. But for now, I need your input.

ANN
(Finding *Moses and Monotheism's* publication date.)
Aaron, *Moses and Monotheism* was published in 1939.

AARON
Right! The year Freud died, His mouth and jaw eaten up with cancer, he completed it the summer before, in exile in London.
(Mimes Freud in pain, penning last sentence.)

ANN
Leaving Vienna at the last possible minute. It's as though he had a death-wish—

AARON
He gave up the ghost on Yom Kippur. He was 83—

ANN
The Day of Atonement? That's uncanny. That is, if Freud was really out, as you claim, to destroy the Torah. But, Aaron, there's a problem with your detective work, isn't there? A big one—

AARON
And that is?

ANN
Freud's explanation for anti-Semitism
(Replacing *Moses and Monotheism* on bookshelf.)
hit the bookstores in 1939, over a quarter of a century after both fainting spells.

AARON
Ann, Freud was a concealer! When he broadcasts his explanation for anti-Semitism means absolutely nothing!—

ANN
If you say so.

AARON
Let's sum up so far. In Freud's eyes, given his understanding of that perpetual scourge, there is no alternative—the Law must go.
(Emphasizing with fingers.)
No Torah, No Judaism, no Christianity, no miserable anti-Semitism.

Ann and Aaron Pore Over Freud's Fainting Spells . . .

ANN

Had they known his elegant solution to the Jewish Question calls for the destruction of their Tree of Life, Freud's B'nai B'rith lodge brothers would have stoned, if not castrated him.—

> (Mimes throwing stones at AARON/FREUD, who protects his head and genitals.)

That is, if they could have gotten away with it.

AARON

That he'd suffer their hatred and contempt, Freud understood only too well. . . . In April 1900, two days after Passover, he dreamt that these "brethren," as he called them,

> (Looking up the dream in *The Complete Letters of Sigmund Freud to Wilhelm Fliess*.)

were, quote, "unkind and scornful of me."

ANN

Aaron, what does Freud say about their scorning him?

AARON

That's just it, he doesn't reveal his interpretation, not even to Fliess. At any rate, the dream's never been published. And, Ann, if dreams are, as he claims, wishes, why on earth would Freud wish for the disdain of his "brethren," other Sons of the Covenant? Well? . . . Ann, how about?: 'At long last I am making my move, showing my hand.'

ANN

For the sake of argument, say you're right. Still, he persisted, didn't abandon his, his project?—

AARON

Right! Otherwise, he'd lose the will to live!—

ANN

"Lose the will to live"? Aaron, that's pretty strong!

AARON

Well, that's the case—as you'll see, that is, if you'll stay with me—

ANN

A deal. . . . But, Aaron, without God or His visitations, wouldn't everything be allowed?—Rape, murder--anarchy—would prevail.

AARON (Gets a book.)
Not in Freud's Promised Land. He alludes to it here in *The Future of an Illusion*—the illusion, Ann, being religion—

ANN

Why am I not surprised?

AARON (reads:)
... New generations, who have been brought up in kindness and taught to have a high opinion of reason, and who have experienced the benefits of civilization at an early age .... will feel civilization as a possession of their very own and will be ready for its sake to make the sacrifices as regards work and instinctual satisfaction that are necessary for civilization's preservation ... If no culture has so far produced human masses of such a quality, it is because no culture has yet devised regulations which will influence men in this way, and in particular from childhood onwards.—(Skips pages)

ANN

And this is Freud the supreme realist?! Why, he's a dreamer, a deluded utopian dreamer!

AARON (resumes reading:)
By withdrawing their expectations from the other world and concentrating all their liberated energies into their life on earth, they will probably succeed in achieving a state of things in which life will become tolerable for everyone and civilization no longer oppressive to anyone. Then, with one of our fellow-unbelievers, the great poet Heine, they will be able to say without regret:
 "We leave Heaven to the angels and the sparrows."
(HE mimes releasing sparrows.)

ANN

(Taking *The Future Of An Illusion* from Aaron.)
And he actually believed he could this pull off, an enlightened secular world?

AARON

Ann, this was his Promised Land! A brotherly world grounded in reason, where at long last the seed of Abraham can move freely across frontiers.
(HE mimes crossing over frontiers.)
As for his pulling this off, let's say he hoped against hope... And, after all, he was born in a caul, a membrane on his head ...

Ann and Aaron Pore Over Freud's Fainting Spells . . .

          (Miming the newborn Sigismund struggling with his hand against the 'blinding light.')
which his mother, Amalia, never let her firstborn son forget.
          (Now HE mimes Amalia Freud:)
My "*goldener* Sigi," you are destined to become a Great Man!
Little did his proud mama know that to become a Great Man, her undisputed darling, her "*goldener* Sigi," must kill that Great Man, Moses.
          (Laying *Moses* figurine on the carpet.)

ANN

Aaron, you know this, this, reading of yours is,
          (Mimes a Talmudic sage bent over a text.)
well, it's hard for me to accept.

AARON

Ann, already by 1900, the noose has been tightening . . . For Freud, as with Theodor Herzl—and for any Jew with eyes to see—the return of the Middle Ages, when our people were blamed for all epidemics, is around the corner.
          (Miming going around corner)—
Just a few of the miserable signs . . . (Emphasizing with fingers:)
The miserable Dreyfus Affair in 'fraternal' France; the ever popular Mayor of Vienna, "I say who is a Jew!," Herr Doktor Karl Lueger!— the first politician ever elected on an anti-Semitic platform!; the sentencing to death in Czechoslovakia of Leopold Hilsner, a young Jewish shoemaker's assistant, for 'killing' a 19-year-old Christian woman for her blood to bake the Passover matzohs—

ANN

The blood libel?! (Horror!)

AARON

          (Offers a matzoh to ANN, who, repulsed, turns head away.)
You sure?   (Taking a bite.)
It's fresh and quite tasty, just the right amount of—

ANN

Aaron!

AARON

Salt.
          (Suddenly, AARON sinks on to footstool:)
     By the waters of Babylon we sat and wept!
          (Flooded with tears.)

ANN (To self:)
The hate-filled lament of the Babylonian captivity.

AARON
O daughter of Babylon, who art to be destroyed—
(Becoming enraged.)

ANN
(Concerned, ANN rushes to AARON, who resists her.)
Aaron! Aaron!

AARON
Happy *shall he be,* that rewardeth thee as thou hast served us.
Happy *shall he be,* that taketh and dasheth thy little ones against the stones.
(As AARON pounds the floor, ANN rushes to him.)

ANN
Aaron, don't you see what you are doing to yourself!? Leave Freud to the psychoanalysts!

AARON (Massaging his painful hands)
Ann, you don't understand. Psychoanalysts, when it comes to their father, they blind themselves!—
(Mimes plucking his eyes out.)

ANN
(Facing him, holding him by the shoulders.)
Aaron, face it! You're losing it!

AARON
On *Pesach,* the season of our deliverance? No way!
(With her help, AARON seats self on couch.)

ANN
(On her knees before Aaron, takes his hands.)
Aaron, at least take a break . . . Freud won't go away.

AARON
Promise?

ANN
You have my word.

Ann and Aaron Pore Over Freud's Fainting Spells . . .

AARON

Not your heart? (Touching her breast.)

ANN

That, too.   (Placing HER hand over his.)

AARON

Then we continue? . . . Just a few more minutes—

ANN

On one condition. You call Klein.

AARON

You think his couch—my *Zoftig* Sophie—misses me?
(Mimes a patient on the couch squeezing cushion.)

ANN

Aaron, *I* miss you!

AARON

First thing in the morning, promise!... (Mimes phoning)
(Getting up from couch.)
Now, Ann, unlike Theodor Herzl, Freud doesn't broadcast his ambition. You see, for his Promised Land to be realized, secrecy is essential.

ANN

Concealing this even from Martha?

AARON

From everyone—

ANN

Everyone, except you.

AARON

May I continue? Now, just as it got the better of Dostoevsky, his bad conscience or guilt got the better of Freud—

ANN

Filial piety?

AARON

Right! Freud loved his gray-haired, Talmud-reading papa.

ANN (Lifting the legal pad.)

Nu, this all-important fainting spell?

THE UNKNOWN FREUD: FIVE PLAYS . . .

AARON

As I said, the first fit happened in 1909—in Bremen, Germany. At the time, Jung *hakens a chainik,* keeps going on and on, about prehistoric corpses recently discovered in marshes of Northern Germany, confusing these naturally preserved bodies with mummies stored in lead cellars in Bremen.

ANN

And the topic of mummies, you believe, called up in Freud's mind Egypt and Moses?—

AARON

Did you hear me say that?! This fit happened on August 20th, the day before Freud and Jung are to sail on *The George Washington* for America. That invitation to lecture at Clark University was a recognition of consequence!—the first such for Freud and psychoanalysis. Freud could almost taste *his* Promised Land—

ANN

Where do you suggest we hang the shingle,
    (Miming looking for a suitable place.)
"Reb Handel, mind-reader extraordinaire!"?

AARON

You through? According to Jung, Freud told him that his "chattering about corpses" meant that Jung had unconscious death-wishes against him.

ANN (Again, lifting legal pad.)

And this second spell?

AARON

Like the earlier one, this spell happened when they were dining. At the time, Jung was tearing into a recent paper by another of Freud's disciples, Karl Abraham. In the paper, Abraham, whom Freud greatly valued, claims that a particular pharaoh—because he ordered his father's name chiseled out from monuments—had had death-wishes against his father.
    (Mimes this chiseling behavior on *Moses* figurine.)
Now, Ann, according to Freud, it was from this Pharaoh, Pharaoh Akhenaten, that Moses got his monotheistic religion—

ANN

But, Aaron, it's only at the end of his life that Freud asserts this.

AARON

Ann, I'll say it again! Freud's a concealer, a careful concealer. It matters not

Ann and Aaron Pore Over Freud's Fainting Spells . . .

when he reveals something.

ANN

A regular Kabbalist. You seek! You find!

AARON

A Kabbalist, am I?!
>(Agitated, AARON lifts the Menorah from the mantle, holding it up ANN's face.)

Ann, what is this?!

ANN
>(Rising, ANN mimes an unsure charades participant.)

A remake of *Dracula* by Mel Brooks?

AARON

Even our precious little Miriam knows! Well, doesn't she?!

ANN (Mimes Miriam)

"I want to wight the wymnora." She was so cute.

AARON
>(Replacing the Menorah, AARON opens *The Letters of Sigmund Freud*, edited by his son, Ernst; HE hands Ann the book.)

Ann, just the underlined part. You'll understand why . . . It's to Martha.

ANN (Reads reluctantly:)
>Until nightfall I was...in the Christian and Jewish catacombs. In the Jewish catacombs the inscriptions are Greek, the candelabrum—I think it's called Menorah—can be seen on many tablets—

"*I think* it's called Menorah"?!   (Shaking HER head in disbelief!)
How can he not know for sure it's called a Menorah?

AARON

That's just it!

ANN

What's just it?!

AARON

A 51-year-old Jew whose beloved Talmud-reading father not only instructed him at age seven in Torah but also conducted the Passover Seder in Hebrew—and without the aid of a Haggadah—(Holds the Haggadah.) cannot not know for sure this is (Lifting the Menorah) a Menorah!

ANN

Okay?

AARON

Ann, here's how I see it: Freud, knowing that his correspondence—especially letters to his wife—will be pored over, is trying to keep his biographers off-track—

(Retrieving the book from ANN, AARON mimes poring over the text.)

ANN

By concealing his knowledge of Judaism? But for what purpose?

AARON

Ann, what have we been talking about?!

(Searching his file and book-cluttered desk)

His creation, psychoanalysis, must not be identified with Judaism. It's got to be seen as a science, an objective discipline, one that could have been created by anyone, Gentile as well as Jew. Ah! Here it is.

(Lifting a sheet from his yellow legal pad.)

Ann, have I your attention?!

ANN

Full!

AARON

Now what riled Jung especially was Abraham's claim that monotheism, Akhenaten's great creation, originated in Akhenaten's unconscious hatred of his father, that is, in his negative Father complex.

(AARON gets *Memories, Dreams, Reflections*.)

Here, in his 1961 memoir, Jung relates that Freud slides off the chair, faints,

(Mimes Freud sliding off chair, but catches self)

just as Jung is pointing out to Freud that Pharaohs other than Akhenaten had also chiseled out or crossed off their father's name from monuments, yet they—Ann, this is a direct quote—"yet they had inaugurated neither a new style nor a new religion."

ANN

Okay?

AARON

(Pointing to it, HE re-quotes the phrase:)

". . . they had inaugurated neither a *new style* nor a new religion."

Don't you see, Ann, Freud faints just as his Promised Land is called up in his mind—

ANN

Aaron, that's a stretch.

Ann and Aaron Pore Over Freud's Fainting Spells . . .

AARON

An enlightened, socially just world grounded in Reason, a brotherly world in which the seed of Abraham can at last move freely across frontiers—
  (Miming doing so)
this is not a radically new style?! And in the magnetic Jung, Freud believed he had his Joshua, who, by knocking down the resistances of the *goyim* to psychoanalysis and its findings, would be instrumental in ultimately instituting his Promised Land.
  (Quickly lifting a sheet of paper.)
Several months after Jung had entered the psychoanalytic fold, Freud, in May 1908, wrote Abraham:

> . . . as a Christian and a pastor's son Jung finds his way to me only against great inner resistances. His association with us is the more valuable for that. I nearly said that it was only by his appearance on the scene that psychoanalysis escaped the danger of becoming a Jewish national affair.
>   (AARON hands the letter to ANN, who gestures for it;
>   ANN studies the letter.)

Ann, don't you see?

ANN

What?! That Freud's other followers were all Jews?

AARON

The very first ones were, Ann, but you miss the point.

ANN

And that is?

AARON

Freud here is all but confessing to Abraham that psychoanalysis, like Theodor Herzl's Zionism, is at bottom
  (Pointing to the phrase on the sheet.)
"a Jewish national affair"—that is, it's a political movement to deliver the Jews—
  (ANN Hands Aaron back the letter.)
And as with all others, Freud kept Jung in the dark—and a good thing that he did. After the breakup he called Freud, "The Pope in Vienna"—
  (Extends right hand for ring to be kissed.)

ANN

Well, at least he didn't call him the Jewish Pope.

AARON

In his first editorial of a Nazi-controlled psychiatric journal, his erstwhile Joshua will put down psychoanalysis, claim that its "Jewish categories" do not apply to Gentiles. And he all but swoons over National Socialism with its mighty "Germanic soul."

ANN

Aaron, when was this?

AARON

In January 1934—

ANN

Just as Freud feared, psychoanalysis dismissed as a Jewish science—

AARON (Gets *Totem and Taboo*)

And all the while Freud continues preparing the ground, especially with his radical notion, here in *Totem and Taboo,* that religion can be traced back to the first patricide, the killing of their father by the sons of the primal horde.—

ANN

"The first patricide" . . . "sons of the primal horde"?! You know how your would-be Moses sounds?—This primal horde business, just why is it so significant?

AARON (Raising *Totem and Taboo*)

Because with this revolutionary account of the beginnings of religion, Freud, in 1913, prepares the way for the essential hypothesis of *Moses and Monotheism*—

ANN

His *farshtunkeneh* speculation that Moses was actually a high-born Egyptian?

AARON

Ann, that's not the essential premise. Rather, it's Freud's hypothesis that the Israelites repeated that first patricide—that is, banding together, they killed Moses,   (Mimes stabbing *Moses* figurine.)
And here is the key point—

ANN (Raising the Bible)

Now he rewrites Deuteronomy! Moses died when he was 120. And for this desert fantasy Freud, I suppose, has evidence?

AARON

Not really, he's clutching at straws.
            (ANN presses palms on temples, as though a headache is
            coming on.)

Ann and Aaron Pore Over Freud's Fainting Spells . . .

Now, Freud goes on to claim—and this, Ann—
        (HE notices ANN holding her head.)

                    ANN

Aaron, all this is giving me a headache.

                    AARON

Ann, we're almost there. Okay?   (Places his arm around her shoulder.)

                    ANN

Okay.

                    AARON

Now, Ann, here is the key point: like Akhenaten's monotheism, Jewish monotheism is nothing but a reaction-formation stemming from the Jews' guilt and remorse over the killing of Moses.

                    ANN

The *alleged* killing of Moses. And this is how Freud accounts for Judaism?—

                    AARON

Not only for Judaism but also, against all odds, its persistence. You see, according to Freud, from generation-to-generation each and every Jew possesses indestructible unconscious memory traces of that traumatic event and terrible deed—along with the related patricidal sense of guilt and remorse.—

                    ANN

Such torturous speculation. Aaron, I'm sorry, but he sounds like a crank. A deluded, opinionated crank.

                    AARON

That may be, but to bring it back home: Ann, in my unconscious, I'm one of the rebellious Israelites who had banded together to kill Moses—
        ('Stabbing' *Moses*, to the floor.)

                ANN (Raising hand, hesitantly)

I'm afraid to ask: Just how does this account for Judaism's persistence?

                    AARON

Ann, consider me transgeneration Everyman Jew. Understand, all this is unconscious: by abiding by the Law I expiate having taken part in the murder of Moses; hence Judaism endures—

(Dusting the Tablets of the Law, and raising *Moses* high, AARON kisses the Law.)

ANN

And if Judaism is just a, a, reaction-formation, then the Law, being a mere creation   (Points to the Tablets)
of man, is not divine—and Christendom and anti-Semitism are no more—

AARON

You got it—that's his secret game plan.
(Replacing *Moses* on the bookshelf.)

ANN

A game plan that is fatally flawed: Aaron, the unconscious memory traces of the killing of Moses are, as you have just said, indelibly imprinted in the Jew's DNA—never to be erased or destroyed—forever stamped!
('Stamping' with hand Aaron's forehead.)
According to his own theory then, Freud's 'messianic ambition' is doomed from the start, isn't it?

AARON (wincing.)

Ann, Freud pinned his hopes on Reason or the Intellect prevailing. To quote Freud, "The voice of reason is a soft one, but it does not rest until it gains a hearing . . ."—

ANN

That'll be the day!
(Doing a two-step, her headache returns; SHE holds her head.)
Oy! I hope I can still work on my papers.

AARON

I'll help grade them.

ANN

Aaron, that's all I need!

AARON

Anyway, we're almost through . . . The powerful Jung has just lifted and carried Freud from the hotel dining room to a couch in the lounge. Here, Jung relates what happened next. (AARON reads:)
   Freud half came to, and I shall never forget the look he cast at
   me. In his weakness he looked at me as if I were his father.
". . .as if I were *his father.*"

ANN

I got "father" without your help. Aaron, if, as you say, Freud is bent on destroying the Torah, then his sense of guilt at the time of the fit has got to pertain to Jakob—

AARON

Freud's guilt of course pertained to Jakob, his beloved first instructor in Torah. But, Ann, during the fit, Freud's Promised Land was called up, the realization of which, again, requires what? . . . That Moses die, once and for all, right?! So, Freud's guilt had to pertain as well to the great man who—to re-quote Freud—"created the Jews," Moses.

(Again, AARON lays the *Moses* figurine on floor.)

Or, to paraphrase Freud on Dostoevsky:

The attacks have the value of a self-punishment. Freud wished Moses dead, and now this impious striver who would be Moses *is* Moses.

(Miming Freud, AARON falls away to rug next to *Moses*. and is dead himself; with fingers closes his eyes.)

ANN

(Dusting and replacing *Moses* on bookshelf.)

And Freud's terrible guilt from childhood? It's time, Aaron, don't you think?

AARON (Getting up)

After Sol's, er, Jakob's death at age 81 in 1896, Freud, feeling as though he had been torn up by the roots, begins his systematic self-analysis, mainly by studying his dreams.

(Mimes Freud at desk with pen in hand, over large writing pad.)

Only to discover to his horror,

(Miming Freud, anguished, hunched over desk, his left hand covering left eye in the manner of one of the doomed in Michelangelo's *Last Judgment*.)

that he is a Cain!

ANN

A Cain?—

AARON

Psychoanalysts call it a "return of the repressed." Freud believes that his jealous, hateful wishes had killed his baby brother, Julius—

ANN

When was this?

AARON

In his birthplace, the little Catholic town of Freiberg, in Moravia, and where the good Christian had humiliated Jakob. Freud was 23 months old, and Julius was either six or eight months old.

ANN
... "six or eight months old?"

AARON
Ann, the date of Julius's birth hasn't been determined.

ANN
His birth record is lost?

AARON
Right! We only know when Julius died, April 15, 1858—

ANN
As brilliant as he was, Freud continued to believe his hateful wishes had killed his baby brother?

AARON
He just couldn't shake it—

ANN
How he must have suffered . . .

AARON
And in silence . . . Freud's atheism, I am convinced, can be traced back to Julius's death—

ANN
'If there *is* a God in Heaven, would He have allowed Julius to die?'—

AARON
You got it, Ann—Freud's atheism wasn't reasoned out. It was that of a tormented, lost soul... Now, soon after the second spell, here is what Freud related to another disciple, Sandor Ferenczi. . . . It's relevant.
(AARON hands Ann Vol. 2 of Ernest Jones's authorized biography of Freud.)

ANN (Reads:)
Freud expressed the opinion that all his attacks could be traced to the effect on him of his younger brother's death—

AARON
And what more fitting way for this haunted Cain to redeem himself than by, by—? Come on, Ann . . . Think! (gesturing, encouraging . . .)

ANN
By delivering *der Kinder,* other Juliuses . . .
(Heads for a large wall photo of their granddaughter.)
and Miriams. . . .

Ann and Aaron Pore Over Freud's Fainting Spells . . .

AARON

That, Ann, is his salvation—

ANN

Aaron, I hate admitting it, but I'm intrigued.

AARON

It's contagious, isn't it?

ANN

Aaron, a thought. Couldn't it have been the case that just as he had wanted Julius out of the way, that Freud wanted Jung out of the way?, that rather than Jung wanting to kill Freud, that Freud, at the dinner
 (Eyeing and handling the knife-shaped letter opener.)
was sorely tempted to sink his steak knife into Jung?

AARON

Ann, this helps! (He jots feverishly.) Were the increasingly rebellious Jung to defect, as seems just a matter of time—Jung especially resented Freud's making the Oedipus Complex into a dogma—Freud's redemptive Promised Land could be nipped in the bud. (Snaps pencil in half.)

ANN

Reason enough for Freud to want his "Joshua" dead! . . .

AARON

Which would make his death-like spell purposeful—it kept Freud from acting on his increasingly aroused murderous feelings.

ANN

A most effective defense, no? . . . Of course! (Slapping her head!) It's the other way around! (Massaging her pained head.)

AARON

The other way around?!

ANN

Freud wanted Jung to murder him!

AARON

Hm! . . ."How sweet it must be to die."
 (Lifts Vol. I of Jones's biography of Freud.)
Those were Freud's first words upon awakening. "How sweet it must to die." . . . Finally, this Cain would be out of his misery . . . no more inner torment—

ANN

Some psychologist! The father of psychoanalysis killed by one of his rebellious sons. . . . Think generations!— . . . Think primal father of the clan—

AARON

Freud . . . the new Moses!—

ANN

No longer "seen from afar," his redemptive Promised Land realized at last. And for all eternity!

AARON

(Rapidly jotting bold letters with a felt-tipped pen on a blank sheet of the yellow legal pad, HE says:)

Ann, as the great Maimonides said, "The gates of interpretation are always open!"

(Tossing the pen, AARON, *now manic,* and armed with his yellow pad or 'tablet,' cries:)

From Moses to Moses who is like unto thee!

(Turns 360 degrees for all to see in bold letters the new 'Law.')

"Know Thyself!"

(Suddenly grief-stricken, the 'Law' slipping from his hands, AARON lowers himself on to the footstool.)

Ann, I miss Sol. (Breaking down.)

ANN

(Like a mother, comforts Aaron.)

I know, Aaron. Aaron, I know.

AARON

Klein keeps telling me I've got to bury him . . . How the hell do you bury your father? . . .He was a milkman—All Jews have money. Right?!

ANN

Aaron, Sol was rich in other ways.

AARON

What do I do? Sit *shiva* another two years?! (In pain.)

ANN

You realize, Aaron, that's almost how long—

AARON

I've been working on Freud! (An awareness; lost in thought . . . .)

Ann and Aaron Pore Over Freud's Fainting Spells . . .

ANN

Aaron, have I your attention?
> (Taps AARON's shoulder; HE jumps.)

Even as you were analyzing or dissecting Freud, you were taking him in to yourself.
> (Closing eyes, ANN swallows piece matzoh, like a Roman Catholic at Mass taking Communion Wafer.)

And because not even Freud can replace Sol, this, this, cannibalism has naturally failed to fill the hole in your heart—
> (ANN puts down remainder of the matzoh.)

AARON

Last session, suddenly at the hour's end, Klein, like a Hebrew prophet of old, stands over me in the half-gloom—
> (AARON mimes Klein, with German or Austrian accent:)

Aaron, you cannot be blind—To no avail have you been internalizing Freud. Aaron, you must your longing embrace! Your sorrow, it must flood you—

ANN

And so you bolted!—So, it wasn't the two-hour drive to the psychoanalytic institute after all! Freud, I see, is not the only Jew who is a careful concealer—

AARON (Now lying on couch)

While Klein is embracing air, quiet as a mouse, Jakob, I mean Sol, appears, wearing his black pea coat and favorite Cubs cap, *The Courier-Journal* folded in his pocket and carrying a milk gallon from the plant.

> (In a trance-like tate, AARON—re-experiencing his acute longing for Sol which had 'broken through' or surfaced that session—rises, tries in vain to embrace 'Sol'; overwhelmed by grief, AARON breaks down, as he sinks on to the foot stool . . .)

ANN
> (To self, as SHE restrains herself from comforting him:)

Ann, don't you dare! He *must* go through this!

AARON
> (Steadying self and wiping his eyes, HE heads for the file cabinet, from the top of which AARON lifts a nondescript pipe, fondling it as HE examines it; bending His head,

AARON 'inhales' the pipe bowl, as if trying to 'take in' Sol's spirit . . . Coughing, HE 'comes back.')
Ann . . . I feel lost.
(Now, smelling Sol's Chicago Cubs cap.)
I don't want his smell to go away. Does that make sense?
(As HE again breaks down, ANN hands him tissues.)
(AARON, collecting self, replaces the Cap tenderly.)
Emotionally drained, catching myself drifting off at the wheel, I—
(Mimes trying to stay awake.)

ANN

Over the phone, I could hardly hear you.
(Mimes holding phone, trying to hear.)
Spending the night in Cincinnati was the sensible thing to do.

AARON

(Looking at Ann out of corner of his eye, AARON opens up:)
Ann, in the Ramada I had a distressing, but eye-opening dream . . . it was all but transparent.
(HE seats self at 'hotel room' desk and writes, 'analyzing' his dream:)
A large black labrador with a long leash is running free. Frantically, as though it's a matter of life and death, I try getting hold of his leash. . . ."Black Labrador"—black dog—Churchill's "Black dog!" "Black dog" is what Churchill called his bouts of depression. Hm! I've been trying to reign in or choke off my huge black dog, my depression. . . . Black, black, Sol's black pea coat. The black dog of the dream is as elusive as Sol was this afternoon in Klein's gloomy office—
(HE mimes attempting to embrace Sol.)
Is the elusive black dog of the dream then also Sol, whom I've been trying so desperately to hold on to, "as though it's a matter of life and death"?—
But if I don't let Sol go, if I don't face head-on my grief, I'll never come back to myself, never be whole, never rid myself of my "black dog" depressions. But to be whole, to have a life without Sol, how's that possible? (Anguish) Let alone not to crack-up?
(ANN resists comforting him, an inner struggle.)
So, naturally—to use your apt term, Ann—your brave husband—"bolted."
(AARON, as wipes his glasses:)
I left my good glasses at Klein's office. Freud says there are no accidents—
(HE goes to wall calendar; writes:)
"Call Klein." Ann, this might not look like it, but it's written in stone!

Ann and Aaron Pore Over Freud's Fainting Spells . . .

ANN

Already, I'm jealous of *Zoftig* Sophie.

AARON

I confess, I do tell her things I don't tell you.
        (Starts pouring Mogen David into two wine glasses.)
But it's just talk.

ANN

That's a relief!
        (AARON laughs, almost spilling the wine.)
Careful! What's so funny?

AARON

I was just seeing myself being wheeled into Our Lady of Peace:
        (Bent over like Groucho, wine glass in each hand, HE stretches arms laterally.)
"*Schwesters, Schwesters,* make way for the *rebbe!* . . . Sisters, make way for the *rebbe!*—

ANN

Aaron, that *is* funny! (Giggling)

AARON

After two thousand years, a fitting reversal—the Church making way for the Jew!
        (AARON hands glass to Ann.)

ANN

Nu, meschugganah lunatic, when do we broadcast?—

AARON

A *rebbe and rebbetzn* from Louisville, Kentucky, who'd listen?

ANN & AARON (THEY toast)

L'Chaim! L'Chaim!
To life! To life!

ANN

Next year in Jerusalem!

AARON

Not the fleshpots of Egypt?! . . .
        (THEY kiss passionately.)

THE UNKNOWN FREUD: FIVE PLAYS...

ANN

This was some session, don't you think?!

AARON (Looks at watch.)
Worth every Shekel!... My Ann, an analyst. Who'da thunk it!?
('Belly dancing' backward, ANN, blowing a kiss, EXITS.)

(Spotting the yellow "Know Thyself!" legal pad, HE raises it—)

"Know Thyself!" Yes, Ann, my love, it was quite a session!
(Gathering his research pages.)
That's all we need, Sol—Good Christians armed with yet another club.
(HE rips the papers...)
(From the top of the file cabinet, HE takes the Cubs cap; smells and returns it. And then dials...)

Dr. Klein, this is Aaron Handel... Yes, those are my glasses—

END of PLAY

This play was given a staged reading at the Cincinnati Playwrights Initiative on September 14, 2010.

*"The Struggle is
Not Yet Over"*

Freud and members of the Committee: (left to right seated) Freud, Sándor Ferenczi, and Hanns Sachs; (standing) Otto Rank, Karl Abraham, Max Eitingon, and Ernest Jones—1922

"The Struggle is Not Yet Over"
A Play in One Scene

...What took hold of my imagination immediately is your idea of a secret council composed of the best and most trustworthy among our men to take care of the further developments of psycho-analysis against personalities and accidents when I am no more....

I daresay it would make living and dying easier for me if I knew of such an association existing to watch over my creation.

First of all: This committee must be *strictly secret* in its existence and in its actions.

—Sigmund Freud to Ernest Jones, letter dated August 1, 1912; in Jones, 1955, p. 153.

I started my professional activity as a neurologist trying to bring relief to my neurotic patients. Under the influence of an older friend and by my own efforts, I discovered some important new facts about the unconscious in psychic life, the role of instinctual urges, and so on. Out of these findings grew a new science, psychoanalysis, a part of psychology, and a new method of treatment of the neuroses. I had to pay heavily for this bit of good luck. People did not believe in my facts and thought my theories unsavory. Resistance was strong and unrelenting. In the end I succeeded in acquiring pupils and building up an International Psychoanalytic Association. But the struggle is not yet over.

—Sigmund Freud, BBC interview at his last residence, 20 Maresfield Gardens, in Hampstead, London, on December 7, 1938.

CAST OF CHARACTERS

DR. DONALD CUNNINGHAM, M.D.:
> Born in 1929, in Sheffield, England, a graduate of Cambridge University Medical School, Dr. Cunningham is a child psychoanalyst at London's Travistock Clinic, where he doubles as a training analyst. Analyzed by Anna Freud, he has authored well-received books on child psychoanalysis. He's wearing an expensive but worn tweed jacket.

DR. PIETRO LUZZATTI, M.D.:
> Born in 1944, in Naples, Italy, a graduate of the University of Perugia Medical School, where he is Professor of Psychiatry. A psychoanalyst, he has

written several books and numerous articles on psychoanalysis and art history. Stylishly dressed, he could be a museum curator.

DR. SOLOMON MAIER, M.D., Ph.D.:
Born in 1938 in the Bronx, a graduate of Yeshiva University and N.Y.U., receiving both a Ph.D. in clinical psychology and a medical degree. A training and supervising analyst at the New York Psychoanalytic Institute, Dr. Maier is Professor of Psychiatry at the Albert Einstein College of Medicine. He is on the editorial board of *The Journal of the American Psychoanalytic Association.* Conservatively dressed, he is a cigar smoker and bearded.

DR. MIMI ROSENTHAL, M.D.:
Born in 1950 in Queens, a graduate of Hunter College and Stanford University Medical School. A training and supervising psychoanalyst at the Boston Psychoanalytic Institute and clinical professor of psychiatry at Yale Medical School, she specializes in the treatment of children. She is attractive and of average height.

SIGMUND FREUD'S GHOST:
The ghost of the father of psychoanalysis (1856–1939) looks like a vigorous 45-year-old. The 5-foot-7-inch, 126-pound Freud has penetrating brown eyes—eyes that have been known to strike terror in disciples who crossed him. Impeccably groomed and carrying a gold-handled cane, he is wearing a 3-piece gray suit with a blue gardenia in its lapel.

SETTING

Sigmund Freud's study, Berggasse 19, Vienna, Austria. The set should approximate Rita Ransohoff's description in E. Engleman's book of photos, *Berggasse 19, Sigmund Freud's Home and Offices, Vienna 1938,* University of Chicago Press, 1981:

The couch is piled high with pillows so that the patient would be in a near-sitting position, but eminently comfortable . . . The patient could cover himself with the shawl at the foot of the couch to protect against a possible draft. Freud would sit behind the couch in an easy chair with a footstool. The room is cluttered in late-Victorian style, but in an organized and "interesting" manner. The antiquities have their place; they do not take over. The wall-covering is plain, almost dark; pattern and color come from the Oriental rugs on the floor, the couch, and its adjacent wall.

TIME:
Several minutes before midnight, September 23, 1989.

(PROLOGUE MUSIC—a Violinist plays the opening bars of *Kol Nidre*.)
 (Outside it is storming. DRS. LUZZATTI, MAIER and ROSENTHAL
 are clearing the antiquities-covered desk for the funerary urn
 in DR. CUNNINGHAM's hands.)

DR. CUNNINGHAM
When Anna Freud, on her deathbed, told me of her father's last wish, well, it took my breath away . . .
 (Places the urn on the desk.)

DR. ROSENTHAL
But, Don, he had been interested in the paranormal—

DR. LUZZATTI
In 1913, he even held a séance here at Berggasse 19.

DR. CUNNINGHAM
But, Pietro, it was Sandor Ferenczi's idea.

DR. MAIER
Don, since when did a disciple—even a member of his inner circle, the Committee—tell Sigmund Freud what to do, and in his own home and office?

DR. LUZZATTI (Examines a marble Venus)
Donald, we, of all people, know the critical role of early life experience. And from his faithful nanny, little Sigi learned about our immortal souls—

DR. ROSENTHAL
Then there's the other side of the coin. At the Passover Seder his Talmud-reading father, Jakob, set aside a large wine cup for Elijah, just in case the Messiah were to show up—

DR. MAIER
That'll be the day!

DR. CUNNINGHAM
There, that's plenty of room. (Placing the urn on the desk.)

DR. ROSENTHAL
The death of his infant brother, Julius, I'm willing to bet, disposed him to believe in survival after death.

DR. MAIER
How?

DR. CUNNINGHAM
Sol, I believe Mimi's on to something, especially given Catholicism's emphasis on the saving of souls.

DR. LUZZATTI
Hm! Little Sigi wondering whether baby Julius is with Jesus in Paradise or burning in everlasting Hell—

DR. MAIER
Pietro, it's Sigmund Freud, the ultimate atheist—the self-described "completely godless Jew"—that we're talking about, not a 23-month-old toddler whose baby brother had just died—

DR. ROSENTHAL
Sol, just the month before, Freud's mother, Amalia, lost her younger brother, who, strangely, was also named Julius—

DR. LUZZATTI
Do you not see, Solomon?

DR. MAIER
See what?!

DR. LUZZATTI
With his young mama overcome with double grief—she was but twenty-two—his devout nanny became little Sigi's mama—

DR. CUNNINGHAM
Giving her a free hand to shape him—

DR. LUZZATTI
And in the plastic stage.... Can this then be behind his putting off Rome for so long—fear that in the seat of Catholicism, with its many moving religious works of art, that his stirred up Roman Catholic sensibility would overwhelm him?

"The Struggle is Not Yet Over"

DR. MAIER

Sigmund Freud bend the knee? Pietro, return to the couch; she misses you.—

DR. LUZZATTI

Have you a better explanation for his Rome phobia?—

DR. CUNNINGHAM

There, that's plenty of room.
        (Removing an envelope from his jacket pocket—)
To keep this evening from getting out, Freud wanted just four persons, all psychoanalysts, present. He wanted America represented, Mimi and Sol, because it was there that he received his first recognition of consequence.

DR. MAIER

His series of lectures on psychoanalysis at Clark University in 1909—
        (DR. CUNNINGHAM replaces envelope on desk.)

DR. ROSENTHAL

William James was there. He even got an honorary degree of Laws.

DR. CUNNINGHAM

Italy, Pietro, because of his many fond memories of Rome.

DR. LUZZATTI

The pagan Rome, not the Christian Rome.
        (Studies a figurine of classical antiquity.)

DR. CUNNINGHAM

And because he lived out his last year in London in freedom, Freud wanted England represented. (Removes handkerchief from jacket pocket.)

DR. MAIER

Leaving Vienna at the last minute in June 1938, it's as if he had a death-wish—

DR. ROSENTHAL

Anna's full day interrogation at Gestapo headquarters decided it for him. He even handed her Veronal tablets—
        (DR. CUNNINGHAM unfolds the handkerchief on the desk,
          revealing a gold ring with an intaglio bearing the head of
          Jupiter.)

DR. LUZZATTI

Freud's Jupiter head ring? May I?
    (DR. CUNNINGHAM hands it to him.)
    (DR. LUZZATTI goes to the light to better see the ring; he mocks sliding it on his right ring finger.)
You think some of our papa's charisma might rub off?

DR. MAIER

Wear it, Pietro, and the Chair at the University of Perugia is yours. Here, let me try.   (Getting ring from Dr. L., HE slips it on.)
It won't come off!—
    (Struggling.)

DR. LUZZATTI

A sign, perhaps, Solomon?
    (DR. MAIER removes the ring; relief.)

DR. CUNNINGHAM

Well, shall we?
    (DR. MAIER places the ring in DR. CUNNINGHAM'S outstretched hand. DR. ROSENTHAL seats self in the chair opposite Freud's desk chair. Placing the ring on the desk, DR. CUNNINGHAM pulls up a chair beside DR. ROSENTHAL and sits down.)

DR. LUZZATTI

    (Beating DR. MAIER to the footstool at the right head of the desk, DR. LUZZATTI sits.)
I am afraid, Solomon, you will have to try to fill our papa's seat.
    (Hesitantly, DR. MAIER seats self in the sacred chair of psychoanalysis.)

DR. CUNNINGHAM

    (Carefully removing a letter from the envelope, he puts on his glasses. and reads:)
My Dear Colleagues,
On the occasion of the fiftieth anniversary of my death, from my study at Berggasse 19, Vienna, you are to try to make contact with me. Just before midnight you are to place my cinerary urn on my writing desk. Next, the Italian among you will place my ring on his right ring finger.
    (Surprised, DR. LUZZATTI obeys.)

Then, as the four of you clasp hands, the Italian will cry out: "Sigmund Freud," followed by "Professor." If, after ten minutes, I don't make contact, consider this experiment over. And enjoy the Roman red wine.
Yours Freud
> (The FOUR clasp hands;
>> the clock begins chiming twelve times.)

DR. LUZZATTI

Sigmund Freud . . . . Professor! . . . . Contact us. Professor!—
> (FREUD'S GHOST APPEARS,
>> holding his gold-handled
>> cane in the manner of a staff.)

> (The sight of FREUD'S ghost terrifies DR. MAIER, the only one seeing it.)

DR. LUZZATTI

Solomon, you are hurting me!

DR. CUNNINGHAM

Sol, you're pale . . . like you've seen a—

DR. ROSENTHAL

Sol, Sol! What is it?!
> (DRS. ROSENTHAL, LUZZATTI and CUNNINGHAM turn to see what DR. MAIER is reacting to.)

DR. LUZZATTI

Holy Mother of God! (In Italian.)
> (In disbelief, DRS. LUZZATTI, CUNNINGHAM & ROSENTHAL stare at FREUD.)

Professor, if I may? A question—

FREUD

My ring, please. I am naked without it.

DR. LUZZATTI

But of course, Professor.
> (Obliges)

FREUD
(Studies ring before slipping it on his right ring-finger.)
You and the others, you do have names?
(Spreading and closing fingers as he gazes at ring.)

DR. LUZZATTI
Forgive me, Professor. I am Pietro Luzzatti and am from Perugia.

DR. ROSENTHAL
Mimi Rosenthal, Professor, from Boston.

DR. CUNNINGHAM
Donald Cunningham, Professor, from London.

DR. MAIER
Solomon Maier, New York City, Professor.

FREUD
Thank you . . . Pietro, you were asking?

DR. LUZZATTI
Professor, you passed away at age 83, and yet you appear my age, 45.

FREUD
You prefer that I return a feeble old Jew so eaten up with cancer of the jaw and mouth that even his chow, Jofi, avoids him because of his smell?

DR. LUZZATTI
To see you as you are, Professor, that is to say, as you appeared in the early days of struggle, this is more than I could have hoped for. But—

FREUD
Ah! You remembered the cigars!
(Pointing his silver cigar clipper at them; HE lights one.)
Smoking was the death of me. I once quit for fourteen months. The trouble was, without my cigars, work was impossible.

DR. LUZZATTI
Professor, one more question.

FREUD
And that is, Pietro?

"The Struggle is Not Yet Over"

DR. LUZZATTI

Professor, what is beyond the veil?—

DR. CUNNINGHAM

Yes, the other world, Professor, what's it like?—

FREUD

(Suddenly enraged, HE lifts cane to cudgel DR. CUNNINGHAM.)

Withholding my cancer from me! By what right, Jones?!

(As the startled DR. CUNNINGHAM struggles to disarm FREUD, DRS. MAIER and LUZZATTI restrain FREUD.)

DR. ROSENTHAL

Professor, the year is 1989. He is not Ernest Jones in 1923—

DR. LUZZATTI

But a later disciple, Donald Cunningham—

FREUD ('Coming to,' he drops Cane.)

Cunningham, I must ask your forgiveness. It must be the accent. For a moment. I was back here at Berggasse 19 with Jones when he informed me that he and the other members of the Committee had withheld my cancer from me in 1923 so that I could take my trip to Rome with my daughter, Anna, in peace.

DR. CUNNINGHAM

Professor, I'd have been enraged, too. (Begins to return cane.)

(Refusing cane, FREUD takes a pad from breast pocket and writes...)

DR. ROSENTHAL

(Whispers to DR. MAIER)

He could have killed Don.

DR. MAIER

Yeah, something's there, Mimi, something explosive, just what, the Professor's not telling.

(Nodding in direction of FREUD returning note pad to pocket.)

FREUD

Cunningham, you were asking?

DR. MAIER (to DR. ROSENTHAL)

Let's not go there again.

DR. CUNNINGHAM
Yes, Professor, the other world...what's it like?

FREUD
Wouldn't you rather know what your "papa" was like?!

DR. LUZZATTI
"Papa"? Then you heard us, Professor?

FREUD
While waiting in the wings, you could say.

DR. MAIER
The Professor is back to form. That's a relief.

FREUD
(Spots 2-headed Roman god Janus.)
Janus, I see that nothing's changed. Your two stone faces still look down on me in superior fashion . . . May I? (Lifting Janus.)
Tell me, O Roman god of new beginnings, have these my children the courage, the moral courage, to see their papa naked?

DR. MAIER
So that's it! He's returned to set the record straight! Maybe even about Rome—

DR. LUZZUTTI
Solomon, careful what you wish for.

FREUD
(Places left Janus mouth to his left ear.)
You just guard the threshold?
(Now places right Janus mouth to his right ear)
You are not psychologists? Thank you both anyway.
(Lightning and thunder; FREUD looks out window.)
On Sunday, July 3rd, 1904, Theodor Herzl died prematurely at the age of forty-four. Jews from all over descended on Vienna for his funeral four days later. The unending procession winding its way through Europe's most anti-Semitic city—I tell you it was a sight to behold. Even for Herzl's Jewish detractors who had dismissed him as just another false messiah—and, also, I suspect, for the ever-popular mayor of Vienna, "I say who is a Jew!," *Herr Doktor* Karl Lueger.

DR. MAIER
Whom Hitler will praise to the high heavens in *Mein Kampf*. But why is he telling us this?

DR. LUZZATTI
Patience, Solomon!

FREUD
In shocked dismay and with mounting irritability I read Herzl's eyewitness account of Dreyfus's court-martial in December 1894. The French General Staff had evidence that one of its officers was selling military secrets to the Germans. The traitor couldn't possibly be a Christian—
(Crossing self with cigar.)

DR. MAIER
(Plays a Jew-hating French General)
Heaven forbid! Ah ha! But of course! It's as plain as his hooked nose, the Judas is Dreyfus, the one Israelite on our staff! ('Wipes' his hands.)

DR. LUZZATTI
An apt scapegoat!

FREUD
In the *Neue Freie Presse,* Herzl also reported on Dreyfus's public degradation on the parade ground of the *Ecole Militaire* a few weeks later, on the fifth of January. Just before being stripped of his honors and his sword broken in two—and with the bloodthirsty mob shouting, "*A la Morte les Juifs*"—"Death to the Jews"—Dreyfus cries, "Soldiers! An innocent is dishonored! Long Live France!"—(*Mental projection: a slide of this incident, with Dreyfus's face superimposed on that of FREUD.*)
And this disgusting behavior took place in the land of "Liberty, Equality"... What was the other? Ah yes! "Fraternity"!
(Gets *The Interpretation of Dreams.*)
Here, in my great confession, I relate a dream-image of mine that was instigated by a train of thoughts concerning Dreyfus on Devil's Island where he—its sole prisoner—was sentenced for life over that fraudulent charge of treason. Ah! here it is. (Hands book to DR. CUNNINGHAM.)

DR. CUNNINGHAM
"A man standing on a cliff in the middle of the sea . . . "

FREUD
Let me see! (Looks at the sentence). James Strachey omitted translating *Steilen*. It was a *steep* cliff!

DR. CUNNINGHAM

Professor, you withhold the thoughts informing this dream-image. But, clearly, Captain Dreyfus's precipitous fall signified to you the precarious standing of Jews in Christendom—Each and every one a potential Dreyfus.

DR. MAIER

The writing was on the wall, the bloody cliff wall.
    (Looks up to the heavens.)
And, Yahweh, your strong hand, where was it?!—I'm still waiting!

FREUD

The miserable plight of that pitiful Alsatian Jew who was as good as dead and the rampant mushrooming of vicious attacks on Jews throughout France—the land of the Rights of Man—were sobering. For, Cunningham, they signaled a return to the Middle Ages, when my people were held responsible for all epidemics.

DR. LUZZATTI

The noose round your increasingly isolated people was being tightened.

FREUD

And nowhere more than in my alleged fatherland. Mark Twain's description of the Austrian Parliament comes to mind (mimes writing):
    They are religious men, they are earnest, sincere, devoted, and they hate the Jews.
Those words penned ninety years ago by Hannibal Missouri's greatest son apply as well, I suspect, to the current members of that august body. . .

DR. ROSENTHAL

In addition to Herzl, there was one other would-be Moses on the Berggasse, wasn't there, Professor?

DR. MAIER

Professor, is that true?—(troubled)

FREUD

My, dear Mimi, your feminine intuition, I see, wasn't analyzed out of you, after all—

DR. MAIER

Oh, but to be a fly on the Berggasse,
When the two Messiahs first they greet.
    (Miming a chance encounter, 'Freud' and 'Herzl' remove their hats and bow to each other.)

"The Struggle is Not Yet Over"

> If not now, when?
> If not us, who?
> (Mimes dancing away arm-in-arm.)

DR. ROSENTHAL

Sol! (A reproof.)

FREUD

You mock me, wicked son?

DR. MAIER

And why shouldn't I!? Taking you at your seductive word, I believed that psychoanalysis—which has been my life—is a science grounded in reason, when, in actuality, you now all but confess to Mimi, it's a political movement—

DR. LUZZATTI

Like Herzl's Zionism, psychoanalysis is a Jewish national affair but cloaked with the mantle of science?

DR. MAIER

You got it, Pietro—it's a covert political movement to deliver the Jews from anti-Semitism. Our great revolutionary 'science' is grounded in shifting sand—our papa's grandiose messianic wishes!

FREUD

Pietro, an irresistible feeling of solidarity with my people was mounting in me... In 1898, Leopold Hilsner was sentenced to death in Czechoslovakia for allegedly killing a 19-year-old Christian woman for blood to bake the Passover matzos—

DR. CUNNINGHAM

The charge of ritual blood-sacrifice—it was actually argued—and successfully—in a modern court of law?

DR. MAIER

You heard, Don... Just one more Dreyfus.

FREUD

That young Jewish shoemaker could have been any one of my three boys.

DR. CUNNINGHAM

Professor, like Herzl, you would institute your own Promised Land?

FREUD

Yes, my dear Cunningham, a socially just world where that neurosis of humankind, religion, is unknown.

DR. LUZZATTI

But this envisioned Promised Land of yours, Professor, it is purchased at a dear price—Judaism itself.

DR. ROSENTHAL

Yes, but Abraham's seed, (Gently touching statuette busts of a boy and a girl) Juliuses and Sarahs, are no longer plagued by that miserable anti-Semitism—

FREUD (Breaking down.)

Julius! Julius! Julius! If there is a God in Heaven, would He have allowed you to die? Cause me to suffer so? - All I wanted was for you to just go away.
> *(FREUD projects: We hear Kaddish, the prayer for the dead. Clutching her dead infant, AMELIA FREUD, 22, looks for answers in JAKOB'S eyes—Why? Why?—as JAKOB, 42, tries comforting her.)*

DR. MAIER

What should we do?

FREUD

> (As FREUD begins to faint, DR. CUNNINGHAM catches him; briefly coming to in his arms as they head for the couch, FREUD looks up at DR. C., as a boy might to his father.)

How sweet it must be to die!

DR. MAIER

Mimi, why in hell did you mention Julius!?

DR. LUZZATTI

Wicked son, you should talk! —

DR. ROSENTHAL

"Julius" just came out.

FREUD

> (On the couch, moaning like a young child; in German, says:)
> *Resi, Resi, all ich wollte nur das er weggeht. Resi, erzaehl noch mal uber Julius und Jesus. Resi, Resi, Sag's mir noch mal, bitte! Noch mal!* (Anguish).

"The Struggle is Not Yet Over"

[All I wanted was for him to just go away. Resi, tell me again about Julius and Jesus. Resi, Resi, tell me, tell me it again, please! Again! (For the English, an off-stage VOICE can be heard.)]

DR. ROSENTHAL
(As the OTHERS look on helplessly, SHE heads for couch and cradles 'little Sigi'; in German. says:)
Sei still mein Sohn, dein klein bruder Julius ist mit Jesus in dem Himmel.
[And then in English]
Hush, my son. Your baby brother Julius is with Jesus—in Paradise with Jesus.
(FREUD drifts off at HER breast.)

DR. MAIER
(Abruptly turning DR. ROSENTHAL'S face towards him.)
Mimi, when our papa awakens—and recalls your playing his Catholic mama to his little Sigi—you'll have hell to pay, especially for that pap about his baby brother Julius being in heaven in the loving care of Jesus—

DR. ROSENTHAL (As if back from a trance.)
That wasn't me!

DR. CUNNINGHAM
In my arms, when the Professor half came-to in his weakness he looked at me as if I were his father. . . . I'll never forget that look.

DR. ROSENTHAL
The sooner this is over, the better—

FREUD
(Slowly coming to, on couch.)
Minna? Minna?

DR. ROSENTHAL
Now, he's calling for his sister-in-law. In 1895, several years after her fiancé passed away, the Professor and his wife, Martha, took her in. Is he confusing me with her?—

DR. CUNNINGHAM
She took more of an interest in his ideas and work than Martha, who was four years older.—

DR. LUZZATTI (Pouring water in a glass.)
They went on trips to Italy together—

DR. ROSENTHAL

That he should call out for Minna, not Martha. Did he, then, marry the wrong sister?

DR. CUNNINGHAM

According to Carl Jung, when visiting Freud here, Minna took him aside and confided that she and Freud had had an affair.

DR. MAIER

That's bull! Consider the source.

DR. LUZZATTI (Beside FREUD)

Professor . . . Professor, it's me, Pietro, your Roman rock.

FREUD

(Refusing assistance, HE sits up, accepts the glass of water; HE seems very old, bent.)

Thank you, Pietro. . . . I suppose the heart rebelled. (To ALL) I beg your forgiveness.

DR. LUZZATTI

Professor, are you up to continuing?

DR. MAIER

Pietro, the Professor has been through enough . . . We all have—

FREUD

Shouldn't I be the judge of that?!

DR. LUZZATTI

Professor, you fell away at the mention of Julius, the name of your deceased infant brother—

FREUD

(*Mental projection: Two year-old SIGI sees his MOTHER nurse JULIUS; both JAKOB and AMALIA make over JULIUS.*)

I was jealous of Julius, hated him—This is difficult. . . I wanted my mother for myself.

(*Mental Projection: Mama, und Ich?! Mama, und Ich?!*
["*Mama, What about me?!*" "*Mama, What about me?!*"])

My hateful thoughts—I believed, had killed him . . . thoughts of knocking him from her breast and kicking him in the head, over and over again.

"The Struggle is Not Yet Over"

Julius was an intruder, a rival . . . Well, I got my hateful wish . . . His death left the germ of guilt in me.

>(Lifting a clay figurine of a seated boy, FREUD *projects: Cradling her dead infant in her arms, AMALIA FREUD looks for answers—"Why? Why?"—as JAKOB tries comforting his young wife*.)

DR. LUZZATTI
It left its mark, that of a Cain!
FREUD
From childhood, I suffered from spells of deep depression. I couldn't account for my black moods and debilitating headaches.
>(Replacing the boy figurine, HE rubs the 'heel' of left hand into his forehead.)

He returned to me, you know?—

DR. CUNNINGHAM
Professor, what are you saying?!

DR. MAIER
Who returned to you, Professor?
FREUD
My brother Julius . . . in the form of another Julius, a brilliant surgeon—

DR. MAIER
Oy, the superstitious belief in the transmigration of souls!
>(HIS head in his right hand, his left leg shaking up and down.)

You can take little Sigi out of the *shtetl*
>(Taps left Janus head)

but not the *shtetl* with its Jewish mysticism out of big Sigi.
>(Taps right Janus head.)

DR. ROSENTHAL
Insolent son, be warned, this evening is young yet!
>(In a voice not HER own, an older, authoritative voice, like that of a Sibyl.)

DR. MAIER
Ooh, you got this *boychik* peeing in his britches!

DR. CUNNINGHAM
Sol! Can't you see Mimi's not herself?!

DR. MAIER
Like a bat out of hell!

DR. LUZZATTI
Mimi, are you all right?

DR. ROSENTHAL (Collecting self, nods)
The sooner this is over, the better—

FREUD
In the Carl Theatre (lights darken), I sat engrossed, marveling at Arthur Schnitzler's intimate, detailed knowledge of the unconscious.
 (on edge of his seat):
It's uncanny, I could have written this play . . . That's it,
 (an 'ah ha!' experience)
he is my double! And his younger brother Julius—my Saturday afternoon card partner—he is Julius come back to me!
 (THE OTHERS, taken by surprise, look at one another!)
 (FREUD gets Taroc deck from desk; cuts & deals)
Feeling obliged to explain my not making his acquaintance—more so since my Anna had taught his daughter, Lili, in elementary school—I wrote Schnitzler on the occasion of his 60th birthday, May 14, 1922.

DR. CUNNINGHAM
Professor, the letter survived.

FREUD (Oblivious, mimes writing)
. . . I will make a confession, which for my sake I must ask you to keep to yourself and share with neither friends nor strangers. . . . I think I have avoided you from a kind of reluctance to meet my double. (Puts pen down.)
 (Schnitlzler's photo is now superimposed on Freud's face.)

DR. LUZZATTI
But, naturally. For to meet one's double signals death, one's own death.

FREUD
Saturday afternoons I play a lively game of taroc with my dead brother, Julius. (Mimes dealing cards.)
And, I, I, would lead humankind to the Promised land of Reason!—
 (Lies down on Couch)

"The Struggle is Not Yet Over"

Tell me, which of you would have accepted me as a patient? No takers?
>(Gets up.)

DR. CUNNINGHAM
Professor, if one person was your dreaded double, that person was Herzl—

FREUD
Correct, Cunningham, but can one ever be sure just who one's double is? When that other felt double, Herzl, was still alive my afternoon walk was a trial.   (Walks tentatively, on the lookout.).
You see, I couldn't afford to die prematurely—

DR. ROSENTHAL
Not before preparing the ground for your own Promised Land, Professor?

FREUD
Correct, my dear Mimi, a world where *der Kinder* move freely across streets—I meant to say, "frontiers.". . . A brotherly world where *der Kinder* move freely across frontiers. . . . (To self:)
Why this slip of substituting "streets" for "frontiers"? Ah! that horror! The Sunday walk with father when I was 10 or 12—"Move freely across streets," indeed!
>(Freud heads for painting of Aeneas holding his son's hand and carrying his father on his back, with Troy in flames in background.)

DR. LUZZZATTI
The Professor, he relives that terrible event, the walk with his papa that he relates in his dream book.

FREUD
>*(A FLASHBACK: FREUD, 10, & JAKOB, 50—Their VOICES sound as if in an echo chamber:*
>*—Schlomo, one **Shabbos** when I was a young man in your birthplace, Freiberg, a Christian came up to me as I was walking and with a single blow he knocked my new **Shabbat** hat from my head and shouted, "Jew get off the sidewalk!"*
>*—And, Papa, what did you do?*
>*—I went into the roadway and picked up my **Shtreimel**—*

The strong man holding my hand changed before my eyes—

DR. LUZZATTI
As if, then and there, God, Himself, died . . .The Professor's atheism, can it have stemmed from here? (More to self.)

FREUD
> (Studies a print of the famous bronze equestrian statue of Garibaldi by Gallori in Rome.)

And, yet, on his deathbed, he looked like your people's greatest hero, Giuseppe Garibaldi:
> I am going out from Rome. Let those who wish to continue the war against the stranger come with me. I offer neither pay, nor quarters, nor provisions, I offer hunger, thirst, forced marches, battles and death. Let him who loves his nation in his heart and not with his lips only, follow me.

Many of his red shirts, Pietro, were Jews, you know—

DR. LUZZATTI
Yes, Professor, I know, out of proportion to their number. But, Professor, you misspoke. Garibaldi cried, "Let him who loves his country follow me in his heart," not "Let him who loves his nation . . ."

FREUD
That slip I'll own, Pietro. If only in life he had behaved like your glorious freedom fighter. . . One night when I was about 7, I urinated on the rug of that very room, my parents' bedroom:
> (Then, another *FLASHBACK: Jakob, 47, is rebuking Sigmund, 7; Amalia, 27, is in her nightgown; there is a fire in the fireplace; we hear their voices as if in an echo chamber:*
> —*Amalia, that boy will come to nothing!*
> —*Jakob, he's only a child.*)

In the course of his reprimand, my father let fall words that were a frightful blow to my ego, "That boy will come to nothing!" In many of my dreams I roll off my achievements and successes, as though to say, "You see, Papa, I have come to something!"

DR. MAIER
Yeah, like becoming the Messiah of the Jews!

DR. ROSENTHAL
Sol!

"The Struggle is Not Yet Over"

FREUD (Oblivious)

When I was on my high horse he loved to say, "My brilliant son there are more things in heaven and earth than are dreamed of in your philosophy." And, my brilliant children, he was right. He meant a lot to me. After his death, I felt uprooted. (Heads for the desk containing artifacts.)
I studied myself in detail, especially my dreams . . . And became my most interesting patient.

(Seated, he mimes writing with a pen in his right hand. In his left hand he has a cigar. Behind him is a bookcase, from which Janus, the 2-headed God, looks down on FREUD. Janus' shadow falls across his face. Adjoining the bookcase is a table with more of his antiquities collection; on the table behind those figurines and against the bookcase there is a large print of Michelangelo's *Moses,* with only the top of the head visible. The rest of *Moses'* head is hidden by the figurines A peal of thunder and brilliant lightning startle Freud.)

DR. LUZZATTI

And, Professor, soon after, in the following year, 1897, you discover the Oedipus complex, the boy's passionate wish to kill his papa so as to possess his mama—

FREUD

On our second move, on the overnight train from Leipzig to Vienna, I saw my mother naked; I was four.
*(FREUD projects: A slide of Botticelli's **The Birth of Venus** is projected: FREUD'S lips and tongue move; the slide then lands on FREUD as he reaches up to touch his own breast.)* (Venus' breasts are superimposed on his. He fondles his breast, catching himself before his passion overwhelms him: A BIG moment; there could be music.)

(DR. LUZZATTI touches Freud's shoulder gently.)

(FREUD 'comes back'.)
Oh, Pietro, where were we? . . .

DR. LUZZATTI

Discussing our shibboleth, the Oedipus complex. And from which, Professor, you derive your mighty weapon to destroy religion.

FREUD
Right, Pietro. After my sense of guilt over Julius's death surfaced, tormented, I resolved to redeem myself by eradicating anti-Semitism. And that very year, 1897, I discover that God the Father once strode the earth in bodily form (Walking with authority)—a projection, pure and simple, out on to the universe of the young boy's idealized perception of his own father—

DR. LUZZATTI
That is to say, the all-knowing, all-powerful oedipal papa.

FREUD
This revolutionary discovery that religion can be traced back to the longing for the father, I keep close to my breast—

DR. CUNNINGHAM
Close to your breast, Professor, until you gain recognition, become the authority on so-called civilized man—

DR. LUZZATTI
For were you to trumpet prematurely God the Papa's humble beginnings ('blows' horn of plenty), psychoanalysis would be dismissed as but a Jewish science—

DR. MAIER
The anti-Semites would have a field day:
> This filth that God is a mere wishful illusion could only have sprung from the diseased mind of a syphilitic Godless Jew!—

DR. LUZZATTI
Psychoanalysis, it would be nipped in the bud—

DR. ROSENTHAL
And, Professor, you kiss goodbye your redemption, the realization of your Promised Land.

FREUD
I must say you've captured me back then—

DR. MAIER
But not fully. Professor, may I play you?

FREUD
And, Schlomo—you don't mind if I address you by your Hebrew name?—are you not already playing me?

"The Struggle is Not Yet Over"

(Points to DR. MAIER'S beard, attire, and cigar.)
Or, perhaps, you are my double? One can never be sure. You, of course, do know that Schlomo is my birth name also—
(DR. MAIER almost falls away.)

DR. LUZZATTI

Courage, Schlomo.

DR. MAIER (Overcoming his brief distress:)

Something's bugging, er, nagging at me. Because it promises so much—(enumerating with fingers) the eradication of anti-Semitism; self-redemption; the exacting of vengeance, that is, the destruction of that miserable seed-bed for good Christians like that human trash who had symbolically castrated my beloved papa, the hated Roman Catholic Church—my brilliant revelation about God the Father, must be, as a scientific construct, suspect—

DR. CUNNINGHAM

And then there is also, Schlomo, er, Sol, the little matter of eternal fame, which the Professor lusted after. For the realization of his Promised Land—a brotherly world grounded in Reason—would leave him in possession of the field—Moses, Jesus, and now the latest comer, the new moral authority, the new Moses, Sigmund Freud—

DR. ROSENTHAL

With but one Law, "Know Thyself!"

FREUD

This takes me back to the weekly meetings held here of the Vienna Psychoanalytic Society.
(Studying his Jupiter ring).
But, truth to tell, it was a mediocre lot, except for a handful. There was, however, one star during these early days of struggle, a Christian star—
(Projection: Photo of Carl Jung)

DR. LUZZATTI

Carl Jung—

FREUD

In 1910, as you probably know, I proposed that he be made president for life of the International Psychoanalytic Association.

DR. LUZZATTI

But in the face of the storm of protest by the Viennese analysts, this extraordinary proposal you withdraw. And a very good thing, too. For your charismatic "crown prince" and "heir", your setting in stone—making into a dogma—the Oedipus complex was increasingly vexing him.

FREUD
Our final break in 1913 couldn't be helped. Still it was a heavy blow. For, Jung, I believed, would break down the great inner resistances of the gentiles to psychoanalysis. .. Later, he dubbed me, "The Pope in Vienna."
        (FREUD extends right hand for Jupiter ring to be kissed.)

DR. LUZZATTI
And in time your, your Joshua, he would reveal his true colors—most especially in his six-year editorship of a Nazi-controlled psychiatric journal, beginning in December 1933—a position, moreover, he voluntarily assumed—

DR. MAIER
Professor, how could you have so misjudged that creep who all but swooned over National Socialism with its mighty "Germanic soul"?

FREUD
Truth to tell, Shlomo, your papa's not been a good judge of men. It's a talent I unfortunately never had.

DR. ROSENTHAL
Jungians contend that his "shadow"—whatever that's supposed to be—got the better of him, that, temporarily it eclipsed Jung the man.

DR. MAIER
        (Black comb on upper lip, he does a song and dance.)
"Me and my shadow . . ." My six-year-long ever-darkening shadow.
        (Dance morphs into Nazi kick-step.)

FREUD
Enough about that scoundrel! . . . Now, before setting others free from their religious chains, I must, I understood, set myself free from the Law. So, Pietro, summoning courage, this hero boards the train to your immortal city, where four days later —
        (Plants self defiantly before the large poster of Michelangelo's *Moses*)
        (Bewildered, DRS ROSENTHAL, MAIER & CUNNINGHAM look at one another.)

"The Struggle is Not Yet Over"

DR. LUZZATTI

Ah! I see!

DR. MAIER

I'm glad that you see, Pietro!

DR. LUZZATTI

Some psychologist! Solomon, before setting others free from their religious chains, the Professor would set himself free from the Law. And to deliver himself from the Mosaic legislation, what better object than Michelangelo's magnificent *Moses*?

DR. MAIER

(Cued in, he puts handkerchief on his head; from the back of Dr. R's chair he takes and kisses her shawl as though a *Tallith*; placing it on his shoulders, he plants himself before the *Moses* poster:)

Moses, if Yahweh exists, where is His strong hand? His Chosen People, have they not suffered enough? Why doesn't He put a stop, once and for all, to the perpetual persecution? Moses, given the unremitting suffering, how can you justify governing my life with your 'Divine Law"? What right have you to be in charge of my life? Well, Moses, here I stand! No More! The miserable anti-Semitism must end, become a thing of the past. The time for Jewish martyrdom. it is over!—

(As DR. MAIER removes the "skull cap," there is lightning and thunder with radiance emanating from *MOSES'* face.)

The radiance! I'm doomed!

(Terrified, as if facing a wild, raving beast.)

('Blinded' by *Moses'* radiance, Dr. MAIER tries seeing his own hand.)

I'm blind! I can't see!

(THE OTHERS are of no help, as they, too, are terrified, having averted or covered their eyes from *Moses'* terrible radiance.)

FREUD (By window, views the storm.)

When I, at last, stood before *Moses* that Thursday, it was storming like this . . . A storm that Michelangelo might have made . . .

DR. CUNNINGHAM

The Professor's nanny prepared him well—

DR. MAIER (Recovering)

Don, what are you implying?! Spit it out!

DR. LUZZATTI
May I, Donald?.... If bread can be Jesus, it follows that stone, marble, can be Moses, the spirit of Moses. (Handling 18-inch statuette of *Moses*.)

DR. MAIER
Pietro, that's crazy, simply craz—

DR. LUZZATTI
And, Sol, you, you can speak?! (Mocks DR. MAIER before *Moses:*) 'The radiance . . . I am doomed!'

FREUD (Touching Janus' left head.)
As *meschuggah* as it sounds Schlomo, that is precisely what my non-rational head believes, er, believed. Reason enough, my wicked son, for my so-called Rome phobia?

DR. ROSENTHAL
That's what this is—a dream, a bad dream. (Pinching self.)

DR. CUNNINGHAM
If I may, Professor, I'll spell it out to both my Jewish brother and sister . . . Inasmuch as he aspired to become the new Moses, what's more fitting than the world's greatest representation of that great man to excite the Professor's superstitious tendencies?

DR. LUZZATTI (Gets book, addresses Others.)
The Professor, he even hints at this in "The Moses of Michelangelo," which, as you remember, he insisted be published anonymously:

> . . . I used to sit down in front of the statue in the expectation that I should now see how it would start up on its raised foot, dash the Tables of the Law to the ground and let fly its wrath.

FREUD
A dream, believe me, my lovely Minna, er Mimi, this evening is not. For four years I prepared. In September 1901, it was now or never. You see, I was already forty-five, and my time was running out—

DR. ROSENTHAL
But, Professor, you come from healthy stock. Your father died at eighty-one and your mother was still well and active—

DR. MAIER (an awareness)
That's what it is, the 'critical age' business! According to Fliess' bizarre

"The Struggle is Not Yet Over"

biological theory, fifty-one is a critical age—

                      FREUD (Wilhelm Fliess photo projected)

A fatal age for men.
                      DR. MAIER

Professor, I still can't believe that you swallowed Fliess's, er, numerology. He should have stuck with the nose and throat—

                      FREUD

And yet, my dear Schlomo, here you are contending with a ghost. And if this shade judges correctly, you are just shy of fifty-one, aren't you?
        (Unnerved, DR. MAIER. catches self, as he's about to light cigar.)
                      DR. LUZZATTI

Courage, Schlomo!!
                      FREUD

Having had heart difficulties, I understood that I might not leave that gloomy, deserted church alive. Worse, I could have a psychotic break. Let's say it's August 1901, the month before my departure (Lays on couch):
        Doctor . . . this is so difficult . . . telling you my real reason for going to Rome . . . It's to enter the Church of St. Peter in Chains (Trance-like.) And once inside, to, to, stand defiantly before the shade of Moses, who is there . . . who is there . . . in the form of my personal totem, the terrible *Moses* of Michelangelo. (Sits up.)
        Doctor, tell me, do I need to be put away?

Withholding my diagnosis from me, my brave band? . . . Well, just in case I cracked up—and who's to say I wasn't already a *meshuggunah* lunatic?—I brought my brother Alexander along . . . We were like a book—the brothers, the covers, and the five sisters, the pages.
        (*A mental projection: We hear them all singing at the Passover Seder: **Da-da ye-nu, da-da-ye-nu, da-da ye nu, da—ye-nu, da-ye nu!***—)
                      DR. ROSENTHAL

A book with a missing first page—

                      FREUD

Julius never knew the joy at the Passover Seder of asking that sweet soul, our father, "Why is this night different. . . ?"
        (*ANOTHER mental projection: a Young Boy's voice*:
        Ma nishtanah halailah hazeh mikol haleilot?

(Simultaneously, FREUD also recites:)
Ma nishtanah halailah hazeh mikol haleilot?

> (*JAKOB FREUD, 45, dips his right forefinger into a silver cup of red wine, dropping the wine from his finger onto a saucer which already has some wine on it: The Finger of God. THE LITTLE BOY, about 5, is enthralled. JAKOB is acting out the 8th plague, the LOCUSTS: miming the Locusts gobbling everything.* [For the LOCUSTS we can have a LIGHT SHOW, such as a rock group might put on, with appropriate SWARMING SOUNDS] . . .
> *We again hear the FREUD family of long ago:*
> ***Da-da ye-nu, da-da-ye-nu, da-da ye nu, da—ye-nu, da-ye nu.***)

(FREUD, wiping away tears, 'comes back')

DR. LUZZATTI
Professor, your vast ambition, it is to become not only the savior of your people but also the Lawgiver of humankind—

FREUD
And your point, Pietro? (Studying his 'card hand.')

DR. LUZZATTI
Did you then not fear that by merely being in the statue's presence that you would die? —

FREUD (Folds 'card hand.')
That Thursday, September 5th, 1901, I did die.
(Sensually handling the *Venus* figurine.)

DRS. LUZZATTI, ROSENTHAL & CUNNINGHAM
What?!

DR. MAIER
I understand.   (HE heads for *Moses* print).
The Professor's face-off with *Moses* was transformative. He became his own person. So, in a very real sense he did die.

DR. CUNNINGHAM
Hm! No longer bound by the Law, the Professor is no longer a boy or son, but his own man who is free to act as he himself chooses and to govern his life as makes sense to him and him alone. . . .

"The Struggle is Not Yet Over"

(Enjoying this, FREUD lights a cigar.)

DR. ROSENTHAL

The Professor matured? Okay?—

DR. LUZZATTI

Solomon, Donald, you miss the essential mark!—When the Professor emerged from the Church of St. Peter in Chains, he returned not as a mere mortal, no matter how free. He returned
(Covering his face with a photo of the face of *Moses*.)
as Moses.

DR. CUNNINGHAM

Balderdash!

DR. MAIER

Pietro, you're out of your ever-loving Latin mind!

DR. ROSENTHAL

For our Winter convention, Pietro, please remind me to propose your interesting thesis for a panel—a panel on wild analysis.

DR. LUZZATTI

Follow me.—

DR. MAIER

What?! And risk excommunication from the psychoanalytic fold.

DR. LUZZATTI

Bear with me! In the religions of antiquity, the hero enters a dark pit; there, he kills the bull god, and emerges as the sacred bull himself, endowed with all of that god's qualities. It is through such an initiation rite that Mithras became the Persian god—

DR. CUNNINGHAM

Pietro, Moses may have been a bull of a man, but as great as he was, he wasn't a deity.

DR. LUZZATTI

Donald, that may be so. But the radiance transferred from Yahweh onto Moses and which so terrified the Israelites at the foot of Mt. Sinai, is that not divine?

DR. MAIER

Yeah, as "divine" as the thunderbolts radiating from Zeus—

FREUD

According to the Bible story, "till Moses had done speaking with the Israelites he placed a veil on his face." But, this evening, I have no such veil.

> (Now brilliant lightning—orange-red light with splashes of violet, purple and scarlet; FREUD'S face glows, terrifying the OTHERS, who avert their face or cover their eyes.
> *Then, a mental projection of FREUD'S: A slide of MOSES' scowling, radiant visage superimposed on FREUD'S face.*)

You can open your eyes my children. The terrible radiance of this Moses, it won't blind you—

DR. ROSENTHAL

Professor, for a moment I was a believer!

FREUD

So, too, it appears, dear Mimi, were your brothers.

DR. MAIER

How did you do that, Professor?!

DR. CUNNINGHAM

Professor, you don't really believe that as a consequence of squaring off successfully with your personal totem that you now possess the radiance of the biblical Moses, that it was transferred onto you?

DR. MAIER

Now that's what I call transference!

DR. ROSENTHAL

Sol! (An admonition!)

FREUD

(Glowers at Dr. MAIER.)

It's far better than coming away with a limp, don't you agree, Cunningham? One moment, I'm a 45-year-old Jew boy from the miserable streets of Vienna and the next I'm Moses! Not bad, if I say so myself. And several months after returning to Vienna I have my first adherents.

> (Addressing DR. MAIER:)

Chance coincidence?—Schlomo, why suddenly so shy?. . . Now, of course, my rational head

> (Touching right head of Janus)

didn't believe that by withstanding the radiance of Moses that I, like Prometheus, had stolen fire from the heavens.

"The Struggle is Not Yet Over"

DR. LUZZATTI (Handling left head of Janus)
But not so your non-rational or mystical head. In this regard, Professor, your 'Catholic mama,' she left her impress.

FREUD

Yes, Resi left her stamp. ('Stamping' forehead). After Julius died, Resi took me to Mass regularly—that is, until I was about 2½, when she was jailed for stealing . . . my toy soldiers even. With a grief-stricken young wife in the tiny Catholic town of my birth, Freiberg in Moravia, my 42-year-old father—he was a struggling textile merchant—had more pressing matters to attend to than my traipsing along with my devout nanny to the Church of The Nativity of Our Lady, where I was exposed to the sacrament of the Eucharist, bread and wine becoming the actual body and blood of Christ—and learned also about doomsday, of souls burning in Hell—and about which I dutifully instructed my parents.

> *(Another mental projection; Kneeling at the foot of his bed, LITTLE SIGI makes sign of the Cross; wide-eyed and with expressive motions, he tells his amused parents about how Jesus Christ conducts His affairs and about Heaven and Hell everlasting.)*

(FREUD catches self as he's about to kneel and cross himself.)

DR. MAIER

The Last Judgment, Professor, you didn't believe that?

FREUD

(Oblivious)
The candles, that music . . . the mystery. (To self.) . . .
Now, my brilliant ones let us examine the situation. I am in the Eternal City, in order, ultimately, to do what to Moses, the Moses of the Bible story?

DR. ROSENTHAL

Simple. To bury him in order to take his place—

FREUD

Sound familiar?

DR. LUZZATTI

But the mama you now passionately wish to possess is Mama Earth.

DR. CUNNINGHAM
And, Professor, because the situation before *Moses* is reminiscent of your oedipal days, you are flooded with the feelings you had had when you wanted to murder your father, Jakob, in order to sleep with your mother, Amalia—

FREUD
And with full force. The patricidal rage—

DR. CUNNINGHAM
Along with the fear of paternal retribution, namely castration—
> *(FREUD projects: JAKOB, 43-45 and AMALIA, 23-25, are in bed. A knife in his hand, JAKOB is about to lunge at his little rival, who is not actually in the scene: it might be too traumatic for a child actor.)*

DR. LUZZATTI
Which *Moses'* crown of horns most certainly calls up.
> *(With his fingers as horns, DR. LUZZATTI 'charges' DR. MAIER'S groin, who, in mock horror, holds on to his genitals.)*

FREUD
(FREUD projects: AMALIA giving LITTLE SIGI'S 3- year-old sister ANNA a bath; seeing ANNA naked horrifies LITTLE SIGI, 5.).
The sight of my younger sister Anna . . . without a penis (Shudders). You see, quite naturally, I thought that she had come with one.

DR. ROSENTHAL
And, needless to say, the gruesome expectation, Jakob cutting off his wee-wee made little Sigi abandon his impious ambition.

FREUD
Essentially, yes, Mimi. But little Sigi's love for his papa was also an inhibiting factor. . . Accordingly, before making my pilgrimage to Moses, I anticipate the re-awakening of those earlier feelings, including my love and longing for my grey-haired father—

DR. LUZZATTI
In September, 1901, Professor, when you first face Michelangelo's *Moses* you hold still to the cathartic method of cure, that is to say, a washing away or purging of neuroses by a reliving of the very emotions which sustain them.

"The Struggle is Not Yet Over"

DR. CUNNINGHAM
Professor, care if I take a stab?
FREUD
Only if it's not fatal, Cunningham.

DR. CUNNINGHAM
When taking your stand against *Moses,* as these anticipated early childhood emotions and feelings surface, it is crucial that you contain yourself, recognize them for what they are—
FREUD
Yes, as new editions of those feelings and attitudes pertaining to my father long ago.
DR. CUNNINGHAM
Stay in control as these, these, new editions of your earlier feeling states and attitudes return, and you resolve or master your Father complex; that is, you no longer submit to the Will of the Father—be he Jakob, Moses or the Lord God Jehovah.—
DR. ROSENTHAL
But get carried away or overwhelmed by this 'return of the repressed,' and, Professor, you may as well close up shop.

DR. LUZZATTI
(Handling the 2-headed god, Janus.)
Like Janus, the guardian of the threshold, you must be constantly on guard, ever vigilant. One momentary lapse, and, Professor, it is all over.

DR. MAIER
My God. Don, lie down on the couch!

DR. CUNNINGHAM
Why?
DR. MAIER
It's all right, isn't it, Professor?
FREUD
Jones, er, Cunningham, the couch is not taboo.
(Removing shoes, DR. CUNNINGHAM lies down.)

DR. MAIER
Now, Don, you know the drill. Just say what comes into your head—

DR. CUNNINGHAM
Not on your life!

DR. MAIER
Then fake it.

DR. CUNNINGHAM
Mumble, mumble, mumble, mumble, frikkin, frikkin mumble. I'm sorry Professor, Mimi.—
> (After miming his intention and getting DR. MAIER'S 'okay,' DR. LUZZATTI places the statuette of *Moses* on the easy chair at the head of the sofa, out of DR. CUNNINGHAM's view.)

DR. MAIER
Now, Don, turn and face the Professor's chair.

DR. CUNNINGHAM
Very funny! What am I to make of?—No!

FREUD
> (Arm around DR. CUNNINGHAM's shoulders, HE whispers:)

My dear Jones, my loyal disciple and gifted editor of our journal, what I am about to say you must not tell a soul: I got the neutral or non-responsive stance of the psychoanalyst—the so-called 'analytic incognito'—from my psychologist, old stone-face himself, the *Moses* of Michelangelo.

DR. MAIER
> (Whispers in DR. CUNNINGHAM's other ear.)

Not a lot of people know that! (a la Groucho Marx)

DR. ROSENTHAL
Jones would have *plotzed*.

FREUD
Fortunately, he could have fallen back on a former vocation—teaching figure skating.   (Taking DR. ROSENTHAL's hesitant hand, FREUD mimes instructing her.)

DR. CUNNINGHAM
(To DRS. LUZZATTI & MAIER)

That the transference, the key instrument of psychoanalysis to cure our patients, came from his trials before the statue, this is simply unbelievable.

"The Struggle is Not Yet Over"

(FREUD is oblivious.)

DR. LUZZATTI
This, Donald, is the reason no one has made the connection. It is inconceivable, too incredible even to imagine.

FREUD
One day, during my afternoon stroll, it came to me.
> (Bows to DR. ROSENTHAL: 'skating session' over')

That's it! I'll model my behavior after *Moses*. I'll be stone-faced—a silent blank screen, a shadowy image onto whom my patients can throw—transfer their oedipal feelings and attitudes—

DR. LUZZATTI
And, Professor, in order to facilitate the transference, you even darken this, your chamber here at Berggasse 19.

DR. CUNNINGHAM
So, Professor, had you never faced *Moses*, psychoanalysis as we know it today wouldn't exist?

FREUD
My dear Cunningham, had I not summoned courage and crossed the threshold of that gloomy church only a few persons would remember that such a thing as psychoanalysis had ever existed. (FREUD blows smoke rings.) And you would not be.
> (The stage darkens; brilliant radiance emanates from FREUD's face, momentarily startling the Others. Carefully removing a volume from bookshelf, HE says;)

On May 6, 1891, my thirty-fifth birthday, my father presented me with this, a re-bound volume of the Bible of my childhood, the illustrated *Hebrew-German Philippson Bible*.

> (*A mental projection in sepia tones: A slide based on an actual photo of Freud, at age 8, with his father. In the photo, Jakob is seated, with a book in his lap, and little Sigi, wearing a suit, is standing beside his father, to his left [Freud is reliving this]. But, here, the slide is projected on the back of Freud while that of his father is projected higher on the wall, like a god.*)

('Coming to,' FREUD hands the Bible to DR. MAIER.)

Its plates held me in thrall—
(The Frontispiece is projected)

DR. CUNNINGHAM
Especially, I suspect, the frontispiece, a lithograph of the biblical Moses with rays of light shooting upward from his forehead—

DR. LUZZATTI (Looks at it)
Imagine its effect on precocious little Sigi on Jakob's knee—

DR. ROSENTHAL
And from a Chasidic background, yet.

DR. MAIER
When the Bible was translated into Greek, the Hebrew word for "rays of light" was erroneously translated as horns. This mistranslation was carried over into the Vulgate, the Latin version of the Scriptures, which, of course, was Michelangelo's Bible—

DR. LUZZATTI
So this is the reason for Michelangelo gracing the head of *Moses* with horns? One and the same feature, then—the statue's crown of horns—called up both the dreaded castration and the terrible radiance.

DR. MAIER
Kind of a double whammy. Either you're zapped or snipped—and either way your life is over.

DR. LUZZZATTI
Professor, your papa's dedication, it is in Hebrew—So, it was but a ruse, your professed ignorance of the sacred language—a way to keep psychoanalysis from being identified with Judaism, from it being dismissed as but a Jewish science.

DR. MAIER
May this former Yeshiva *boocher* attempt a rendering, Professor?

FREUD
If you wish, Schlomo.

DR. MAIER
Son who is dear to me, Schlomo—

FREUD
After my paternal grandfather. He was a *Chasid,* you know.

"The Struggle is Not Yet Over"

DR. MAIER
when you were seven the spirit of the Lord began to stir and said, study my Book, from which lawgivers have drawn the waters of knowledge and wisdom . . . For many years, the Book, like Broken Tablets, has been lying in my closet. Re-bound in a new leather cover, I present it to you as a token of love.
From your father, Jakob, who loves you forever. . . .
> (DR. MAIER hands the Bible to DR. LUZZATTI.)

FREUD (Wiping tears away.)
A father's death has to be the most poignant loss of a man's life.
> (FREUD heads for painting of Aeneas fleeing Troy in flames carrying his father on his back and holding his young son's hand.)

DR. LUZZATTI
Mercifully, Professor, your gray-haired papa could not foresee that in 1897, a mere six years after turning this sacred text over to you, that you—his beloved birthday boy—would secretly resolve to destroy the Law, see to it that there would be no remnants of the Torah to restore—
> (Hands Bible to the eager DR. ROSENTHAL.)

DR. ROSENTHAL
Not one leaf, not one law—(Hands Bible to DR. CUNNINGHAM.)

FREUD
Guilt, filial piety, I knew could be my undoing in that gloomy Church. For, again, I loved that sweet soul, my father— (Retrieves Bible)
By assuring us that we are God's chosen people, Moses made us confident, optimistic, and even proud.
> (With the gold cane handle, He lifts Dr. Maier's chin.)

To him, we owe our tenacity of life. But, Schlomo and Minn—er, Mimi, that great man of our people who had molded us into who we are, must be sacrificed in order to save *der Kinder*—

DR. CUNNINGHAM
And, Professor, to save yourself—

FREUD
At the last moment. I almost backed out and left the miserable anti-Semitism to Herzl and his band of Zionists. But an ugly incident near Salzburg, in my

so-called fatherland, settled it. We were on our family vacation. My two older boys were on the lake fishing, when they were jeered—grown men calling them *Yids,* accused the dirty Jew boys of stealing fish . . .

DR. MAIER

That was Christian of them!

FREUD

With that can one live?

DR. LUZZATTI

Such cruelty, it shocks me still.

FREUD

Oliver and Martin were only ten and eleven

DR. LUZZATTI

About the same age as you on that miserable walk with your papa.

FREUD

Well, later that afternoon, Martin and I chanced on those good Christians.
        (Swinging his walking stick.)
The trash made way, let me tell you! And Martin was at the ready.
        (A projection: young Martin, 11, ready to club with his oar.)
My boys didn't have to look for models . . . for fathers–

DR. LUZZATTI

        (By painting of Aeneas holding son's hand.)
And for this in large part, Professor, your boys, they are indebted to Virgil, the singer of Aeneas:

> Son learn fortitude and toil from me . . . When before long you come to man's estate be sure that you recall this . . . let your father arouse your courage.

FREUD

As a schoolboy, for pleasure I read *The Aeneid* in Latin—

DR. LUZZATTI

And from which, Professor, you appropriated your Dream Book motto—and which, I now understand, is actually your very battle cry: *"Flectere si nequeo superos, Acheronta movebo."* ["If I can not bend the heavens, I'll move hell."]

"The Struggle is Not Yet Over"

FREUD (From memory:)
"*Arma virumque cano* . . ." "Of arms and the man I sing ! . . ."

That Virgil is known as "the magician" is no mystery to me. . . For that great poet's hero helped shape this hero, who, too, would save his own wandering and homeless people. . . . Well, the next morning, this Aeneas and his brother Alexander boarded the train for the Holy City—Your questions?

DR. CUNNINGHAM (Gets a volume.)
Professor, in exile in London one year before your death, you complete *Moses and Monotheism*; in this, your last major assault on religion, you account for anti-Semitism—an insight that, it is now clear, you had arrived at before the turn of the century. Professor, may I be frank?

FREUD
Cunningham, I believe I can handle it.

DR. CUNNINGHAM
Professor, your explanation for anti-Semitism has always seemed, well, simplistic. Moreover, not all Christians hate Jews. True, Peter, Paul, the Apostles—all Jews—handed Christians their exacting religion, but to assert as you do here (raising the book) that for this, we, er, I mean, they, loathe the Jews— (Rattled by the slip).
Forgive me, Professor . . . Mimi, Sol.

FREUD
Et tu, Mon Fils? (Mocks having been stabbed.)
Jones, er, Cunningham, you have just confirmed my point vis-a-vis the Christian's undying hatred and perpetual persecution of the Jews. Not having the courage—the moral courage— to acknowledge his hatred for his demanding religion which obliges him to renounce his aggressive tendencies and illicit sexual desires, the Good Christian disavows this hatred or loathing and displaces it on to the ones who had enchained him, the Jews. That is why so long as there is Christianity, my people—as you have just witnessed within your soul just now—will continue to suffer from that miserable scourge, anti-Semitism.

(A PROJECTION: 'FREUD' is bound by the phylacteries and the Torah Scroll to the Cross: the two rollers from the Torah Scroll are positioned to make the Cross to which 'FREUD' is bound: the phylacteries are wrapped around

>*the twisted Scroll enveloping 'FREUD,' who is in full religious garb, including full-length prayer shawl.) (Or Chagall's **White Crucifixion** can be projected...)*

DR. CUNNINGHAM

Accordingly, the Law must be sacrificed.

FREUD

Yes, Cunningham, the Torah must go—

DR. LUZZATTI

And as Judaism goes, so goes what you consider is its toxic shoot, Christianity.

DR. MAIER

Moses...Jesus

> *(Pats each Janus head, then with his tie, DR. MAIER 'hangs' the figurine by its common neck.)*

Caught together, hanged together!

DR. LUZZATTI

> *(Points to Aeneas painting, with Troy in flames)*

And it is precisely here, Professor, that you part company with your classical double. For, in order to save his homeless and wandering people, Aeneas, upon landing in Italy, entered the underworld to *receive* instructions from his father, Anchises. But you, by contrast, in order to save your homeless and wandering people, you, on your fourth day in Rome, descended into the underworld to *destroy*, ultimately, the Instructions of your father, your father Moses—the Torah!

FREUD

Yes, Pietro, in this regard my identification with Aeneas was a twisted one . . . more so, since that pious hero entered the underworld on the orders of the supreme Roman god, Jupiter—and,

> (looking at his Jupiter ring)

of course, from Yahweh I received no such divine command... Still, like my classical double whose mother was Venus, I, too, was favored by that sign of greatness, an exceptional birth—

> (FREUD PROJECTS, showing AMALIA in the scene related below:
>
> *Infant Sigi is in a wicker cradle. Initially, for a moment, the slide does not find the right place, and AMALIA is*

"The Struggle is Not Yet Over"

projected on Freud, who struggles with his hand against the 'blinding' light, as if the light were a caul.)

One day in a pastry shop, in my birthplace in Moravia, a Czech peasant-woman informed my mother, who was only twenty, that because I born in a caul, a membrane on my head, that she had brought a great man into the world.... "You are destined to become a great man, my golden Sigi."

DR. MAIER
Which, apparently, she never had let her *goldener* Sigi forget.

DR. ROSENTHAL
But, Professor, little did your proud mother know that to fulfill your great destiny that, you, her undisputed darling, would murder that great man our people, Moses.

FREUD
(Gold-handled cane raised, HE heads for the *Moses* print.)
To assure safe passage, Aeneas was obliged to pluck a Golden Bough to shield him in the underworld. Well, *this* Aeneas entered his underworld, the gloomy chamber of *Moses* armed with his own 'Golden Bough'"—

DR. CUNNINGHAM
Which you had plucked seemingly by chance, your brilliant illumination that God the Father is nothing but an exalted father—that is to say, the oedipal father transformed, magnified a thousand-fold.

DR. LUZZATTI
Professor, may I reconstruct?
FREUD
Pietro, as our great Jewish sage Maimonides said, "The gates of interpretation are endless." Is that not so, Schlomo?

DR. LUZZATTI
Grazi, Professor. Some time in late 1897, your mystical head,
(touching left Janus head)
excited by your vast ambition, senses that Michelangelo's terrible *Moses* embodies or possesses the shade of the biblical Moses.
(Mimes *Moses*/Moses transformation: animated)—

DR. MAIER
Pietro, the pantomime we can do without.

DR. LUZZATTI (Oblivious)

And after four years of detailed preparation, and armed with your hell's charm, that is, your golden notion of how the God-idea came to be, and hoping against hope that it, itself, is not what you assert God to be—a mere hollow wish fulfillment—you gather courage, and with fear and trembling, enter that dreaded, shadowy chamber to stand defiantly before Yahweh's Messenger. And after delivering yourself from the Mosaic legislation you then deliver humankind from its religious shackles and institute your atheistic Promised Land. This, Professor, is your game plan, your secret game plan—

DR. MAIER (With mock megaphone)

Visitors to the Freud Museum, good news: Now, in the consulting room, for this night only, is the latest comer, *Goldener* Sigi! But a caution! The beaming countenance of this ambitious little *pisher,* it is not veiled.

DR. CUNNINGHAM

Sol, you're again out of line!

DR. LUZZATTI

Line? Line? (An awareness.) Excuse me, Professor, Aeneas' son, he was named Julius.

(Pointing to the boy whose hand Aeneas holds).

Did you not also find that uncanny?

DR. MAIER

What nonsense now?!

DR. LUZZATTI

Solomon—or should I say, Schlomo—according to legend, it was from this boy, Iulus Ascanius, that Aeneas' great line descended, the Romans, and it was the Professor's intention to have as descendants his very own Julius or Julian line—a line, as the great Virgil portrays, "who are just—not by constraint of law, but by choice."—

DR. MAIER

You mean us, the psychoanalysts?

DR. ROSENTHAL

Professor, if I may?

FREUD (Nods approval)

I am not here.

DR. ROSENTHAL

Sol, we're to be the midwives—the models for and educators of the Professor's Julian line—a line of enlightened unbelievers, a self-aware line

"The Struggle is Not Yet Over"

that chooses to control both its aggressive tendencies and illicit sexual impulses—

DR. LUZZATTI

Because they do not disown or repress their anti-social tendencies, this enlightened line does not throw or project onto others their own lust and aggressive inclinations, Accordingly, they identify one with the other. And with identification, love follows —love even for the so-called stranger. It is this line, the Professor's Julius or Julian line—a line which of its own volition controls its asocial inclinations—that would institute the Professor's Promised Land, an atheistic brotherly kingdom where the Professor's "Know Thyself!" is taken to heart and where Jesus' "Love one another" is unknown, for to love on command, well, it is just not possible.

DR. MAIER (Gets a book.)

Here, in his 1927 attack on religion, *The Future of an Illusion,* the Professor suggests that such an atheistic utopia is possible, but since he never mentions it again, I believed that it was an aberration—that, later, coming to his senses, he dismissed it as a fantasy:

> . . . New generations, who have been brought up in kindness and taught to have a high opinion of reason, and who have experienced the benefits of civilization at an early age . . . will feel it a possession of their very own and be ready for its sake to make the sacrifices as regards work and instinctual satisfaction that are necessary for its preservation. They will be able to do [this] without coercion from their leaders—

DR. LUZZATTI

These "new generations" or new people, they sound like the Professor's Julian line, do they not?

FREUD (Quotes by heart, as if in a trance.)

> . . . As honest smallholders on this earth they will know how to cultivate their plot in such a way that it supports them. By withdrawing their expectations from the other world and concentrating all their liberated energies into their life on earth, they will probably succeed in achieving a state of things in which life will become tolerable for everyone and civilization no longer oppressive to anyone. Then, with one of our fellow-unbelievers [Heinrich Heine], they will be able to say without regret:
>
> > "We leave Heaven to the angels and the sparrows."

DR. LUZZATTI
And   (Pointing to the above quote),
Professor, the grandest wish promised you by your Golden Bough, it is here, is it not!? That is the say, not immortality, which you most definitely craved, but the undoing, at long last, of having played Cain to Julius' Abel. For, so long as your brotherly Julian line lives, Julius lives!

DR. MAIER
I guess I could give Hebrew lessons. (Gallows humor)

FREUD
(Hands DR. MAIER open folder & points.)
Schlomo, please read; these are minutes from the early years.

DR. MAIER (Reads:)
Scientific meeting on April 15, 1908. The society, which . . . is to appear before the public for the first time, is named: Psychoanalytic Society—

FREUD
Thank you, Schlomo. This name-change—from the Psychological Wednesday Society to the Vienna Psychoanalytic Society, a moment, you will agree, significant in the history of psychoanalysis—was made on my carried motion . . . That date, April 15, 1908, was the 50th anniversary of Julius's death.
(ALL FOUR register surprise.)

DR. LUZZATTI
In this manner, Professor, you secretly dedicated to the memory of Julius the psychoanalytic movement—

DR. MAIER
One more shock, and I'll be wheeled out.

DR. LUZZATTI
Courage, Solomon. Your constitution, it is stronger than you suspect. . .

DR. CUNNINGHAM (Gets book; addresses Freud)
In this famous passage of your 1914 essay on the statue, you write, "no piece of statuary has ever made a stronger impression on me." Professor, did it have the same powerful impact when you stood before it on your last trip, the one taken with Anna in 1923?—

"The Struggle is Not Yet Over"

DR. MAIER

Some analysts never learn—(to self)
> (Suddenly enraged, FREUD, again, lifts cane to cudgel DR. CUNNINGHAM.)

DR. ROSENTHAL

Oh no, not again!
> (As the startled DR. CUNNINGHAM tries to shield self, DRS. MAIER and LUZZATTI intervene.)
> (DR. CUNNINGHAM picks up cane and, again, hands it to FREUD.)

DR. MAIER (To DR. ROSENTHAL)

The beauty part, Mimi, is that we might now find out what really had set the Professor off —

FREUD
> (Goes to painting of Aeneas, holding his son Iulus Ascanius's hand.)

The visitations, they had already begun—

DR. MAIER

He saw his cancer as a punishment, as divine retribution?—

DR. LUZZATTI

So, this then is behind the Professor's fury towards Jones?—the cancer, it aroused fear, fear that Yahweh with His Visitations actually exists after all—

FREUD

Earlier that year, 1923, on the 19th of June—my daughter Sophie's younger son died of miliary tuberculosis. Heinele was 4½ . . . I was sure I had killed him.
> (SLIDE of Heinele's photo)
> [FREUD *projects, VOICE OF GOD* (Exodus 20:5):
> *. . . I the Lord Thy God am a jealous God, visiting the iniquity of the fathers upon the children unto the third and fourth generation of them that hate me.*]

DR. LUZZATTI

'The sins of the papa' . . .

FREUD

Heinele was of superior intelligence and indescribable spiritual grace, and repeatedly said that he would die soon!—How did he know such a thing?!

245

THE UNKNOWN FREUD: FIVE PLAYS . . .

(Breaks down)

DR. MAIER
At bottom, then, his homicidal rage towards Jones
(Raising Freud's cane over his head)
was due to the Professor's sense of guilt over the death of his most beloved grandchild.

DR. ROSENTHAL
Imagine the inner torment—

FREUD
Nothing mattered. I withdrew, quit attending meetings. Three days earlier, on June 16, the *Shabbat* reading portion in synagogues the world over was Numbers 16, covering the rebellion by Korah and his cohorts against the authority of Moses—

> *[A mental projection: "They, and all that appertained to them went down alive into the pit."; then a SLIDE of Botticelli's **The Punishment of Korah, Dathan, and Abiram** (Numbers 16:33), which shows Moses, rays emanating from the top of his head, calling down Yahweh's wrath on these Hebrews who rebelled against his, Moses', authority.*

[FREUD covers his eyes to protect himself from the radiance of Botticelli's *Moses,* which is superimposed on FREUD.]

DR. MAIER (Quotes Numbers 16: 32)
And the earth opened her mouth, and swallowed them up, and their houses, and all the men that *appertained* to Korah and all *their* goods.

FREUD (Turns to the FOUR.)
Heinele's mother, Sophie, my beautiful Sunday child, had died of influenza three years earlier.
(Photo of Freud with Sophie.)

DR. LUZZATTI
The visitations, they seemingly had begun. And with a vengeance! And yet, and yet, Professor, you continue defying Jehovah—

FREUD
I must, I must, save *der Kinder*!

DR. MAIER
And all the while conning us into believing that psychoanalysis is an objective discipline, a science—

"The Struggle is Not Yet Over"

FREUD

For misleading you and betraying your trust, my children, I am truly sorry. But secrecy was essential—My time with you is about up. Your questions. Be quick!

DR. CUNNINGHAM

Professor, for 16 years you suffered the mouth and jaw cancer stoically, refusing pain medication in order to be clear-headed; you had had thirty-three torturous operations. And yet, you ask Dr. Schur to put you out of your misery—

DR. ROSENTHAL

It was his life. He was in constant pain. To avoid needless agony, why shouldn't the Professor have . . . ?

FREUD

Please, my dear Min, er, Mimi, I don't need any help . . . It's a good question. I was wasting away, shrinking. At the most, I had a few days left . . .

>(Disoriented, he's back there:)
>My dear Dr. Schur, now it's nothing but torture and makes no sense anymore . . .
>(extending arm for the 'injection,' taking it stoically.)

I thank you . . . Tell Anna about this.

DR. CUNNINGHAM

It's a flashback—the Professor is on his deathbed at 20 Maresfield Gardens in London.

DR. LUZZATTI

Choosing to end his life with poison . . . like Hannibal.

FREUD

Minna, Minna.
>(DR. ROSENTHAL approaches FREUD; takes his hand.)

Heinrich Schliemann's autobiography, *Ilios*. The third shelf in the corner.
>(DR. CUNNINGHAM hands it to DR. ROSENTHAL, who begins handing it to FREUD—)

You have it, good. Where it is cracked. He will speak for me, Schliemann, this big dreamer and discoverer of Troy, Aeneas' Troy. Minna, you will know the place.

DR. ROSENTHAL (Reads:)

>I was now sure that Minna still loved me, and this stimulated my ambition. Nay, from that moment I felt within me a boundless energy, and was sure—

THE UNKNOWN FREUD: FIVE PLAYS ...

(Colorized photo of FREUD and MINNA.)

FREUD (By heart)
—and was sure that with unremitting zeal I could raise myself in the world and show that I was worthy of her . . .
To arouse his courage, Schliemann had his Minna and I, . . . my Minna.
(Patting her hand.)
(Tears trickle down DR. ROSENTHAL'S face.)
Without you—hold me, hold me. I am so cold. (She comforts him.)
(Drifting off, FREUD paraphrases Goethe's *Mignon:*)

"Kennst du das Land wo die Citronen bluhen?" "Know'sth thou the land where lemon-trees bloom, where golden oranges glow and from the blue sky a soft wind blows? Do you know it, perhaps?" It is there to Italia, to the delicious land of Italy, that I brought my beloved . . . my beloved Minna.

(DR. CUNNINGHAM is now comforting DR. ROSENTHAL, as DRS. MAIER and LUZZATTI look after FREUD, who 'coming back,' spots DR. LUZZATTI.)

Oh, Pietro. And your question, my Roman rock?—your question! Be quick!

DR. LUZZATTI
Professor, in the dream book you relate that you were born on the birthday of a Jewish general of Napoleon exactly one hundred years later. The date that Dr. Schur administered the fatal morphia, was it—?

FREUD
As it turns out, Pietro, I was mistaken: Marshall Massena wasn't Jewish. But I get your point. You are asking if my deathday fell on a special date. Dr. Schur did his good deed—his *mitzvah*—on Thursday, September 21, the anniversary of Virgil's death. (ALL register surprise.)
Not only did the great poet breathe life into Aeneas. He, also, as you know, breathed life into this would-be Aeneas or savior of his homeless, wandering nation. Virgil's deathday is then a fitting day for me to die, wouldn't you say, Pietro, my rock?—

DR. CUNNINGHAM
But, Professor, you passed away two days later, on Saturday, the 23rd.

"The Struggle is Not Yet Over"

FREUD
Did I, Cunningham? The Lord's ways, they are mysterious. . . . In His merciful wisdom, He saw to it that I died on a Saturday—and the Sabbath, indeed, any Jewish holy day is a good day to give up the ghost. Is that not so, Schlomo?

DR. MAIER
Yes, Professor, it means you led a righteous life.

FREUD (The Jupiter ring is flashing)
Well, my children, I'm afraid it's time . . . . Minn, er, Mimi, will you give this hated old Jew a kiss?

DR. ROSENTHAL
Thought you'd never ask.

>(Before THEY know it, their tender kiss is passionate; embarrassed and pleased, THEY disengage.)

FREUD
My one regret . . . This is not Rome. (Kisses Mimi's hand.) On May 25th, 1913, the Sunday I handed out intaglios to the Committee to be mounted into a gold ring like this—

(Showing her his ring)

it seems so long ago—that day fell on *Lag b'Omer,* which is considered to be a lucky day, for this minor harvest festival of the Counting of the Sheaves or bundles of grain celebrates, as you may know, the end of a plague that was killing our people—

DR. LUZZATTI
Which is apt, Professor. For you aspired to eradicate a plague, the miserable anti-Semitism—

FREUD (Searching his pockets, oblivious.)
Where is it? I know it came with me.

DR. CUNNINGHAM
Working behind the scenes in London, Budapest, Berlin and Vienna, under the Professor's leadership, secretly policed, directed, and protected the psychoanalytic movement.—Sol, did you know that the Professor dispensed the engraved stones to the six members of the Committee on this Jewish feast day? —

>(Mental Projection of the famous 1922 photo of The Committee: Freud is superimposed on FREUD; four of the original five Committee members are superimposed on the OTHERS.)

DR. MAIER

This is the first I've heard of it. Rabbi Akiba's disciples had been dropping like flies when, suddenly, the dying stopped on *Lag b'Omer* or the thirty-third day of the counting of the sheaves—

DR. LUZZATTI

Rabbi Akiba, he supported Bar Kochba in his three-year revolt against the Romans.

DR. MAIER

Right, it was the last Jewish war of independence. Ah ha! Despite himself, the Professor did leave a trail—a date trail. Listen! Not only did Reb Akiba proclaim that Bar Kochba was the Messiah. (Bending back his pinky). He gave that Jewish freedom fighter his name, Bar Kochba, which means "Son of a Star." –It's an allusion to the Messiah to come as predicted in the Book of Numbers: "There shall come a Star out of Jakob"... (Propelling his open left hand upwards.)

DR. LUZZATTI

Jakob, like Jakob Freud!

DR. CUNNINGHAM

No doubt about it, the Professor was a concealer, a careful concealer—

DR. MAIER

Either that or we chose to blind ourselves. Those of us who are Jews most of all. How long have I been researching, and lecturing on, the Jewish roots of psychoanalysis? In his memoir, Dr. Schur mentions the Professor's exquisite sensitivity to dates, like his getting engaged to Martha on the 17th of the month because in Hebrew the letters of the word "good" add up to 17—and yet I ignore this significant detail, the date of his dispensing of the intaglios, which for the Professor, it's now only too clear, was on a par with Jesus breaking bread with his disciples that fateful Passover.

FREUD
(Finding the engraved ringstone in his inside jacket pocket, he addresses Dr. Rosenthal.)

Here, please take this stone. (Trying to hand her the intaglio.)
It was meant for another. She, I believe, would understand . . . Do not deny me this special pleasure.

DR. ROSENTHAL (Takes intaglio to bosom.)

I feel my brothers' jealousy. It's lovely. Thank you, Professor.

"The Struggle is Not Yet Over"

FREUD
No, my child, it is for me to thank you. . . . Now, there is one last confession. Pietro . . . come close. It has to do with Rome, Christian Rome.

DR. LUZZATTI
I know, Professor.

FREUD
You do? Well, my Roman son, tell me!

DR. LUZZATTI
You not only *feared* that in the seat of Catholicism you would be unable to resist acknowledging Christ, but also *wished* that, overwhelmed, you would be unable to resist—

DR. MAIER
Professor, you didn't?!

FREUD
Why so perplexed, Schlomo? This seemingly simple act promised your papa redemption—His anguish over Julius's death would be behind him forever. Moreover, if Resi was right, he'd be reunited with Julius—

DR. MAIER
I can't believe I'm hearing this! Professor, say something!

DR. CUNNINGHAM
Don't you see, Sol? (Extending arms laterally.) In Rome, the Professor would be coming home, home to his nanny, home to Jesus Christ whose blood cleanseth us from *all* sin—

DR. LUZZATTI
This evening we've just focused on the Jewish side of the religious coin—

DR. MAIER
Rome, the Professor's road to Damascus? Pietro, You can't be serious—

DR. ROSENTHAL (To DR. MAIER)
Sol, as we well know, behind a phobia, there is not only a fear but also a wish.

FREUD
Five days before Christmas, 1883, I visited Dresden, where for the first time I viewed Titian's *The Tribute Money* and was immediately captivated by the head of Christ. Far from beautiful, this noble human countenance is

full of seriousness, intensity, profound thought, and deep inner passion... Lost in wonder, I found myself saying, "This is Christ."...—

        (Titian's head of Christ is now projected on FREUD'S head.)

Where that sensation came from, I didn't then know. I would love to have gone away with it, but there were too many people about.... So I left the Zwinger Museum with a heavy heart.

DR. MAIER
I'm feeling weak.

DR. CUNNINGHAM
Life Saver, Schlomo?

        (Offers a Life Saver to DR. MAIER, who rejects it.)

Anyone?

FREUD
        (Takes one; swallowing it a la Communion Wafer)

Lemon?

DR. CUNNINGHAM
Butterscotch, Professor.

FREUD
Hm! Cunningham, this is all right!

        (Getting a decanter, HE begins pouring red wine into five glasses.)

The most unnecessary expenditure I know of is for all the coal that's needed for hell-fire. It would be so much better to follow the usual procedure, have the sinner condemned to so many hundred thousand years of roasting, then lead him to the next chamber and just have him sit there. The waiting would soon become a worse punishment than being actually burned.... Minna, er, Mimi?

        (FREUD hands her a poured glass.)

DR. ROSENTHAL
Thank you, Professor.

FREUD
Cunningham? (Hands him a glass)

DR. CUNNINGHAM
Thank you, Professor. (Hands him glass)

DR. LUZZATTI
Grazi, Professor. (Hands him glass)

"The Struggle is Not Yet Over"

FREUD

Schlomo? (Hands him glass)

DR. MAIER

Thank you, Professor. (Looks at his wine glass.)
"Roman red wine"! The blood of Christ!
(Horrified, HE drops the glass.)
Over my dead body, I'll swallow that!—

FREUD

(Pours another glass; before DR. MAIER knows it, it's in his hand. FREUD then offers a toast.)
My children, *L'Chaim!* To Life!

DRS. LUZZATTI, CUNNINGHAM & ROSENTHAL

To life! (They drink up.)
(Without having toasted, the full glass in his hand, DR. MAIER rushes to open a window for air.)

FREUD (His ring flashes)

My time is galloping—Cunningham, (Extends hand)
for making this extraordinary evening possible, I thank you. And, oh, yes, my Anna sends you her warmest regards. . . Thank God I remembered. My Anna-Antigone never would have forgiven me . . .
(FREUD's ring flashes; now urgently.)
Pietro, when you and your young wife, Francesca, with her blooming good looks next visit the Eternal City, do stay at the Hotel Eden at Via Ludovisi. It more than lives up to its name. And, one more thing, my Roman rock, you will remember to say "Hello" to *Moses* for me.

DR. LUZZATTI

With pleasure, Professor. And in the tongue of Virgil.

FREUD

My dear, dear Schlomo, rest assured
(Placing his hand on DR. MAIER's shoulder.)
your papa, he did not bend the knee in Rome.

DR. MAIER

I knew that, Professor. Deep down, I really did.

FREUD (Takes coin from breast pocket)
This ancient coin bearing a Hebrew inscription was minted in 133, one year after Bar Kochba's short-lived revolt against the Romans—
    (Hands the coin to DR. MAIER.)

    DR. MAIER (Taking the coin, HE translates:)
"The Redemption of Israel."
    FREUD
Schlomo, this silver denarius from the land of our fathers is yours.
    (Pressing coin into DR. MAIER's hand).
A token of your papa's love.
    DR. MAIER (Trying to contain self.)
Thank you, papa, er, Professor!—
    FREUD
    (HE places hands on Dr. MAIER'S head; the Jupiter head ring flashes; DR. MAIER bursts into tears; FREUD gently tilts DR. MAIER's head; looks him in the eye.)
Verstanden?

    DR. MAIER
But, Professor, you're a poor judge of men—

    FREUD
Verstanden?! Verstanden?!

    DR. MAIER (Still collecting himself.)—
I understand.
    DR. CUNNINGHAM
Mimi, Pietro, what's going on? I'm lost.

    DR. LUZZATTI
Do you not see, Donald? It is a Bible re-enactment: "And Joshua . . . was full of the spirit of wisdom; for Moses had laid his hands upon him . . ." Which is to say, 'If I am Moses who is about to leave this world, then you, Schlomo, are Joshua'—
    DR. ROSENTHAL
Who'd carry on the struggle, and lead humanity to the Professor's Promised Land? Good God!
    DR. LUZZATTI
Exactly!—The staff, it is being passed.

"The Struggle is Not Yet Over"

FREUD
(To DR. MAIER now somewhat composed.)
Good. . . . *Der Kinder*, remember, *der Kinder*!
(Jupiter ring flashing urgently, He now turns to OTHERS.)
My children, you will keep this night to your selves and share it with neither friends nor strangers—

DR. CUNNINGHAM
You have my word, Professor—

DR. LUZZATTI
Mine, also, Professor.

DR. MAIER
Mine you already have, Professor. ('Lost' in the coin.)

(DR. ROSENTHAL 'seals' lips with her Jupiter stone.)

FREUD
Good. Remember, dear ones, the struggle is yet not over; it is still miserable outside— (Looks out window). The voice of reason is a soft one, but it does not rest until it gains a hearing—
(Now, lost in thought)

DR. CUNNINGHAM
May I, Sol? (Gesturing for the denarius, HE does a 'double take')
The Professor could have sat for this head of Bar Kochba.
(Hands coin to Dr. Luzzatti, who, too, does a 'double take.')

DR. LUZZATTI
The likeness, it is striking.

DR. ROSENTHAL (To Freud in low voice)
It is for this that you have returned, isn't it, Professor? For a trustworthy Joshua, unlike Jung—

FREUD
That scoundrel!
(Becoming enraged and about to fall away, HE collects self...)
To remain steadfast, Minna, er, Mimi, he will need you—

DR. ROSENTHAL
You have to ask?

FREUD (Holding her hand.)
Spoken as a true daughter.—

DR. LUZZATTI
(Reaches for *The Aeneid*; approaches FREUD.)
Scuzi, Professor, at crucial moments my papa, he would consult Virgil—

FREUD
The practice of Virgilian lots?

DR. LUZZATTI
Professor, from all sides we are assailed, not only by believers and religious institutions, but also by critics—many distinguished scientists—who attack us, asserting that we have yet to show the validity of our concepts or even the efficacy of our treatment—Please, this is a time critical for psychoanalysis—

FREUD
(Wipes hands on handkerchief before taking *The Aeneid,* HE feels the title; oblivious to time.)
My father who was a very happy man with a peculiar mixture of deep wisdom and fantastic lightheartedness often chided me for spending money on books. You see, for this bookworm, the smell .. the taste of books . . . reading was sensual.
(HIS ring flashes urgently; DR. LUZZATTI gets a gold pen from pocket.)
The boatman is getting impatient. Apparently, he has never heard of Jewish time—
(Eyes closed, FREUD extends hand for DR. L's pen.)
Let it fall where it will!
(Arriving at a lot, he opens his eyes, reads it with pleasure, savoring the words; as he recites, he seems to be praying, *davening,* as do Jews in the synagogue, moving upper body back and forth):
revocate animos, maestumque timorem mittite—
Now call back your courage, and have done with fear and sorrow.
Someday, perhaps, remembering even this time of struggle will be a pleasure.
(Lost in the 'realization' of his Promised Land, FREUD holds the book to his breast.)
Oh, fair moment, linger awhile!

(The room darkens; then there is brilliant lightning with a bluish haze; and a thunderclap; then silence.)

(When we can see clearly, FREUD is gone.)

"The Struggle is Not Yet Over"

DR. CUNNINGHAM
Professor, wait!—

DR. LUZZATTI
(Examines *The Aeneid's* binding.)
No crack in the spine . . . uncanny.

DR. MAIER
"Oh, fair moment, linger . . . " The Professor had to have been seeing our, er, his Promised Land—

DR. ROSENTHAL
Psychical reality was in play. In the Professor's mind, his dream of establishing a brotherly world had been realized.

DR. LUZZATTI
Mimi, the Professor's viewing his 'Promised Land from afar' need not have been a delusion but an instance of peering into the future—

DR. CUNNINGHAM
Precognition? Isn't that a stretch?!

DR. LUZZATTI
And this night, Donald, has it not been a stretch—a stretch beyond what is commonly thought possible.

DR. CUNNINGHAM
Now, we'll never know if the Professor believed it was all worth it—

DR. ROSENTHAL
Including his sacrificing—as had Aeneas—personal happiness with the woman he loved—

DR. MAIER
Why, suddenly, does this 'Joshua' feel he's being had? You set this all up, didn't you, Don?! A *goyische* smoke and mirrors con—

DR. LUZZATTI
Solomon, your Jewish victim complex, you've not worked it through. What purpose would there—?

DR. MAIER (To Dr. LUZZATTI)
Pietro, you're in on this, too! Jew-hatred oozes through the pores of your smooth papal skin. This 'Joshua' can smell it.— (Sniffs his own wrist.)

257

DR. ROSENTHAL
Sol, you're on edge. We are all are. This is pure paranoia.

DR. LUZZATTI
Solomon, that you sniff yourself is apt, for the Jew-hatred you detect—it is yours—

DR. MAIER (Shoving Dr. LUZZATTI aside)
Bloody Papist! Out of my way!

DR. LUZZATTI
Do you not see, Solomon? Anti-Semitism has so poisoned your soul that you have become—like not a few of our patients—a specimen of Jewish self-hatred—

DR. MAIER
For this enlightening session, this rare denarius should be sufficient payment.
    (Prying open Dr. LUZZATTI's hand, HE places the coin in it.)—
    (Now, turning abruptly to DR. CUNNINGHAM)
Don, the letter. I want to see it! I know the Professor's handwriting—

DR. CUNNINGHAM
Not in the state you're in!

DR. MAIER
Then his alleged ashes will do!— (Rushes for the urn—)

DR. ROSENTHAL
Sol, get hold of yourself!—

DR. CUNNINGHAM
No, you don't!
    (Places hand over DR. Maier's hand, now on the urn lid.)

DR. LUZZATTI
Donald, your finger!

DR. CUNNINGHAM
Good God, the Jupiter ring!—
    (Astonished, DR. CUNNINGHAM loosens grip on Dr. Maier's hand.)
But it was on the Professor's finger—

"The Struggle is Not Yet Over"

DR. LUZZATTI

One is on my hand.

DR. MAIER

On mine, also . . . (Starts removing his hand from urn lid) How did he do that?!

DR. ROSENTHAL

Like manna from heaven.

DR. LUZZATTI

You think that this is his resting place, Paradise?

DR. MAIER

What kind of a question is that?!

DR. CUNNINGHAM

Sol, how can you deny, after this evening, that there's 'something more'?

DR. LUZZATTI

Faust made a compact with Lucifer and yet his soul, it was raised to Paradise:
> Whoever aspiring struggles on,
> For him, there is salvation.

DR. MAIER

Salvation! My God, Pietro, that's poetry! And Christian to boot!

DR. ROSENTHAL

Pietro, you're not saying that the Professor made a pact with the Devil?

DR. LUZZATTI

Mimi, what had this Cain to lose? His inner torment?

DR. MAIER

Pietro, you're spouting drivel—

DR. LUZZATTI

(Gets *The Interpretation of Dreams*.)
The Professor, was he not fond of saying that nothing is alien to him?—The Dream Book motto, it even hints at his considering such a compact, "If I cannot bend the heavens, I'll move hell!"

DR. ROSENTHAL

But, Pietro, exchange his soul for what?

DR. LUZZATTI

For (bending back one finger) that infinite something which attracts followers, charisma; (bending a second finger) for time to prepare the ground and (bending third finger), most importantly, for the means to purchase his personal redemption, which had come to him in the form of his 'Golden Bough', his dazzling notion regarding the beginnings of the idea of God the Papa, universal acceptance of which would eradicate the miserable anti-Semitism, would it not?

DR. MAIER

Pietro, stay with Judaism, not Catholicism. Because our life belongs to the Almighty, it's forbidden to shorten one's life by even a split second, let alone be cremated or reduced to ashes like Aeneas (Pointing to the urn). And the Professor defied Jehovah. No matter the reason for the defiance or how seemingly noble the cause, he defied Him. He'd have to be punished. That much I know—

DR. LUZZATTI

But from a Jewish perspective solely—
> (Now, there's brilliant lightning and an ear-shattering peal of thunder. A book, *The Comprehensive Hebrew Calendar,* crashes to the floor.)

DR. CUNNINGHAM

What on God's earth was that?

DR. LUZZATTI

The urn!

DR. MAIER

It's not the urn.

DR. CUNNINGHAM

Pietro, you scared the hell out of me. (lifting the urn.)

DR. LUZZATTI

I'm sorry, Donal-

DR. ROSENTHAL

Look!! It was a book.
> (Pointing to the book on the floor.)

DR. LUZZATTI

Mimi, that cannot be it, a mere book falling open on a rug. No, something shattered—

"The Struggle is Not Yet Over"

DR. ROSENTHAL (Bending over the open book.)
It's the Jewish calendar. . . But it was on the bottom shelf—

DR. MAIER (Reaches down)

Good Lord! (Clutches his heart.)

DR. ROSENTHAL
Sol, what is it? Sol, what's the matter?!
(DRS. CUNNINGHAM & LUZZATTI rush to DRS. ROSENTHAL & MAIER.)

DR. MAIER
(Oblivious, his left forefinger now 'glued' to a page, HE prays, moving upper body back and forth.)

Blessed art Thou, Lord our God, King of the Universe who has kept us in life and sustained us—

DR. ROSENTHAL
Sol! Sol! I can't reach him.

DR. MAIER
And enabled us to reach this season.—

DR. CUNNINGHAM
"Season"? What's he—?

DR. LUZZATTI (Looking at the page.)
Mary, Holy Mother of God (In Italian). . . The Professor, he died on the Tenth Day of the Hebrew month of *Tishri, Yom Kippur* —

DR. CUNNINGHAM
What?! The anniversary of Moses' descent from Mt. Sinai with the Tablets . . . when he gave the Israelites the Law? No!

DR. LUZZATTI
From to Virgil's deathday to the Day of Atonement, it is a time span which bridges the two worlds of the Professor—worlds which formed, which shaped, him—

DR. MAIER
Our God and God of our fathers, pardon our iniquities on this Day of Atonement; blot out our transgressions and our sins, and make them pass away before thine eyes—*Shema yisrael, adonai elohainu adonai ehad*—

DR. ROSENTHAL
(Tries getting DR. MAIER's attention.)
Sol! For God's sake!—

DR. MAIER
Hear O Israel, the Lord is Our God. The Lord is One. You shall Love the Lord your God will all your heart.—

DR. ROSENTHAL
Sol! Sol! Get hold of yourself! This isn't *shul* at Yom Kippur—You're at the Freud Museum in Vienna—

DR. MAIER
What happened?

DR. CUNNINGHAM
(Raising the page)
You lost it when you saw that the Professor gave up the ghost on Yom Kippur.

DR. MAIER
Now, I remember. The Yeshiva *boocher* in me took over.

DR. LUZZATTI
And, in me, the altar boy.

DR. CUNNINGHAM
A religious remnant remains... If I can speak for myself, an unruly remnant.

DR. MAIER
I feel like a heel. Don, Pietro, can you forgive your Jewish brother? I thought, I really thought, I had worked it through.

DR. CUNNINGHAM
Sol, at the end of his life, in exile in London, didn't the Professor conclude that analysis is endless, interminable?

DR. LUZZATTI
And, Schlomo, for a Jew to be wary, is that so terrible? After all, outside remains miserable... I believe this is yours.
(Returning the Denarius to DR. MAIER, he hugs him, as

"The Struggle is Not Yet Over"

does DR. CUNNINGHAM; DR. MAIER tears up.)

DR. ROSENTHAL

Can girls play?

    (ALL embrace—a mirroring of the séance circle—with DR. ROSENTHAL beside DR. MAIER.)
    (A SHOFAR blast startles ALL FOUR.)

DR. MAIER

The Shofar? (high-pitched). Am I losing it again?—
    (In the background, a VIOLINIST plays *Kol Nidre.*)

FREUD'S VOICE

Courage Schlomo, one day you will remember this time of struggle as the best . . . *Shalom.*

    (After looking up in terror and awe, DRS. CUNNINGHAM, LUZZATTI and MAIER each examine his Jupiter ring, while the pleasantly surprised, DR. ROSENTHAL places her Jupiter stone, now miraculously attached to a gold necklace, over her heart. The four Jupiter stones glow, followed by FREUD'S ringstone, now atop the urn.)

    (Another SHOFAR blast! We now see a brilliant sky, signaling the dawning of a glorious new day.)

    (In single file, the FOUR exit, stage front, DRS. CUNNINGHAM and LUZZATTI; ROSENTHAL gazes at the Jupiter stone cupped by her hands, lets it fall over heart, and walks straight ahead. DR. MAIER—now armed with FREUD'S gold-handled cane in the manner of a staff—moves with new resolve or purpose.)

END of PLAY

Earlier versions of the play were given staged readings at The Actor's Edge Workshop in Elizabethtown, KY (July 2004) and at the Floyd County Playhouse in New Albany, Indiana (August 1989).

Essay Section

NOTE: The five papers in this section contain much of the research upon which the plays are based. I recommend that they be read in the order presented.

—Robert L. Lippman

ESSAY I

FREUD'S BOTANICAL MONOGRAPH
SCREEN MEMORY REVISITED

[The following has been previously published in *The Psychoanalytic Review*, 96 (4), August 2009, and appears here with the requisite rights and permissions and with the permission of the National Psychological Association for Psychoanalysis.]

> Another presentiment tells me, as if I knew already—though I don't know anything at all—that I am about to discover the source of morality.
> —Letter of Sigmund Freud to Wilhelm Fliess, dated 31 May 1897.
> (*The Origins of Psychoanalysis: Letters to Wilhelm Fliess*)

> . . . the realization of a secret wish . . . might mature at the same time as Rome . . .
> —Letter of Sigmund Freud to Wilhelm Fliess, dated 2 March 1899.
> (*The Origins of Psychoanalysis: Letters to Wilhelm Fliess*)

In his 1958 essay, "Psychoanalysis—Science or Party Line?," Erich Fromm asserts:

> unconsciously [Sigmund Freud] . . . wanted to be . . . one of the great cultural-ethical leaders of the twentieth century. He wanted to conquer the world . . . and to lead man to the only—and very limited—salvation he was capable of: the conquest of passion by intellect. To Freud, this—not any religion or any political solution like socialism—was the *only* valid answer to the problem of man [In Fromm, E. (1963, p. 143)].

Freud, however, eludes Fromm. The following paraphrase of the above conveys the present author's quite different reading of the father of psychoanalysis: *consciously* [Sigmund Freud] wanted to conquer the world and to lead man to the only—and very limited—salvation he was capable of: the conquest of passion by intellect. To Freud, this was the *only* valid answer to *the Jewish problem.*

In other words, like Theodor Herzl, Sigmund Freud was bent on delivering his people from anti-Semitism—but secretly so. Herzl's

Promised Land was a sovereign Jewish State; Freud's Promised Land, on the other hand, was an enlightened secular world, a brotherly world where the seed of Abraham can move freely over frontiers.

The author was cued in to Freud's conscious messianic ambition by his dream of the Botanical Monograph—more accurately by a scene purportedly from his chldhood which came to Freud while he was analyzing this short dream. According to Freud, this recollected scene is "intimately related" to "the ultimate meaning of the dream, which," he adds, "I have not disclosed" (Freud, 1900b, p. 191).

But first, the dream itself, which Freud dreamt in the second week of March 1898, while working on his masterpiece, *The Interpretation of Dreams* (1900b), and in which it is included. Here is James Strachey's translation in the Standard Edition:

> I had written a monograph on a certain plant. The book lay before me and I was at the moment turning over a folded coloured plate. Bound up in each copy there was a dried specimen of the plant, as though it had been taken from a herbarium (Freud, 1900b, p. 169).

And here is the all-important scene, the key to this short but significant dream:

> . . . It had once amused my father to hand over a book with *coloured plates* (an account of a journey through Persia) for me and my eldest sister [Anna] to destroy. Not easy to justify this from the educational point of view! I had been five at the time and my sister not yet three; and the picture of the two of us blissfully pulling the book to pieces (leaf by leaf, like an artichoke, I found myself saying) was almost the only plastic memory that I retained from that period of my life (p. 172; Freud's italics, for he was associating to "colored plate").

Now in *The Interpretation of Dreams,* Freud (1900b) asserts, "in every language concrete terms, in consequence of the history of their development, are richer in associations than conceptual ones" (p. 340). And in the original edition [*Die Traumdeutung* (1900a)], the plates or illustrations in this "account of a journey through Persia" are denoted by *Tafeln,* which commonly signifies the Decalogue or the Ten Commandments [cf. "*Die (mosaischen) Gesetztafeln,* decalogue" (*The New*

ESSAY I: Freud's Botanical Monograph...

Cassell's German Dictionary, 1962, p. 193)]. After redacting the Torah in Babylon, Ezra, in 458 B.C.E., journeyed with the *Tafeln*-filled Torah to another city in the *Persian* Empire Jerusalem, where, in a public ceremony thirteen years later (445 B.C.E.), he read the Law to the people, establishing the Torah as the Book of Books. The "account of a journey through Persia" then can easily signify the Persian travel book of every Jew's childhood, the Torah—in Freud's case, in the form of the illustrated German-Hebrew Philippson Bible, a rebound volume of which his father, Jakob, gave him on his thirty-fifth birthday, May 6, 1891. Mercifully, Jakob wasn't able to foresee that, in 1897, the year following his death, his brilliant son would secretly resolve not to preserve, but to destroy the Law—see to it that there'd be no remnants of the Torah to rebind, not one leaf, not one law. (Cf. "the picture of the two of us blissfully pulling the book to pieces . . . leaf by leaf.")

According to Freud, the Botanical Monograph dream was instigated by a conversation he had the night before with his friend, the ophthalmic surgeon Leopold Konigstein. The subject matter of this conversation, Freud, however, doesn't disclose. Nor will he ever do so. On February 14, 1911, eleven years after publication of *Die Traumdeutung,* Freud's disciple Carl Jung, who was then conducting seminars on dream interpretation, writes Freud, expressing his displeasure at Freud's withholding "the crucial topic of the conversation with Dr. Konigstein, which is absolutely essential if the dream is to be understood properly. Naturally, one cannot strip oneself naked but . . ." (Freud & Jung, 1974, p. 395). Three days later, on the 17th, Freud, under perceived pressure, replies:

> . . . the crucial conversation . . . dealt with the very topic we touched on in Munich. . . the Egyptian statue allegedly costing 10,000 kronen. . . .When I was a young man my father chided me for spending money on books, which at the time were my higher passion. As you see all this is not for the common people (Freud & Jung, *Ibid.,* p. 395).

But, as I shall show, a close reading of two pertinent passages in *Die Traumdeutung* reveals that Freud is once again holding back—the crucial topic of the conversation cannot have been the pricey "Egyptian statue" which he couldn't afford to add to his collection of antiquities:

> ... my dream was connected with an event the previous evening. I had walked home with Dr. Konigstein and had got into conversation with him about a matter [*angelegenheit*] which never fails to excite my feelings [*lebhaft erregt*] whenever it is raised.... (Freud, 1900b, p. 171; [1900a, p. 177]).

Since *erregend* (cf. *erregt*) means "irritability" and *lebhaft* means "strong" or "vigorous" *(The New Cassell's German Dictionary,* 1962), the "matter which never fails to excite [Freud's] feeings" is repugnant to him. Moreover, it is repugnant to Dr. Konigstein as well:

> ... in the course of [the conversation] I had given [Dr. Konigstein] some information [*ihm Andeutungen gemacht*] which was bound to affect both of us closely... [*beiden nahe gehen mussen*] ... (p. 174, [p. 180]).

Strachey's translation here is misleading. Freud did not give Konigstein "some information." He gave Konigstein an interpretation. [*The New Cassel's German Dictionary* (1962) defines *deutung* (cf. *Andeutungen,* above): "interpretation, meaning, signification." Here, then, is a more valid rendering:

> ... in the course of [the conversation] ... I had given [Dr. Konisgstein] an interpretation [about a matter] which was bound to affect both of us closely...

Moreover, the original wording suggests strongly that Freud views this aversive or repulsive subject matter as an ominous sign. [*Die Vorbedeutung* (cf. *ihm Andeutungen gemacht,* or "I had given him [an interpretation]") means "foreboding, omen, augury" and *vorbedeuten* means "to forebode, presage" *(The New Cassell's German Dictionary,* 1962, p. 543)].

According to Strachey, Freud (1900b, p. 172, ed. n.1) dreamt the Botanical Monograph on or about 10 March 1898. And in early March 1898 there was one "matter" (or *angelegenheit*) that "was bound to affect," that must move both (*beiden nahe gehen mussen* ...) Freud and his fellow Jew profoundly: the miserable Dreyfus Affair. (*Angelegenheit,* which Strachey translates as "matter," also means "affair.") Less than three weeks earlier, on February 23rd, Emile Zola was sentenced to a year

Essay I: Freud's Botanical Monograph...

in prison for libel vis-à-vis "*J'accuse!*", his bold Open Letter (January 13th) in defense of Captain Dreyfus (convicted on the false charge of treason on December 22, 1895) in which the 57-year-old writer accused specific members of the French General Staff of covering up "one of the greatest crimes of the century," the railroading of Dreyfus. [A player in the Dreyfus Affair was Gabriel Hanotaux, the French Minister of Foreign Affairs or *der auswartigen angelegenheiten*. Moreover, *angeklagt* means "a man accused" or "defendant"—like Capt. Dreyfus or Emile Zola.] On February 9th, the second day of Zola's seventeen-day libel trial, Freud wrote Fliess, "Zola keeps us breathless. He is a fine fellow, a man with whom one can get on" (Freud, 1954, p. 245) [in 1898, date unknown, Freud recruited Konigstein for his B'nai B'rith lodge (Klein, 1985, p. 87)]. The militant anti-Jewish violence in the land of the Declaration of the Rights of Man portends for Freud the resurfacing of virulent anti-Semitism throughout Christendom—each and every Jew a potential Dreyfus. Almost three years earlier, on July 5, 1895, Theodor Herzl, who had witnessed and reported on Dreyfus's public degradation on the parade ground of the Ecole Militaire, penned the following to the Chief Rabbi of Vienna, Rabbi Moritz Guedemann—as you listen to Herzl, please imagine that Freud is speaking to Konigstein during their "crucial" talk:

> I have been watching [the anti-Semitic] movement in Austria and elsewhere with the closest attention. These are as yet mere rehearsals. Much worse is to come (Pawel, 1989, p. 242).

Freud's book-destroying accomplice in the recollected scene, his sister Anna, who was born on December 3, 1858, just eight months after his infant brother Julius died (April 15). Several months prior to dreaming the Botanical Monograph, Julius's death surfaced, returned to Freud, in his systematic self-analysis which Freud had begun in response to the death of his father, Jakob, on October 23, 1896, which had left him feeling uprooted:

> ... I welcomed my one-year-younger brother (who died within a few months) with ill wishes and real infantile jealousy, and ... his death left the germ of guilt in me (Letter to Wilhelm Fliess of 3 October 1897; Freud, 1954, p. 219).

Oppressed by his fratricidal sense of guilt, Freud secretly vowed to make an atonement by delivering the children—other little Juliuses (and Sarahs)—from the scourge of anti-Semitism. And that very year, 1897, Freud discovered not only the Oedipus complex but also a dazzling derivative: the God-idea stems from the Father complex. That is, God the Father is a projection out on to the universe of the oedipal boy's idealized perception of his father. With this godsend (or God-send) which for now he keeps close to his chest, Freud would redeem himself from having played Cain to Julius's Abel: no God, no Judaism, no Christianity, no miserable anti-Semitism to distort or destroy the lives of the children. [Or, as the Root (Judaism) goes, so goes the miserable Branch (Christianity).] At the cost of Judaism, he would redeem the children—and himself.

But before setting others free from their religious chains, it is essential, Freud understands, that he set himself free from the Law, from Judaism's hold. In this light, please consider the following:

> The thoughts corresponding to [Botanical Monograph] dream consisted of a passionately agitated plea on behalf of my liberty to act as I chose to act and to govern my life as seemed right to me and me alone. . . . (Freud, 1900b, p. 467).

In order to get on with his messianic ambition it is essential that Freud set himself free from the Law and become his own person. But how? Helpful here is Freud's gloss on his free-associations to "artichoke" [cf. "blissfully pulling the book to pieces (leaf by leaf, like an *artichoke,* I found myself saying")]:

> Behind 'artichokes' ["leaf by leaf, like an artichoke"] lay, on the one hand, my thoughts about Italy [which, as Strachey notes, Freud doesn't specify] and, on the other hand, a scene from my childhood . . . (Freud, 1900b, p. 283).

"[O]n the one hand . . . on the other hand" indicates an equivalency, doesn't it? Because the childhood scene ("on the other hand") is bound up with Freud's desire to "govern [his] life," Freud's "thoughts about Italy" ("on the one hand") should also pertain to his desire for personal freedom. Now, by this time Freud has been "longing for Rome" (letter to Fliess of December 3, 1897, three months before the dream). So, it is safe to read "my thoughts about Italy" as "my thoughts about Rome."

Consider:

"On the one hand," Rome	"On the other hand," Vienna
I, Sigmund, take my stand before that terrible Symbol, the *Tafeln*-bearing *Moses* of Michelangelo (in the Church of St. Peter in Chains).	I, Sigismund, 5, destroy a token of the Torah given me by my father Jakob, the *Tafeln*-filled Persian travel book.

In his 1914 essay, "The Moses of Michelangelo," which at his insistence was initially published anonymously, Freud will confess, "no other piece of statuary has ever made a stronger impression on me than this [*Moses*]" (p. 213). And, as we shall see, it is for good reason that the statue impresses him so.

Now, at the time of the dream Freud still holds to the cathartic method of cure for neuroses:

> ... [we] lead the patient's attention back from his symptom to the scene in which and through which that symptom arose; and having thus located the scene, we remove the symptom by bringing about, during the reproduction of the traumatic scene, a subsequent correction of the psychical course of events which took place at the time (Freud, 1896, p. 193).

In other words, when a patient in the safety of the psychoanalyst's office relives a traumatic event, there is a purging of the emotions which sustain the neurotic symptom which arose from that event; hence, the symptom collapses. Freud's neurotic symptom is submission to the Will of the Father, be the father Jakob Freud, Moses or Jehovah. And because the situation before Michelangelo's *Moses* would be reminiscent of his oedipal days when he wanted to kill his father to possess his mother, Freud who is secretly bent on killing Moses (by destroying the Law) in order to possess Mother Earth understands that there would be uprushes of feelings and attitudes from his childhood concerning his father, Jakob. It is essential that they not overpower him, that he stay in control as these resurface, especially the parricidal rage and the terror while awaiting the anticipated retribution, i.e., castration. Indeed, in "*Der Moses des Michelangelo*" (throughout which "*die Tafeln*" denotes the two Tablets or Tables of the Law), Freud (1914) unwittingly reveals his castration anxiety before *Moses*/Moses, who, enraged, glowers at the backsliding Israelites worshipping the Golden Calf:

> ... Sometimes I have crept cautiously out of the half-gloom of the interior as though I myself belonged to the mob upon whom his eye is turned—the mob which can hold fast no conviction [*das keine Uberzeugung festhalten kann*] ... (p. 213 [p. 175]).

In the phrase "the mob which can hold fast no conviction," Freud uses "*uberzeugung*" to denote the word "conviction," and since *zeugungslied* means "penis" (*Cassell's*, 1982), the following rendering of Freud's recounted experience is reasonable (that is, if, as I maintain, Freud intends to kill and succeed Moses):

> "[It's] as though I myself belonged to the mob unto whom [Moses'] eye is turned... the mob which [can not hold on to their penises]."

Moment by moment Freud must stay alert, recognize that he is experiencing but new editions of feelings and attitudes from his childhood pertaining to his father, Jakob. Maintaining his emotional balance is essential if he is to set himself free from the will of the father; again, whether that father be Jakob Freud, Moses or Jehovah.

Because he loved his father, Freud understands that guilt or filial piety could sabotage his intention to destroy the Law and replace Moses, both as Lawgiver ("Know Thyself!") and as deliverer of the Jews. Moreover, not having surmounted his belief in what he will call "the Bible Story," Freud (1925, added 1935, p. 8) fears Yahweh and His terrible Justice or vengeance, especially that his little ones, his three boys and three girls, will suffer, pay for their father's rebellion. When he was a boy, Freud, dreading retribution, abandoned his ambition to kill his father, Jakob, in order to take possession of his mother, Amalia; four decades later, would Freud, dreading Yahweh's retribution, abandon his ambition to kill his father Moses in order to take possession of mother earth? Would he risk Yahweh's avenging Himself upon his little ones, and unto "the third and the fourth generation"? (Exodus 20:5). The death of one child, his brother Julius, is already on his hands—or so he believed.

Like Janus, the two-headed Roman guardian of the threshold, Freud must be ever vigilant or he'd never resolve his father problem, never be

Essay I: Freud's Botanical Monograph...

his own person, never govern his own life, forever be bound to the Law. One momentary lapse, and he could kiss his messianic ambition goodbye.

The world's greatest representation of Moses, however, is more than a mere prop for Freud to set himself free from bondage to the Law— much more. For when it comes to his great secret ambition, Freud is superstitious:

> ... My own superstition has its roots in suppressed ambition (immortality) and in my case takes the place of that anxiety about death which springs from the normal uncertainty of life .... [Freud's jottings in the interleaved copy of the 1904 edition of *The Psychopathology of Everyday Life* (Freud, 1901, [1904], p. 260, ed. n.)

Because 'murdering' the biblical Moses (by destroying the Law) and supplanting him, both as the new moral educator of humankind and as deliverer of his defenseless people, guarantees Freud immortality, Michelangelo's 8-ft, 4-inch bull-horned representation of that great man of his people so excites Freud's superstitious tendencies that the statue is his personal totem, that is. Moses himself (or the shade of Moses). In this regard, consider the following from Freud's 1914 anonymously published essay, "The Moses of Michelangelo":

> I can recollect my own disillusionment when, during my first visits to San Pietro in Vincoli [St. Peter in Chains], I used to sit down in front of the statue in the expectation that I should now see how it would start up on its raised foot, dash the Tables of the Law to the ground and let fly its wrath. ... (Freud, 1914, p. 220.)

Feeding Freud's 'totem' superstition is, I suspect, his Roman Catholic sensibility thanks to his devout Czech nanny who took him to mass regularly at Freiberg's Church of the Nativity of Our Lady: If bread, a Communion Wafer, is Jesus, what's to keep stone, Michelangelo's marble *Moses,* from being Moses? Here it is worth noting that when Freud was growing up in the small Catholic Moravian town of Freiberg where he learned that symbols (Wine and Wafer) can be what they represent (the Blood and Body of Jesus), a statue inspired by Michelangelo's *Moses* was stationed in its town square: this imposing Israelite writes on a stone tablet and wears a helmet with horn-like projections (Lippman, 2003, p. 34, n.9).

For a sense of Freud's uncanny experience in the gloomy church before the statue, we turn to the famous passage from "The Moses of Michelangelo":

> ... How often have I mounted the steep steps from the unlovely Corso Cavour to the lonely piazza where the deserted church stands, and have essayed to support [*standzuhalten*] the angry scorn of the hero's glance [*Blick des Heros*]! ...
> (Freud, 1914b, p. 213 [1914a, p. 175]).

According to *The New Cassell's German Dictionary* (1962), *blick* ("glance") means "touches of light," and *blicken,* in addition to meaning "to glance," means "to *shine*" (cf. Exodus 30:35: "... the skin of Moses' face *shone*"). And in the *Cassell's* edition of 1914 (Bruel, 1906 [rev. 1914]), the year that "*Der* Moses *Des* Michelangelo" was published, we find that *anblitzen,* which stems from the same root, in addition to meaning "to cast a furious look upon," means "to throw a *ray* upon." (In the frontispiece of the Freud family Bible, the illustrated German-Hebrew Philippson Bible, rays emanate upward in 'bundled' fashion from both sides of the forehead of the Tablet-bearing biblical Moses.) The year before, 1913, in *Totem and Taboo,* Freud quoted a pertinent observation by the anthropologist, Northcote W. Thomas:

> ... 'Persons or things which are regarded as taboo may be compared to objects charged with *electricity;* they are the seat of a tremendous power which is transmissible by contact and may be liberated with destructive effect ...' (p. 20; italics mine).

This mysterious force or *mana* is comparable, then, to lightning or *blitz.*

Turning from *blick,* we now look at the word, *standhalten* (to "support," above). The 1914 edition of *Cassell's* defines *standhallten* as follows: "To withstand; to resist; to hold one's own; to stand firm." Freud's 'choosing' *standhalten* suggests strongly that whenever he entered the Church of San Pietro in Vincoli that Freud—his superstitious tendencies excited—attempted to resist the *blick* or *mana* of *Moses*/Moses (cf. "How often have I ... essayed to support ..."). Applying this decoding of *blick* and *standhalten* back to the time of the Botanical Monograph dream

Essay I: Freud's Botanical Monograph...

(March 1898), three and one half years before he will first set eyes on Michelangelo's *Moses,* we arrive at the following rendering:

> Vis-à-vis the *mana* [*blick*] of *Moses*/Moses, I intend to [*standhalten*] withstand, resist, hold my own, stand firm.

On the other hand, when he writes about the Israelites at Mt. Sinai vis-a-vis Yahweh, instead of using *standhalten,* which implies active resistance or opposition, Freud uses *ertragen* which implies passive submission. ("To bear; to suffer; to tolerate; to put up with"):

> ... Even Moses had to act as an intermediary between his people and Jehovah, since the people could not support [*ertruge*] the sight of God; and when he returned from the presence of God his face shone-some of the *mana* had been transferred on to him ... (Freud, 1921b, p. 125 [1928, p. 140]).

Whereas *ertragen* suggests resignation (the Israelites), *standhalten* suggests resistance or defiance (Freud). Unlike the Israelites who passively suffered the will of Yahweh, this Israelite would defiantly hold his ground, stand up to *Moses*/Moses, ultimately to Yahweh. Again, *Cassell's* defines *standhalten* as follows: "To withstand; to resist; to hold one's own; to stand firm." In his last major attack on religion, *Moses and Monotheism,* Freud (1939) will add a pertinent note:

> It is historically certain that *the Jewish type was finally fixed* as a result of the reforms of Ezra and Nehemiah ... (p. 42n; italics mine).

It was Ezra, of course, who brought the Torah, the Five Books of Moses, from Babylon to the Israelites in Jerusalem in 458 B.C.E. And if the Law of Moses "finally fixed" the Jews, then Moses is *the* ancestor of the Jews. By withstanding the sight of *Moses*/Moses, Freud intended to "unfix" himself, set himself free from the Law, and, thereby, become a person in his own right. (Cf. the lead quote: "... the realization of a secret wish ... might *mature* at the same time as Rome ...")

Having been born in a caul (Jones, 1953, p. 4), which is a sign of greatness, and which his mother, Amalia, never let her "*goldener* Sigi" forget, it is probable that Freud superstitiously believes that he, himself, possesses *mana* from birth, and, so, may be able to withstand the terrible *mana* or supernatural power of *Moses*/Moses:

> ... kings and chiefs are possessed of great power, and it is death for their subjects to address them directly; but a minister or other person of greater *mana* than common can approach them unharmed.... This power is attached to all *special* individuals, such as kings, priests or newborn babies, to all *exceptional* states, such as the physical states of menstruation, puberty or birth, and to all *uncanny* things . . . (Sigmund Freud, *Totem and Taboo,* 1913, p. 20; p. 22, Freud's italics.)

Moreover, if Freud were to withstand *Moses*/Moses' terrible charge or *mana,* then not only would he deliver himself from the Law. He would possess the *mana* of Moses—the terrible radiance would be transferred on to him, the new Moses:

> . . .The strangest fact seems to be that anyone who has transgressed one of these prohibitions himself acquires the characteristic of being prohibited-as though the whole of the dangerous charge had been transferred over to him. (*Ibid.*, p. 22).

At this point I'll backtrack and quote from Freud's "longing for Rome" letter to Wilhelm Fliess of December 3, 1897, which, again, was three months before the Botanical monograph dream:

> I dreamt I was in Rome. . . . Incidentally my longing for Rome is deeply neurotic. It is connected with my schoolboy hero-worship of the Semitic Hannibal, and this year in fact I did not reach Rome any more than he did Lake Trasimeno. Since I have been studying the unconscious, I have been so interesting to myself. It is a pity *that one always keeps one's mouth shut about the most intimate things.*
>
> ["The best that you know you must not tell to the boys".] (Freud, 1954, p. 236; Bracketed quote from Goethe's *Faust,* as translated by James Strachey; italics mine.)

In this guarded letter to Fliess, who was then his best friend and confidant, Freud writes, "Since I have been studying *the* unconscious..."

Essay I: Freud's Botanical Monograph...

—Not "*my* subconscious." What he is alluding to is universal, pertaining not just to himself but to humankind in general. And armed with "the best" that he knows, his secret theoretical knowledge regarding the humble or oedipal beginnings of God the Father, Freud would annihilate religion and, thereby, eliminate anti-Semitism. Unlike Hannibal, not only would this Semitic avenger enter Rome; he would eventually crush the Romans, the new Romans, the Roman Catholic Church, the breeding ground for anti-Semites like the Christian thug who knocked his father Jakob's new *Shabbat* fur cap into the mud and ordered him off the pavement, with Jakob meekly complying and not defending himself.

In *The Interpretation of Dreams,* just before mentioning the fateful Sunday stroll when Jakob related his encounter with the Christian in Freud's birthplace (Freiberg in Moravia), Freud refers to his boyhood identification with Hannibal:

> To my youthful mind Hannibal and Rome symbolized the conflict between the tenacity of Jewry and the organization of the Catholic church. And the increasing importance of the effects of the anti-semitic movement upon our emotional life helped to fix the thoughts of those early days. Thus the wish to go to Rome had become in my dream-life a cloak and symbol [*Deckmantel und Symbol* (1900a, p 202)] for a number of other passionate wishes . . . (1900b, pp. 196–197).

This is a veiled confession: In order to ultimately eliminate Christendom, especially the Catholic church, Freud would journey to Rome, enter the Church of St. Peter in Chains, and, there, set himself free from the Law by standing up to that terrible *Symbol,* the *Moses* of Michelangelo. In Luther's Bible, which Freud references in his works, "*Decke*" [as in *Symbol und Deckmantel*] denotes the veil which cloaks the dangerous supernatural radiance or *mana* of Moses:

> "And till Moses had done speaking with [the terrified Israelites at the foot of Mount Sinai], he put a veil on his face" [Exodus 34:33—". . . *legte er eine Decke auf sein Angesicht*"].

To repeat: The arousal of his ambition to be the successor to Moses excites Freud's superstitious side; at such times, Michelangelo's *Moses* is, for Freud, a symbol in the same manner that the Host is a symbol for devout Catholics like his early instructress in the faith, his devout Czech nanny—the statue is Moses or the shade of Moses. And if the dangerous charge or supernatural radiance of this terrible *Symbol,* Michelangelo's *Moses,* were 'transferred over' to Freud in the gloomy church, he would assume the mantle or *Mantel* of Moses, again, both as Lawgiver ("Know Thyself!") and as deliverer of his oppressed homeless people. Cf. Elisha succeeding the Prophet Elijah:

> He [Elisha] took up the mantle [*den Mantel*] of Elijah that fell from him . . . And the sons of the prophets . . . said, The spirit of Elijah doth rest on Elisha. And they . . . bowed to the ground before him (II Kings 2:13; 15 [2. KONIGE 2:13; 15]).

[The description of Elisha's brethren bowing to Elisha is reminiscent of Joseph's dream of his brothers' sheaves making "obeisiance to my sheaf" (Genesis 37:7). In *The Interpretation of Dreams,* Freud (1900b) acknowledges identifying with Joseph—not because Joseph was the savior of his people, but because Joseph was "an interpreter of dreams":

> . . . the name Josef plays a great part in my dreams. . . . My own ego finds it very easy to hide itself behind people of that name, since Joseph was the name of a man famous in the Bible as an interpreter of dreams. (p. 484, n. 2)].

Having had signs of heart trouble dating from 1893, Freud, while readying himself, probably understood that under the strain he could suffer a fatal heart attack in the church. [According to Dr. Max Schur (1972, p. 62), who was his personal physician from 1928 until his death in 1939, Freud had "suffered an organic myocardial lesion" in 1894.] And if his heart were to give out, it would leave his wife, Martha, and their six little ones destitute. And what if he were to suffer a breakdown, have a psychotic break? To have such a great ambition and to believe that he could pull it off, maybe this big dreamer is already a *meschuggana*h lunatic, just another messianic pretender, one more deluded messsiah of the Jews who comes on the scene during times of especial Jewish misery.

Still, summoning courage, Freud at long last entered the Eternal City on September 2, 1901. Three days later, on Thursday, the fifth, he crossed the threshold of the Church of St. Peter in Chains, and took his stand before *Moses*/Moses. Remarkably, like Jakob who had seen "God face to face" and prevailed, Freud came through this dreaded but essential ordeal. At age 45, Freud—who enjoyed quoting the German poet Ruckert's line, "the Book tells us it's no sin to limp"—emerged from the gloomy church transformed; that is, as an exceptional being, possessing the divine and terrible biblical radiance of Moses (or so his superstitious side believed). Fourteen days later, on September 19, Freud (1985, p. 449) will write Fliess: "Rome . . . was a high point of my life." The high point is more like it.

In the fall of the following year Freud gathers disciples (Gay, 1988, p. 136), and is on his way to preparing the ground for his Promised Land, an enlightened brotherly world where the seed of Abraham can at last move freely over frontiers. And is on his way to becoming FREUD.

Seven years later, on April 15, 1908, the fiftieth anniversary of Julius Freud's death, the six-year-old Psychological Wednesday Society is re-named—on Freud's carried motion—the Vienna Psychoanalytic Society (Nunberg and Federn, 1906–1908, p. 373); in this manner, Freud secretly dedicates to the memory of Julius the psychoanalytic movement.

In 1935, the Polish-Jewish writer Bruno Schulz (1990) averred, "certain images in childhood . . . amount to an agenda" (p. 111). Though Freud's image of him and his sister Anna destroying "an account of a journey through Persia" seems to fall into this category, this childhood scene is not a veridical recollection. For as Freud asserts in his 1899 paper, "Screen Memories":

> Whenever *in a memory the subject himself appears* . . . as an object among other objects this contrast between the acting and the recollecting ego may be taken as evidence that *the original impression has been worked over*. It looks as though a memory-trace from childhood had been here translated back into a plastic and visual form at a later date—the date of the memory's arousal. But *no original impression has entered the subject's consciousness* (p. 321; italics mine).

The evoked childhood scene, like the Botanical Monograph dream, is itself a wish fulfillment. By the "date of the memory's arousal," Freud is bent on destroying religion; accordingly, in addition to depicting Freud (and his sister) destroying a fitting Torah symbol ("an account of a journey through Persia"), this "worked over" scene from his childhood contains a mix pointing to his mighty weapon, the oedipal beginnings of the God the Father: (1) infantile sexuality ("pulling . . . artichoke"; see Anzieu, 1986, pp. 285–286), and (2) the age at which the oedipal boy not only abandons his ambition. He also unwittingly transforms his father into God the Father ("I had been five").

Freud's messianic ambition can easily account for his abandoning the seduction hypothesis (adult psychopathology, namely neurotic disorders or symptoms, can be traced back to father-child incest) for the Oedipus complex and its dazzling derivative, Freud's mighty weapon, the origin of the idea of God the Father.

REFERENCES

ANZIEU, D. (1986). *Freud's Self-Analysis.* Translated by Peter Graham. London: Hogarth Press.

BREDIN, J. (1986). *The Affair: The Case of Alfred Dreyfus.* Translated by Jeffrey Mehlman. New York: George Braziller.

BREUL, K. (1906, rev., 1914). *A New German and English Dictionary.* New York: Funk & Wagnalls. *Cassell's German Dictionary, The New.* (1962). New York: Funk and Wagnalls.

DERFLER, L. (1963). *The Dreyfus Affair: Tragedy of Errors.* Boston: D.C. Heath and Company.

FREUD, S. (1896). The Aetiology of Hysteria. In J. Strachey, ed. and trans., *The Standard Edition of the Complete Works of Sigmund Freud,* 24 vols. London: Hogarth Press, 1953–1974, 3.

―――― (1899). Screen Memories. *Standard Edition* 3.

―――― (1900a). Die Traumdeutung. Vienna, G.W. II/III.

―――― (1900b). The Interpretation of Dreams. *Standard Edition* 4–5.

―――― (1901). The Psychopathology of Everyday Life. *Standard Edition* 6.

―――― (1901–1905). Fragment of an Analysis of a Case of Hysteria. *Standard Edition* 7.

―――― (1905). The Essays on the Theory of Sexuality. *Standard Edition* 7.

―――― (1913). Totem and Taboo. *Standard Edition* 13.

―――― (1914a). *Der* Moses *des* Michelangelo. G. W. X.

―――― (1914b). The Moses of Michelangelo. *Standard Edition* 13.

―――― (1921a). *Massenpsychologie und Ich-Analyse.* G.W. 13.

―――― (1921b). *Group Psychology and the Analysis of the Ego. Standard Edition* 18.

―――― (1924). The Dissolution of the Oedipus Complex. *Standard Edition* 19.

―――― (1925). An Autobiographical Study, *Standard Edition* 20.

―――― (1939). Moses and Monotheism, *Standard Edition* 23.

―――― (1954). *The Origins of Psycho-Analysis: Letters to Wilhelm Fliess,*

Draft and Notes, 1887–1902. Edited by M. Bonaparte, A. Freud and E. Kris; translated and edited by E. Mosbacher and J. Strachey. London and New York, Basic Books and Imago.

——— (1959). *Collected Papers.* Authorized translation under the supervision of Joan Riviere, edited by Ernest Jones. London: Hogarth Press.

——— (1960). *The Letters of Sigmund Freud.* Selected and edited by E. Freud. New York: Basic Books.

——— (1985). *The Complete Letters of Sigmund Freud to Wilhelm Fliess, 1887–1904.* Translated and edited by Jeffrey Moussaieff Masson. Cambridge: Harvard Univ. Press.

——— & JUNG, C.G. (1974). *The Freud /Jung Letters: The Correspondence between Sigmund Freud and C.G. Jung.* Edited by William McGuire. Translated by Ralph Manheim & R.F.C. Hull. Bollingen Series XCIV. Princeton: Princeton University Press.

——— & ZWIEG, A. (1970). *The Letters of Sigmund Freud and Arnold Zweig.* Freud, E., ed., Translated by E. and W. Robson-Scott. New York: Harcourt Brace and World.

FROMM, E. (1963). *The Dogma of Christ.* New York: Rinehart and Winston.

GAY, P. (1987). *A Godless Jew: Freud, Atheism and the Making of Psychoanalysis.* New Haven: Yale University.

KLEIN, D. (1985). *Jewish Origins of the Psychoanalytic Movement.* Chicago: University of Chicago.

LIPPMAN, R. (2000). Is Freud in the Dates? *Midstream*, Volume XXXVI, No. 1, January.

——— (2001). Freud's Hypothesis that the Jews Killed Moses. *Midstream*, Volume XXXXVII, No.5, July/August.

———(2002). Sigmund Freud Avoids His Double, Theodor Herzl. *Midstream*, Volume XXXXVIII, No. 7, November/December.

——— (2003). Freud, the Law, and Michelangelo's *Moses. Midstream,* Volume XXXXIX, No .1, January .

NUNBERG, H. & FEDERN, E. (1962). *Minutes of the Vienna Psycho-analytic Society.* Volume I, 1906–1908. New York: International Universities Press.

PAWEL, E. (1989). *The Labyrinth of Exile: A Life of Theodor Herzl.* New York: Farrar, Strauss & Giroux.

SCHOLEM, G. (1971) *The Messianic Idea in Judaism.* New York: Schocken Books.

SCHULZ, B. (1990). *Letters and Drawings of Bruno Schulz.* J. Ficowski, & W. Arndt, eds. & V. Nelson, trans. New York: Fromm International Publishing Corp.

SCHUR, M. (1972). *Freud: Living and Dying.* New York: International Universities Press.

ESSAY II

FREUD'S DREAM CASTLE BY THE SEA

When Freud spoke of his having been greatly influenced by his early reading of the Bible he can only have meant in an ethical sense, in addition to his historical interest. He grew up devoid of any belief in a God or Immortality, and does not appear to have felt the need of it.
—Ernest Jones, 1953, p. 19.

Two months after dreaming the Botanical Monograph, a few days after his 42nd birthday (May 6, 1898), Freud, on the 10th or 11th of May (Anzieu, 1986, p. 314), dreamt Castle by the Sea. To Freud, who has been readying himself for his face-off with *Moses*/Moses, the dream must have been transparent:

> A castle by the sea; later it was no longer immediately on the sea, but on a narrow canal. The Governor [*der Gouverneur*] was a Herr P. I was standing with him in a big reception room—with three windows in front of which there rose buttresses with what looked like crenellations [battlements]. I had been attached to the garrison as something in the nature of a volunteer naval officer. We feared the arrival of enemy warships, since we were in a state of war. Herr P. intended to leave, and gave me instructions [*Instruckionen*] as to what was to be done if the event that we feared took place. His invalid wife was with their children in the threatened castle. If the bombardment began, the great hall was to be evacuated. He breathed heavily and turned to go; I held [*halte*] him back and asked him how I was to communicate with him in case of necessity. He added something in reply, but immediately fell down dead. No doubt I had put an unnecessary strain upon him with my questions. After his death, which made no further impression on me [*Nach seinem Tode, der mir weiter keinen Eindruck macht*], I wondered whether his widow would remain in the castle, whether I should report his death to the Higher Command [*dem Oberkommando*] and whether I should take over command of the castle as being next in the order of rank. I was

> standing at the window, and observing the . . . merchant vessels rushing past rapidly through the dark water, some of them with several funnels and others with bulging decks . . . . Then my brother was standing beside me and we were looking out of the window at the canal. At the sight of one ship we were frightened and cried out: 'Here comes the warship!' But it turned out that it was only the same ships that I already knew returning. There now came a small ship, cut off short, in a comic fashion, in the middle. On its deck some curious cup-shaped or box-shaped objects were visible. We called out with one voice [*rufen wieaus einem Munde*]: 'That's the breakfast-ship [*Fruhstucksschiff*]!' (Freud, 1900b, pp. 463–464; [Freud, 1900a, pp. 466–467]).

According to Freud (1900b),

> The localities in the dream were brought together from several trips of mine to the Adriatic. . . . A short but enjoyable Easter trip which I had made to Aquilea with my brother [Alexander] a few weeks before the dream was still fresh in my memory. The dream also contained allusions to the *maritime war* between America and Spain and to anxieties to which it had given rise about the fate of my relatives in America (p. 464).

Ostensibly, Freud here is concerned about the fate of his sister Anna and her family who live in New York, "as there were fears it might be attacked or bombarded from the sea" (Anzieu, 1985, pp. 314–315). On the other hand, the proximity of "Spain and . . . anxieties about the fate of my relatives" to "Easter trip" suggests strongly that Freud's concern over anti-Semitism informed this dream whose "dream-thoughts dealt with the future of my family [*Zukunft der Meinigen*] after my premature death" (Freud, 1900b, p. 465; [Freud, 1900a, p. 468]). Here it is worth noting: "*die Meinigen,*" in addition to "my family," means "my people" (*The New Cassell's German Dictionary*). On March 31, 1492, the Catholic Sovereigns Isabella and Ferdinand signed the Edict of Banishment: Jews had until the 31st of July to leave Spain (the alternatives, death or conversion). In the Hebrew Calendar this deadline date was the 7th of Ab, but, according to Jewish tradition, the departure deadline was the 9th of Ab, which was the date, in 586 B.C.E. of the Chaldean or Babylonian destruction of the First Temple. By historical coincidence, the 9th of Ab was also the date that the Romans destroyed the Second Temple in 70 C.E.

Essay II: Freud's Dream Castle by the Sea

(Donin, 1972, p. 263). It is on the Fast of Ab or Tisha b'Av. that Jews lament the destruction of both Temples. (For Freud's familiarity with this the most tragic day in the Hebrew Calendar, see his July 23, 1882, letter to Martha Bernays; in Freud, 1960, p. 16.)

At this point it is worthwhile to revisit the following passage:

> I held [*halte*] him back .... but he immediately fell down dead. No doubt I had put an unnecessary strain upon [the Governor] with my questions. After *his death,* which *made no further impression on me* . . . (emphasis added).

With the above in mind, visualize Freud standing before *Moses*/Moses in the Church of St. Peter in Chains (cf. "a big reception room—with *three* windows") defiantly removing the phylacteries or *tefillin* from his forehead and left arm, as an unseen narrator reads from the Book of Deuteronomy:

> Therefore impress these My words upon your very heart: bind them as a sign on your hand and let them serve as a symbol on your forehead . . . Deuteronomy 11:18.
> *The Torah: The Five Books of Moses.*

> (The above translation accords with the traditional Hebrew or Masoretic text. In the King James Version, the verse is, "Therefore ye shall lay up these My words in your heart and in your soul, and bind them for a sign upon your hand, that they may be as frontlets between your eyes.")

Now consider this reading: having succeeded in confronting *Moses*/Moses with his plaint or charge against Yahweh regarding the perpetual persecution of his people (cf. "[fatal] strain upon [the Governor] with my questions"), Freud has set himself free from Yahweh's stamp, the Law (cf. "his death ...made *no further impression [Eindruck]* on me"); accordingly, he proceeds to free others—Jew and Gentile alike—from their religious shackles by destroying the Torah, signified by the death of the screen for the biblical Moses, the Governor. Thus, this haunted Cain's most passionate wish, the wish driving the dream, his wish to redeem himself by delivering his besieged nation—*der Kinder* especially—has been realized: No Torah, no Judaism, no Christianity, no miserable anti-Semitism. It seems, then, that Freud needn't have feared that he would die prematurely (cf. "... my premature death"), that is, before preparing the soil for his Promised Land, a socially just world grounded in reason where the seed of Abraham—Juliuses and Sarahs—at long last, can develop their talents and satisfy their needs.

"no further impression on me, I wondered whether his widow would remain in the castle..."

On the 9th of Ab or Tisha b'Av, the fast day commemorating the destruction of both the First and Second Temples, Jews recite verses from the Book of Lamentations; in the first of its five laments or dirges, fallen Jerusalem is likened to a grieving widow:

> 1. How doth the city sit solitary, *that was* full of people! *how* is she become a widow! she *that was* great among the nations, *and* princess among the provinces, *how* is she become tributary!
> 2. She weepeth sore in the night, and her tears *are* on her cheeks...
> 3. Judah is gone into captivity...

Given his familiarity with Tisha b'Av. it is not a stretch to surmise: "I wondered whether his widow would remain in the castle" alludes, ultimately, to Freud's concern for his besieged nation were it to "remain in their castle" or fortress, the Torah; note: Torah means instruction (cf. "The Governor ... gave me instructions [*Instruckionen*]....")

"We [my brother and I] called out with one voice [rufen wieauseinem Munde]: 'That's the breakfast-ship'"

"The English word 'breakfast,' means," Freud (1900b) notes, "'breaking fast'"—as in, he makes clear, breaking a fast (p. 466). According to Maimonides, when the Messiah appears fast days will become a thing of the past. Having (in the dream) destroyed Judaism's miserable shoot, Christianity—albeit at the terrible double cost of Judaism and Moses—Freud has broken for all time the Fast of the 9th of Av (Tisha b'Av), including all that that most tragic day in the Jewish calendar signifies; accordingly, "breakfast-ship"—"a small ship, cut off short, in a comic fashion, in the middle," symbolizing the castration or destruction of Christendom—evokes a "memory of the most cheerful *joie de vivre*":

> ... And while the little mail steamer made its way slowly ... we, who were the only passengers, ate our breakfast on deck in the highest spirits ... and we had rarely tasted a better one. This, then, was the 'breakfast-ship'. ... (p. 466).

Accompanied by "excellent" wine, this joyous 'breaking a fast' meal with his brother Alexander occurred on Easter Sunday, April 10th (Freud, 1985, p. 308), or the fourth day of Passover, the season the Messiah is to appear—and five days before the fortieth anniversary of Julius's death. Because Freud's messianic ambition stems from his fratricidal sense of guilt, it is reasonable to assume: in the dream, Alexander is a screen for Julius, that is to say, it is Freud and Julius who "[call] out "with *one voice*": "That's the breakfast-ship!" At the family Seder, Jakob Freud, as per tradition, had set aside a wine glass for the Messiah's herald, Elijah, not suspecting that the long-awaited deliverer of his people was possibly already in his home.

Then again ...

"I wondered ... whether I should report his death to the Higher Command"

Yahweh, dem Oberkommando, may actually exist; if so, were Freud to stay on his path, then dismal indeed would be the *Zukunft* or future of his children "unto the third and fourth generation" (Exodus 20: 5). Formerly, under the imagined threat of castration, Sigismund abandoned his intention to kill his grey-haired father, Jakob, to possess his young mother, Amalia; under the imagined threat of even more horrific visitations would Sigmund abandon his impious intention to kill each and every Jew's venerable father, Moses, to possess Mother Earth?

REFERENCES

ANZIEU, D. (1986). *Freud's Self-Analysis.* Transl. Peter Graham. London: Hogarth Press.
The New Cassell's German Dictionary (1962). New York: Funk and Wagnalls.
DONIN, RABBI HAYIM HALEVY. (1972). *To Be a Jew.* New York: Basic Books.
FREUD, S. (1900a). *Die Traumdeutung.* Vienna, G. W. II/III.
——— (1900b). The Interpretation of Dreams. In J. Strachey, ed. and trans. *The Standard Edition of the Complete Works of Sigmund Freud*, 24 vols. London: Hogarth Press, 1953–1974, 4–5.
——— (1960). *The Letters of Sigmund Freud.* Selected and edited by

E. Freud. New York: Basic Books.

——— (1985). *The Complete Letters of Sigmund Freud to Wilhelm Fliess, 1887–1904.* Jeffrey M. Masson. ed. & trans. Cambridge: Harvard Univ. Press.

JONES, E. (1953). *The Life and Work of Sigmund Freud.* New York: Basic Books.

TORAH, THE (1962). *The Five Books of Moses: A new translation of The Holy Scriptures according to the Masoretic Text.* Philadelphia: The Jewish Publication Society of America.

ESSAY III

FREUD'S FAILURE TO RECALL THE SURNAME OF JULIUS MOSEN

> You know what [Josef] Breuer told me one evening? I was so moved by what he said that in return I disclosed to him the secret of our engagement. He told me he had discovered that hidden under the surface of timidity there lay in me an extremely daring and fearless human being. I had always thought so, but never dared tell anyone. I have often felt as though I had inherited all the defiance and all the passions with which our ancestors defended their Temple and could gladly sacrifice my life for one great moment in history.
> —Sigmund Freud to Martha Bernays, letter dated February 2, 1886; Freud, 1960, p. 202.

> My Dear Ones:
> *"Kennst du das Land wo die Citronen bluhen?"* [Know'st thou the land where the lemon trees bloom?]....The darkest green...belongs ...to orange and lemon trees with green fruit, and when I stand up and look down into the garden I can see on the farthest trees the great orange-yellow balloons *'im dunkeln Laube gluhend'* [And oranges like gold in leafy gloom]. One of these trees has achieved a strange color effect...
> —Freud, September 3, 1902, from Sorrento; Jones, 1955, pp. 21–22.

> Dressed in a stiff straw hat, and carrying a gold-headed cane, Freud and his company climbed a steep ridge ... (Gifford, 1972, p. 30).
> —Freud at James Jackson Putnam's Adirondack camp, following his lecture series on psychoanalysis at Clark University.

On August 26, 1898, three months after he dreamt Castle by the Sea, Freud pens Wilhelm Fliess a guarded account of his recent failure to recall the surname of the German-Jewish poet Julius Mosen (ɔ. Julius Moses):

> You know how you can forget a name and substitute part of another for it; you could swear it was correct, although inevitably it turns out to be wrong. That happened to me recently

> with the name of the poet who wrote *Andreas Hofer* ("Zu Mantua in Banden [To Mantua in Chains]"). It must be something with an au—Lindau, Feldau, of course, the man's name is Julius Mosen; the "Julius" had not slipped my memory. I was able to prove (i) that I had repressed the name Mosen because of certain associations; (ii) that infantile material played a part in the repression; and (iii) that the substitute names that were pushed into the foreground were formed, like symptoms, from both groups of material. The analysis of it turned out to be complete, with no gaps left; unfortunately, I cannot expose it to the public anymore than my big dream (Freud, 1985, p. 324).

For ease of presentation of the following reconstruction, selected components of the guarded account are re-arranged.

"the 'Julius' had not slipped my memory . . . infantile material."

As both McGrath (1986, p. 291) and Anzieu (1986, pp. 358–359) intimate, "infantile material" suggests strongly that Freud's sense of guilt over his infant brother Julius's death (Freud, 1985, p. 268) was evoked at the time of the lapse. To repeat: against his better judgment, Freud continued to believe that when he was 23 months old he had killed his baby brother with his hostile wishes; tormented by this conviction, Freud secretly resolved to redeem himself by delivering *der Kinder*, Juliuses and Sarahs, from the scourge of anti-Semitism.

"I can not expose [the analysis] to the public anymore than my big dream."

Two months earlier, in response to Fliess's reservations about his including his "big dream" in his ongoing work, *The Interpretation of Dreams*, Freud penned:

> So the dream is condemned. . . . Let me know at least which topic it was to which you took exception and where you feared an attack by a malicious critic. Whether it is my anxiety, or Martha, or the *Dalles* [poverty or *misery* in Yiddish], or my *being without a fatherland*?

(Letter dated June 9, 1898; in Freud, 1985, p. 315; emphasis added.)

Five months earlier in *"J'accuse!"* (January 1898), Emile Zola denounced *"the miserable* anti-Semitism," and prior to Zola's bombshell, in his famous political tract, *The Jewish State,* Theodor Herzl (1896) referred to anti-Semitism as *Judennot,* "the *misery* of the Jews." Clearly, Freud's deep concern over anti-Semitism informed his "big dream," which never did surface. And given that this lost dream is associated in Freud's mind with his (withheld) analysis of the Mosen slip, it is reasonable to conclude: Freud's distress over that perpetual scourge is implicated in the lapse as well.

The subject of Mosen's poem, the Tyrol's national hero, Andreas Hofer, had rallied his fellow Tyrolese with his cry, "Men, the hour has struck!" (Freud, 1992, p. 229). Similarly, this modern freedom-fighter from Europe's most anti-Semitic city recognizes, with the noose tightening round his people, the urgent need to act; more so, for in nine years he will be 51, "the limit," he fears, "of [his] life" (Freud, 1900b, p. 513)—and he has yet to set foot in Rome.

"Zu Mantua in Banden [To Mantua in Chains]"

In a subsequent letter dated October 23rd, the first anniversary of his father Jakob's death, Freud (1985), after stating that his "yearning for [Rome] is ever more tormenting," alludes in the next sentence to his "big dream" (p. 332). According to the "contiguity rule" of psychoanalysis (Freud, 1905 [1901], p. 39), this proximity indicates that Freud's longing for Rome and his "big dream" are intimately related. And because this lost dream is associated in his mind with the Mosen slip, it is not a stretch to assume: during the lapse, Freud's Rome longing was stirred up. Again, before setting others, Jew and Gentile alike, free from their religious chains, which is essential for the realization of his Promised Land—an enlightened secular world where *der Kinder* live in peace with their neighbors and can move freely across frontiers—Freud would set himself free from the Law in Rome—by taking his stand before his personal totem, Michelangelo's *Moses,* in the Church of S. Pietro in Vincoli, aka the Church of St. Peter *in Chains* (cf. above, "in Banden [*in Chains*]"). Erected to house the two chains which fell from Peter's wrists in his Jerusalem jail cell just before he was to be executed, this church had been the titular church of Cardinal Giuliano della Rovere, who, later, as Pope Julius II (1443–1513) commissioned Michelangelo to create *Moses* for his envisioned tomb. (Despite his expressed wish, Pope Julius is entombed in St. Peter's.) Freud must have thought it ironic that Julius II, dead almost four hundred years, had handed him the task of facing *Moses*/Moses, the successful execution of which—that is, the freeing himself from *his chains,* the Law—could lead ultimately to the destruction of that great Pope's church. This dreaded but essential task in that gloomy Roman church calls up for Freud the fateful descent, in Italy, into the underworld of Aeneas (cf. *And*re*as* Hofer). But only up to a point would he follow Aeneas' path: in order to save his homeless people, that legendary Trojan hero undertook his perilous descent into the underworld to *receive* instructions from the shade of his father, Anchises. By contrast, in order to save his homeless people (cf. "being without a fatherland"), Freud would undertake his perilous descent into *his* underworld—the gloomy Church of St. Peter in Chains—to *destroy* the instructions of his primal or ur-father Moses: the Torah. (Again, at the cost of his people's Tree of Life, this tormented and conflicted Cain would redeem himself.) And, like his classical double, this Aeneas would come armed, armed with a Golden Bough—or "Lindau."

"It must be something with an au—Lindau, Feldau"

Because Virgil (79–19 B.C.E.), the singer of Aeneas, was born near Mantua (cf. "Zu Mantua . . ."), this northern Italian city is often referred to as that great poet's birthplace. In *The Divine Comedy,* with which Freud had an easy familiarity (McGrath, 1986, p. 303), Dante (1952) addresses Virgil's shade as "Courteous Mantuan soul" [Hell, Canto II]. Though it was from an oak tree that Aeneas plucked his Golden Bough, the substitute name "Lindau" is a fitting token of Aeneas' hell's charm whose "leaves [and] pliant twigs are all of gold" (Virgil, 1983, *The Aeneid,* Bk. VI): adorning a lind or linden tree are small yellow flowers; Au, of course, is the symbol for gold. Armed with his secretly plucked dazzling "Lindau" or hell's charm—the oedipal beginnings of the idea of God—Freud possesses, he trusts, his mighty weapon and ticket to personal redemption: universal acceptance of this revolutionary notion that God the Father is but a projection onto the universe of his father as perceived by the oedipal boy would cut the ground out from religion, and, thereby, make anti-Semitism a thing of the past.

"something ending in an au–. . . Feldau"

Armed with his Golden Bough or "Lindau," Aeneas descended into the underworld to the blessed home of the righteous dead or *Manes,* Elysium's Golden Fields or "Feldau":

> Where souls take ease among the Blessed Groves
> Wider expanse of high air endow
> each vista with a wealth of light. (Virgil, 1983, Bk. VI.)

ESSAY III: Freud's Failure to Recall the Surname . . .

Freud's Golden Fields, the gloomy Church of St. Peter in Chains, is his battlefield. For there, he would free himself from the Law by taking his stand before Michelangelo's terrible *Moses*; again, this statue embodies, Freud superstitiously believes, the spirit or shade of the biblical Moses. In other words, the world's greatest representation of that great man is a symbol in the same manner that the Communion Wafer or Host is a symbol for Roman Catholics (such as his Czech nanny who in his tiny Catholic birthplace, Freiberg in Moravia, had instilled her Jewish charge with a Roman Catholic sensibility): *Moses* is Moses; that is to say, this magnificent 8 ft., 4 in. representation of Yahweh's Lawgiver possesses all of that venerable prophet's qualities, including his terrible radiance or *mana* [cf. "Zu *Man*tua"] that had so unnerved the Israelites at the foot of Mt. Sinai (Exodus 30:35)—and which Freud (1921) will refer to in *Group Psychology and the Analysis of the Ego:*

> Even Moses had to act as an intermediary between his people and Jehovah, since the people could not support the sight of God; and when he returned from the presence of God his face shone— some of the *mana* had been transferred on to him (p. 125).

In *The Divine Comedy,* Virgil's shade, acting as Dante's guide to the underworld, informs Dante that because Moses "did not have baptism" the shade of Moses had been suspended in those Golden Fields, that is, until Christ descended and lifted that great man's shade to Paradise (Hell, Canto 1V). At any one time, depending on which of his two religious sensibilities, Jewish or Roman Catholic, is stirred up or operative, Freud's Lord is either Yahweh or Jesus Christ, and inasmuch as he expects his Roman Catholic proclivities to break through in the Church of St. Peter in Chains where everything would come to a head, it is worthwhile to return to the Botanical Monograph (March 1898), specifically to Freud's free-association to the dream-element "a dried specimen of a plant":

> In my preliminary [secondary school] examination in botany I was . . . given a Crucifer [*Kruzifere*] to identify—and failed to do so [*und erkannte sie nicht*]. My prospects would not have been too bright [*Er ware mir schlecht ergangen*], if I had not been helped out by my theoretical knowledge [*wenn nicht meine theoretischen Kenntnisse mir heraus geholfen hatten*]. (Freud, 1900b, pp. 171–172; [Freud, 1900a, p. 177]).

A crucifer, a flowering plant with four equal petals arranged crosswise, is a fitting token of Christ (and of his Church). The evocation of his failure at the Sperl Gymnasium to identify a "Crucifer" ("given a Crucifer to identify"), signifies this haunted Cain's anticipated struggle against acknowledging [*erkannte. . . . nicht*], in the Seat of Catholicism, Jesus Christ as His Redeemer. Freud pins his "prospects" on his secret "theoretical knowledge" [*meine theoretischen Kenntnisse*]. But if God the Father is not merely an "exalted father" (Freud, 1910, p. 12), and He *is* Jesus Christ, then at the Last Judgment when Christ "shall reward every man according to his works" (Matthew 16:27), Freud's "prospects . . . would not [be] too bright"—indeed they would be, as he well knows, *"schlecht"* (Freud, 1900a, p. 177, above) or "wretched" (*Cassell's New German Dictionary*, 1906, rev., 1914). Even though Virgil's shade informs Dante that it had witnessed Jesus lift Moses' shade to Paradise, it's easy for me to imagine Freud envisioning himself encountering that great man's shade in the very setting, the setting of the righteous dead—the Blessed Groves or *Feldau*—that Anchises had directed Aeneas' attention to the future line of his son, Julius (Iulus Ascanius), the Romans. For after all this Aeneas, too, would have an enlightened "Julius" or "Julian" line, a line which is "just—not by constraint of law, but by choice" (Virgil, 1983, *The Aeneid,* Bk VII, p. 202). To repeat: the realization of his passionately longed-for "Julius" line would *undo* Freud's "killing" Julius, for so long as his enlightened brotherly line lives, his baby brother Julius lives! By itself, this—its grandest promise—makes Freud's mighty Golden Bough, the oedipal beginnings of God the Father, as a scientific construct suspect—not to mention the other promises his "Lindau" guarantees: the realization of his avenging Hannibal fantasy, the destruction of the new Romans, that seed-bed for anti-Semites, the Roman Catholic Church; the deliverance of *der Kinder* from anti-Semitism; self-redemption; and, by becoming the new moral authority or Lawgiver ("Know Thyself"), immortality.

This striver, is he then just another deluded messianic pretender?

"Zu Mantua in Banden [To Mantua in Chains]" (another look)

By the time Freud pens his guarded account (August 26, 1898), Herzl's Jewish detractors were denouncing the Zionist leader as a false messiah—a characterization, which, Freud, self-aware as he is, understands may very well apply to him. (The first major Zionist convention, the Second

Zionist Congress will convene three days later in Basle, Switzerland.) In View of the Tiber (date unknown), one of his dreams "based upon a longing to visit Rome," his analysis of which he withholds, Freud (1900, p. 194) views from a railway carriage the Pont Sant' Angelo, a bridge favored by messianic pretenders (Scholem, 1971, p. 12). [In rabbinical lore dating from the second century the Messiah is already on earth: *waiting in hiding,* he sits among the beggars and lepers at the entrance to Rome (Seltzer, 1930, pp. 307–308).] One such pretender who in rags sat by the bridge was Shlomo Molcho (Waagenaar, 1974, pp. 153–154), whose path to martyrdom prefigured that of Andreas Hofer: in 1532, two years after proclaiming himself the Messiah of the Jews in Rome, Molcho, on orders of the Holy Roman Emperor Charles V, was taken *in chains to Mantua,* where, after being condemned by the Inquisition, he was burned at the stake; similarly, almost three hundred years later, Hofer, on orders of Napoleon, was taken *in chains to Mantua,* where, after a sham trial, he was executed by a firing squad on February 20, 1810. (To the very end, in the face of imminent execution, Hofer, as had Molcho, remained defiant.) Though no evidence seems to exist indicating that he was familiar with the son of *Conversos* who became "famous in the annals of Jewish history and martyrdom as Solomon [Shlomo] Molcho, the pseudo-Messiah" (Roth, 1932, p. 68), it is conceivable, if not likely, that as part of his detailed, four-year preparation for *Moses/* Moses, and out of fear that he is just another deluded pretender, Freud would have studied the lives of the various false messiahs—especially one named Schlomo or Shlomo (Solomon). For, as Freud (1913), who was born Sigismund Schlomo, will note, obsessional neurotics believe there is "a transcendental connection between all bearers . . . of the same name" (56; p. 112), and being himself an "'obsessional type'" (Freud, 1974; p. 82), he knows this from personal experience. At any rate, if his Golden Bough is but a hollow wish-fulfillment and there really is a *Gott in Himmel,* then this Schlomo, having lost his way, could expect not redemption but justice, that is to say, either Yahweh's dreadful visitations or, if the Lord is Jesus Christ, hell's wretched torments.

NOTE

In early 1937, Marie Bonaparte purchased Freud's letters to Wilhelm Fliess from Reinhold Stahl, the Berlin bookseller who had acquired them from Fliess's widow, Ida. Soon after, in late February or early March, Freud informed Bonaparte "he wanted the letters burned"

(Bonaparte's notebook entry; in Freud, 1985, p. 9). Aware that they would shed unparalleled light on the origins of psychoanalysis, and knowing that he intended to destroy these letters dating from 1887 to 1904, Bonaparte refused to re-sell them (at half-price) to her friend and mentor. Had she complied, the Mosen lapse would have been lost—as had the "big dream," which "must have been something 'political'" (Schur, 1966, p. 75; Freud, 1985, pp. 318–319, n.1).

REFERENCES

ALTER, R. & KERMODE, F. (1990). *The Literary Guide to the Bible*. Cambridge: Harvard University Press.

ANZIEU, D. (1986). *Freud's Self-Analysis*. P. Graham, trans. London: Hogarth Press.

Cassell's German Dictionary, The New . (1962). New York: Funk and Wagnalls.

DANTE, A. (1952). *The Divine Comedy*. C. E. Norton, trans. Chicago: Great Books.

FREUD, S. (1900a). Die traumdeutung. Vienna, G.W., 2/3.

——— (1900b). The interpretation of dreams. In J. Strachey, ed. and trans. *The Standard Edition of the Complete Works of Sigmund Freud*, 24 vols. London: Hogarth Press, 1953–1974, 4–5.

——— (1901[1905]). Fragment of an analysis of a case of hysteria. *Standard Edition* 7.

——— (1913). Totem and taboo. *Standard Edition* 13.

——— (1921). Group psychology and the analysis of the ego. *Standard Edition* 18.

——— (1927). The future of an illusion. *Standard Edition* 21.

——— (1939). Moses and monotheism. *Standard Edition* 23.

——— (1960). *The Letters of Sigmund Freud*. Selected and edited by E. Freud. New York: Basic Books.

———(1992). *The Diary of Sigmund Freud 1929–1939*. Translated, annotated, and introduced by Michael Molnar. New York: Charles Scribner's Sons.

——— (1985). *The Complete Letters of Sigmund Freud to Wilhelm Fliess, 1887–1904*. Edited and translated by J.M. Masson. Cambridge: Harvard University Press.

——— & JUNG, C. (1974). *The Freud/Jung Letters: The Correspondence between Sigmund Freud and C.G. Jung*. W. McGuire, ed., R. Manheim and R. F. C. Hull.
trans. Princeton: Princeton University Press.

GAY, P. (1988). *Freud: a life for our time*. New York: Norton.

GIFFORD, G.E., Jr. (March/April 1972). Freud and the Porcupine. *Harvard*

Medical Alumni Bulletin, pp. 28–31.

HERZL, T. (1896, 1988). *The Jewish State*. (Based on S. D'Avigdor's 1896 translation. Intro by A. Bein.) New York: Dover.

JONES, E. (1955). *The Life and Work of Sigmund Freud*. New York: Basic Books.

LIPPMAN R. (August 2009). Freud's Botanical Monograph Screen Memory Revisited, *Psychoanalytic Review*, 96(4).

MCGRATH, W. J. (1986). *Freud's Discovery of Psychoanalysis: The Politics of Hysteria*. New York: Cornell University Press.

ROTH, C. (1954). *A Bird's-Eye View of Jewish History*. New York: Union of American Hebrew Congregations.

SCHOLEM, G. (1971). *The Messianic Idea in Judaism*. New York: Schocken Books.

SCHUR, M (1966). Some Additional "Day Residues" of the Specimen Dream of Psychoanalysis. In *Psychoanalysis, A General Psychology; Essays in Honor of Heinz Hartmann*, R. M. Lowenstein, L. M. Newman, M, Schur, and A. J. Solnit, eds. New York: International Universities Press.

SELTZER, R.M. (1980). *Jewish People, Jewish Thought: The Jewish Experience in History*. New York: Macmillan Publishing Company.

VIRGIL (1983). *The Aeneid*. R. Fitzgerald, trans. New York: Random House.

ESSAY IV

THE ALIQUIS LAPSE: PREPARING THE GROUND WITH MINNA

En cas de doute, abstien toi. [When in doubt, abstain.]
—Inscription questionably attributed to St. Augustine by Sigmund Freud's friend Ernst von Fleischl-Marxow, and embroidered in 1883 by Martha Bernays for Freud's room in the General Hospital of Vienna; at Freud's request (Jones, 1953, p. 66).

... when he told me about the [shipboard] dream in which his wife and her sister played important parts, I asked Freud to tell me some more of his personal associations with the dream. He looked at me with bitterness and said, "I could tell you more, but I cannot risk my authority."
—Carl Jung to John M. Billinsky in 1957 (Hogenson, 1983, pp. 167–168).

For each of us fate assumes the form of one (or several) women [sic]...
—Freud to Sandor Ferenczi, letter dated July 9, 1913 (Freud, 1993, p. 499).

In August 1898, Sigmund Freud (42) and his sister-in-law Minna Bernays (33), while vacationing in the Swiss Alps, stayed two nights at the *Schweizerhaus* in Maloja. One hundred and eight years later, after reading Freud's inn entry of August 13, "Dr. Sigm Freud u frau," Dr. Franz Maciejewski concluded, "By any reasonable standard of proof, Sigmund Freud and his wife's sister, Minna Bernays, had a liaison" (Blumenthal, 2006). Three years after the "liaison," Freud (1901) will offer an analysis of a failure to quote correctly Dido's cry, "Let someone arise from my bones as an avenger!" According to Freud, the individual who failed to recall "*Aliquis*," Latin for someone, was a travel companion troubled by the possibility that his lover was pregnant. As Swales (1982) asserts, this young Jew and his Italian lover are actually screens for Freud and his sister-in-law Minna. But given that he is dissembling, Freud may have been fantasizing: '... but were we to make love, Minna could get pregnant!' [Again, Freud had firsthand knowledge of contraceptive failure, the birth, five years earlier, of Anna Freud (Shapiro, 1996, p. 557).]

The lapse occurred in the summer of 1900, while Freud and Minna were on vacation in Italy, which included a visit to Trent in the Tyrol (Jones, 1953, p. 363). A member of the Freud household since late 1895, Minna, whom Freud called "*Schwester*" (McGrath, 1986, p. 280, n.15), followed Freud's work much more closely than did his wife, Martha, who was four years older. Here it is worthwhile to quote Paul Roazen (1975):

> Minna was more intellectual than Martha, read foreign languages easily, was quite literary, and became a real support on his work. . . . Minna . . . really understood his ideas, and he was far more likely to discuss his cases with her than with Martha. . . . In conversation Freud remembered that in his loneliest and yet most creative years, the 1890's, only Minna and his friend Wilhelm Fliess had been able to sustain his faith in himself, for they believed in his intellectual achievement . . . (p. 61).

Presenting this disguised bit of self-analysis, Freud writes:

> . . . [On a holiday trip last summer (1900)] I renewed my acquaintance with a certain young man of academic background. I soon found that he was familiar with some of my psychological publications. We had fallen into conversation—how I have now forgotten—about the social status of the race to which we both belong; and ambitious feelings prompted him to give vent to a regret that his generation was doomed (as he expressed it) to atrophy, and could not develop its talents or satisfy its needs. He ended a speech of impassioned fervour with the well-known line of Virgil's in which the unhappy Dido commits to posterity her vengeance on Aeneas: '*Exoriaire* . . .' Or rather, he *wanted* to end it in this way, for he could not get hold of the quotation and tried to conceal an obvious gap in what he remembered by changing the order of the words: '*Exoriar(e) ex nostris ossibus ultor.*' At last he said irritably: 'Please don't look so scornful: you seem as if you were gloating over my embarrassment. Why not help me? There is something missing in the line; how does the whole thing really go?'
>
> 'I'll help you with pleasure,' I replied, and gave the quotation its correct form: *'Exoriar(e) ALIQUIS nostris ex ossibus ultor.'* ['Let someone (*aliquis*) arise from my bones as an avenger!'] (pp. 8–9; Freud's italics.)

Essay IV: The Aliquis Lapse: Preparing the Ground with Minna

To make it easier to refer back to, I am presenting in dialogue form the core of the remainder of this "conversation" in which "ambitious feelings" were stirred up:

> —How stupid to forget a word like that! By the way, you [Freud] claim that one never forgets a thing without some reason. I should be very curious to learn how I came to forget the indefinite pronoun "*aliquis*" in this case.
>
> — . . . I must only ask you to tell me, *candidly* and *uncritically*, whatever comes into your mind when you direct your attention to the forgotten word without any definite aim.
>
> —Good. There springs to my mind, then, the ridiculous notion of dividing up the word like this: *a* and *liquis*.
>
> —What does that mean?
>
> — I don't know.
>
> —And what occurs to you next?
>
> —What comes next is *Reliquen* [relics], *liquefying, fluidity, fluid*. . . .
>
> I am thinking [," he went on," Freud writes, "with a scornful laugh"] of *Simon of Trent*, whose relics I saw two years ago in a church at Trent. I am thinking of the accusation of ritual blood-sacrifice which is brought against the Jews again just now, and of *Kleinpaul*'s [1892] book in which he regards all these supposed victims as incarnations, one might say, new editions of the Saviour.
>
> —The notion is not entirely unrelated to the subject we were discussing before the Latin word slipped your memory.
>
> —True. My next thoughts are about an article . . . in an Italian newspaper. Its title, I think, was "What St. *Augustine* says about Women." . . . And now . . . . I am thinking of a fine old gentleman I met on my travels last week. He was a real *original*, with all the appearance of a huge bird of prey. His name was *Benedict*, if that's of interest to you. . . . Anyhow, here are a row of saints and Fathers of the Church: St. *Simon*, St. *Augustine*, St. *Benedict*. There was, I think, a Church Father called *Origen*. Moreover, three of these names are also first names, like *Paul* in *Kleinpaul*. Now it's St. *Januarius* and the miracle of his blood that comes into my mind—my thoughts seem to be running on mechanically.

—Just a moment: St. *Januarius* and St. *Augustine* both have to do with the calendar. But won't you remind me about the miracle of his blood?

—Surely you must have heard of that? They keep the blood of St. Januarius in a phial inside a church at Naples, and on a particular holiday it miraculously liquefies. The people attach great importance to this miracle and get very excited if it's delayed, as happened once at a time when the French were occupying the town. So the general in command—or have I got it wrong? was it Garibaldi?—took the reverend gentleman aside and gave him to understand, with an unmistakable gesture towards the soldiers posted outside, that he *hoped* the miracle would take place very soon. And in fact it did take place . . .

—Well, something *has* come into my mind . . . but it's too intimate to pass on . . .

—Well, go on. Why do you pause?

— . . . . Well then, I've suddenly thought of a lady from whom I might easily hear a piece of news that would be very awkward for both of us.

—That her periods have stopped?

—How could you guess that?

— . . . Think of *the calendar saints, the blood that starts the flow on a particular day, the disturbance when the event fails to take place, the open threats that the miracle must be vouchsafed, or else* . . . In fact you've made use of the miracle of St. Januarius to manufacture a brilliant allusion to women's periods.

— . . .Without being aware of it. And you really mean to say that it was this anxious expectation that made me unable to produce an unimportant word like *aliquis*?

—It seems to me undeniable, You need only recall the division you made into *a-liquis*, and your associations: *relics, liquefying, fluid.* St. Simon was *sacrificed as a child*—shall I go on and show how he comes in? You were led on to him by the subject of relics.

—No, I'd much rather you didn't. I hope you don't take these thoughts of mine too seriously, if indeed I had them. In return I will confess to you that the lady is Italian and that I went to Naples with her. . . . (pp. 9–11; Freud's italics).

Summing up, Freud offers the following reconstruction:

Essay IV: The Aliquis Lapse: Preparing the Ground with Minna

> The disturbance in reproduction occurred . . . from the very nature of the topic hit upon in the quotation, since opposition unconsciously arose to the wishful idea expressed. The speaker had been deploring the fact that the present generation of his people was deprived of its full rights; a new generation, he prophesied like Dido, would inflict vengeance on the oppressors. At this moment a contrary thought intruded, 'Have you really so keen a wish for descendants? This is not so. How embarrassed you would be if you were to get news now that you were to expect descendants from the quarter you know of. No: no descendants—however much we need them for vengeance' (p. 14).

"A huge bird of prey . . . . St. Benedict"

According to Gregory the Great (540–604), who is the authority on St. Benedict (480–550), the greatest temptation of the flesh the father of Western monasticism had ever experienced happened on a day when the holy man was alone and the Devil or "Tempter" appeared in the form of "a small [persistent] *dark bird,* commonly called *a black bird*":

> . . . the evil spirit brought back before his mind's eye a certain woman whom he had once before seen. So intensely did the Tempter inflame his mind by the sight of that woman that he could hardly control his passion. He was overcome by sensuality, and almost considered abandoning his solitary retreat . . . [To contain himself] he "flung himself naked upon . . . stinging thorns and burning nettles . . . roll[ing] around there for a long time, and came out with his whole body wounded by them (Gregory, 1977, p. 7).

The extreme measure taken by St. Benedict to "control his passion" strongly suggests that Freud, during their visit in Italy in the summer of 1900, lusted after Minna—as does the proximate evocation of the early Church Father Origen ("St. *Benedict* . . . a Church Father called *Origen*") who, "to work freely instructing female catechumens," purportedly castrated himself (*Encyclopaedia Britannica.* 1973, p. 1094).

"What St. Augustine says about Women"

According to Augustine, women, unlike men, do not possess "the power of reason and understanding" to restrain themselves when sexually aroused; this being the case, he counsels:

> A wife's body should be . . . subject to the sex of her husband as the appetite of action is subjected by reason of the mind, to conceive the skill of acting rightly (St. Augustine, *Confessions,* 1943, pp. 378-379).

Because Freud recalls "What St. Augustine says about Women," it is reasonable to suppose: at the time of the lapse, Freud senses, correctly or not, that Minna on this trip desires him, and, following Augustine, he believes that whether or not they give in to their mutual lust is ultimately up to him, for, being a man, he possesses "the power of reason and understanding" to prevail over sexual desire.

"*St. Augustine, St. Benedict*"

Inasmuch as Freud and his *Schwester* Minna were alone on this trip, it's not a stretch to surmise—especially given St. Augustine's take on women—that the following incident involving St. Benedict and his determined sister, Scholastica, came to Freud while studying the lapse: Scholastica implores Benedict, "Please don't leave me tonight, but let us us talk until morning about the joys of life in heaven." But he answered, "What are you saying, sister? I certainly cannot stay outside my monastery for any reason." Whereupon Scholastica silently prays to God; the fair weather changes to a torrential downpour—and she prevails over Benedict's resistance: he spends the night (Adapted from *Dialogues of Gregory the Great, Book II, St. Benedict,* 1977, pp. 42–43).

"*I am thinking of Simon of Trent, whose relics I saw two years ago . . .*"

In 1475 in Trent, Jews allegedly killed two-year-old Simon for blood to prepare the Passover matzoh. According to Ben-Sasson (1976):

> The entire [Jewish] community was arrested and subjected to torture, which led to conflicting confessions. Those sentenced were promptly executed, while the remaining Jews were expelled. The impact of the [blood] libel was felt far and wide. . . . In 1582 the infant Simon was officially proclaimed a saint of the Catholic Church. [In 1965 the Church withdrew its canonization and acknowledged that a judicial error had been committed against the Jews of Trent in this trial (p. 580).]

Essay IV: The Aliquis Lapse: Preparing the Ground with Minna

In addition to the fourteen Jews who went up in flames in Trent (Wistrich, 1991, p. 34), Dido's funeral pyre could have easily called up in Freud's mind the auto-de-fes of New Christians or *Conversos*, as well as the countless members of his detested "race" burnt to death in the Middle Ages—more so, given Freud's identification with the Semitic queen's *ultor* or avenger.

"a new generation, he prophesied like Dido, would inflict vengeance on the oppressors"

When Virgil (70-19 B.C.) penned Dido's cry for an avenger, he had in mind "the favorite hero of [Freud's] later school days," Hannibal (247-182 B.C.):

> And when in the higher classes I began to understand for the first time what it meant to belong to an alien race, and anti-semitic feelings among the other boys warned me that I must take up a definite position, the figure of the semitic general rose still higher in my esteem. To my youthful mind Hannibal and Rome symbolized the conflict between the tenacity of Jewry and the organization of the Catholic church. And the increasing importance of the effects of the anti-semitic movement upon our emotional life helped to fix [*fixieren*] the thoughts and feelings of those early days (Freud, 1900b, p. 196; 1900a, p. 202).

The above amounts to a confession: " I . . . understand . . . I must take up a definite position [against] . . . the Catholic church, . . . the increasing anti-Semitism . . . fixing these thoughts and feelings." In other words, this modern Hannibal or relentless Semitic avenger is bent on destroying the new Romans, that seed-bed for anti-Semites like the good Christian who had knocked off Jakob Freud's new *shabbos* hat, his *Shtreimel*, into the mud and ordered him off the pavement: the Roman Catholic Church (cf. "ambitious feelings . . . vengeance").

"St. Simon . . . sacrificed as a child"

In the first edition of *The Interpretation of Dreams*, Freud (1900b, p. 197) refers to Hannibal's father (Hamilcar Barca) as Hasdrubal, which was actually the name of Hannibal's *younger* brother. This is an understandable slip: the 'father' of Hannibal/Freud is not so much Freud's beloved humiliated father, Jakob, as it is Freud's infant brother Julius whom Sigismund at 23 months of age had "sacrificed" with his evil wishes (Freud, 1985, p. 268). Again, in 1897, after discovering in his self-analysis that he had played Cain to Julius's Abel in their birthplace, Freiberg in Moravia (now Pribor, in the Czech Republic), Freud, oppressed by his fratricidal sense of guilt, secretly resolved to atone for having "sacrificed" Julius by instituting his ideal Promised Land, an enlightened secular world in which the seed of Abraham—future Juliuses (and Sarahs)—can thrive, can at last "develop [their] talents [and] satisfy [their] needs." Again, at the cost of his people's Tree of Life, the Torah, this haunted Cain would redeem *der Kinder*—and himself.

"so keen a wish for descendants"

Aeneas, through his son, Iulus or Julius Ascanius, will become the ancestor of an enlightened line—a line which is "just by choice" (Virgil, 1983, p. 202). And Freud, too, would have his own humane "Julius" or Julian line, the inhabitants of his socially just Promised Land. St. Benedict's prevailing over his lust enabled him to sire the Benedictines. Similarly, in order to sire his own spiritual line—his "Julius" line—Freud must, he understands, successfully prevail over his desire for his muse and secret love, Minna (e.g., Lippman, November 18, 2009). Benedict's spiritual descendants Christianized Europe (there were as many as 37,000 Benedictine monasteries); Freud's spiritual descendants, on the other hand, would de-Christianize the entire world. [Benedict's Rule—with its demand for *life-long obedience,* under threat of expulsion—enabled Benedict's "children" to Christianize Europe. On the afternoon of Sunday, May 25, 1913, when he formally instituted his secret watchdog council, the Committee, at Berggasse 19, did Freud have Benedict's Rule in mind? After all, for one's counter-movement why not take from the enemy what works?]

In addition to the suffering it would cause Martha and their three young boys and girls, a sexual scandal, especially one involving his wife's sister, would jeopardize the realization of Freud's Promised Land. Given his cruel predicament—being torn between his Promised Land and his desire for Minna—there is no better model for Freud to follow than the legendary Trojan hero who, to save *his* homeless, wandering nation, sacrificed personal happiness; once again, we turn to Augustine:

Essay IV: The Aliquis Lapse: Preparing the Ground with Minna

> Even though passions may disturb the inferior part of the soul, a mind . . . firmly resolved never permits passion to prevail over rational resolve. On the contrary, the mind is the master and by refusing consent and by positive resistance, it maintains the sovereignty of virtue. Such a man, as Virgil describes him, was Aeneas:
>
> > 'With mind unmoved he doth remain,
> > While [Dido's] tender tears run down in vain.'
> > (*City of God,* 1958, Book IX, p. 177.)

Here, it is worth recalling: it was not Aeneas, but Dido who pressed for sex. (Cupid, in the form of Julius Ascanius, had infected her with passion for that legendary Trojan, Freud's classical double.)

Four months prior to the Aliquis lapse, and just three days after Passover, Freud on Tuesday, April 24, 1900, gave a talk on Emile Zola's *Fecondite* (1899) at his B'nai B'rith lodge, which he had joined on September 29, 1897. Because it mirrors his Promised Land, Freud could easily have penned the "divine dream" envisioned in this utopian novel completed by Zola while in voluntary exile in England:

> And the divine dream, the generous utopian thought soars into the heavens; families blended into nations, nations blended into mankind, one sole brotherly people making of the world one sole city of peace and truth and justice! Ah! may eternal fruitfulness ever expand, may the seed of humanity be carried over the frontiers . . . (Zola, 1899 [1925], p. 411).

With regards to the couple who co-founded this brotherly world of "peace, truth and justice," Zola asks rhetorically, "And would they not forever live in their children—forever be united, immortal, in their race?" (p. 410). Similarly, were his envisioned Promised Land to become a reality, wouldn't Freud and his beloved *Schwester* Minna "forever live in their children, forever be united, immortal in their race," that is, in their spiritual children, their "Julius" line—a line "just by choice"? [Not surprisingly, Freud, in 1907, will place *Fecondite* on a list of "ten good books. . . . books to which one owes some part of one's life and philosophy" (Freud, 1960, p. 269)].

Fourteen summers after the Aliquis lapse, Freud will give Sabina Spielrein, then twenty-eight, advice with regards to her longing for her ten-year older former lover, Carl Jung—advice which, vis-a-vis his longing for Minna, Freud adhered to faithfully:

> ... Warm your life's intentions with your fire instead of burning yourself up with it. Nothing is stronger than controlled and sublimated passion. You can achieve nothing while you are at loggerheads with yourself (Letter of June 12, 1914; in Carotenuto, 1982, p. 122).

Which is reminiscent of Pope Gregory's observation regarding St. Benedict: "He had put out the forbidden flame within. ... by transforming the fire" (*op. cit.*, p. 7).

On May 25th of the previous year, Freud handed each member of the Committee an ancient intaglio engraved with a scene from classical antiquity to be mounted into a gold ring like his own. When dispensing these five precious stones that Sunday afternoon did one more 'recipient' come to Freud's mind, arguably the person most deserving of such a stone, a stone, moreover, that had already been set in a gold band?

REFERENCES

AUGUSTINE. (1943). *The Confessions of St. Augustine.* Translated by J.G. Pilkington. New York: Liveright.
——— (1958). *The City of God.* G.G. Walsh, D.B. Zema, G. Monahan, and D.J. Honan, transl. Garden City: Image Books.
BEN-SASSON. H. ed. (1976). *A History of the Jewish People.* Cambridge: Harvard University Press.
BILLINSKY, J. (1969). Jung and Freud (the end of a romance). *Andover Newton Quarterly.*
BLUMENTHAL, R. (2006), Hotel Log Hints at Illicit Desire That Dr. Freud Didn't Repress. *The New York Times.* December 24.
CAROTENU, A. (1982). *A Secret Symmetry: Sabina Spielrein Between Jung and Freud.* (A. Pomerans, J Shepley, J. and K. Winston, trans.). New York: Pantheon Books.
ENCYCLOPAEDIA BRITANNICA. (1973.)
FREUD, S. (1900a). *Die Traumdeutung.* Vienna, G.W. II/III.
——— (1900b). *The Interpretation of Dreams. Standard Edition* 4–5.
——— (1901). *The Psychopathology of Everyday Life. Standard Edition* 6.
——— (1927). *The Future of an Illusion. Standard Edition* 21.
——— (1939). *Moses and Monotheism. Standard Edition* 23.
———(1960). *The Letters of Sigmund Freud.* Selected and edited by

E. Freud. New York: Basic Books.

—— & FLIESS, W. (1985). *The Complete Letters of Sigmund Freud to Wilhelm Fliess, 1887–1904,* translated and edited by J.M. Masson. Cambridge: Harvard University Press.

—— & FERENCZI, S. (1993). *The Correspondence of Sigmund Freud and Sandor Ferenczi, Volume 1: 1908–1914.* Edited by E. Brabant, E. Falzeder and P. Giampieri-Deutsch; translated by P. Hoffer.

GREGORY, (1967). *Dialogues. Book II, Saint Benedict.* Translated by Myra L. Uhlfelder. Indianapolis: Bobbs-Merrill.

HOGENSON, G. (1983). *Jung's Struggle with Freud.* Notre Dame: University of Notre Dame Press.

JONES, E. (1953; 1955). *The Life and Work of Sigmund Freud.* New York: Basic Books.

LIPPMAN, R. (2009). Freud, Minna, and Schliemann's *Ilios.* Online at: www.InternationalPsychoanalysis.Net, Nov. 18.

LOTHANE, Z. (2007). Sensation-Mongering Among Historians: A Response to "Did Freud Sleep With his Wife's sister? An Expert Interview with Franz Maciejewski, PhD " *Medscape Psychiatry News,* June 13. Online at: www.medscape.com/viewarticle/558079.

MACIEJEWSKI, F. (2007). Did Freud Sleep With his Wife's sister? An Expert Interview with Franz Maciejewski, PhD. *Medscape Psychiatry News,* May 4, Online at: www.medscape.com/viewarticle/555692.

MCGRATH W. (1986). *Freud's Discovery of Psychoanalysis: The Politics of Hysteria.* New York: Cornell University Press.

NUNBERG, H. & FEDERN, E. (1962). *Minutes of the Vienna Psycho-analytic Society.* Volume I, 1906–1908. New York: International Universities Press.

ROAZEN P. (1975). *Freud and His Followers.* New New York: Alfred A. Knopf.

SHAPIRO, E.R. (1996). Grief in Freud's Life: Re-conceptualizing Bereavement in Psychoanalytic Theory. *Psychoanalytic Psychology: A Journal of Theory, Practice.*

SWALES, P.J. (1982). Freud, Minna Bernays, and the Conquest of Rome: New Light on the Origins of Psychoanalysis. *New American Review*: 1, 1-23.

VIRGIL, (1983). *The Aeneid.* Translated by Robert Fitzgerald. New York: Random House.

WISTRICH, R.S. (1991). *Antisemitism: The Longest Hatred.* New York: Schocken Books.

ZOLA, E. (1899). *Fecondite. Fruitfulness.* Translated by Vizettely. London: Chatto and Widus, 1925.

ESSAY V

FREUD'S "DISTURBANCE OF MEMORY ON THE ACROPOLIS" REVISITED[*]

> So much for [*Moses and Monotheism*] . . . . I have been very much besought to write something for Romain Rolland's 70th birthday. . . . I managed to write a short analysis of "a feeling of alienation" which overcame me on the Acropolis in Athens in 1904, something very intimate . . . . But combine the two proverbs about the rogue who gives more and the beautiful girl who will not give more than they have [sic] and you will see my situation.
> —Sigmund Freud's letter to Arnold Zweig in Haifa, January 20, 1936; in Freud and Zweig, 1970, p. 119.

On June 5, 1938, en route to exile in England, Freud (1856–1939), his wife, Martha, and their daughter Anna stopped off in Paris, where they had a pleasant twelve-hour visit with his disciple, Marie Bonaparte. By the time they left her home, Freud retrieved from Bonaparte, who had smuggled it out of Austria for him, his 4⅛-inch bronze statuette of Athena (Jones, 1957, pp. 227–228), the Olympian guardian of Athens, where, on his first and only visit to that immortal city, he had an odd experience on the afternoon of September 4, 1904 (Jones, 1955, p. 24):

> When, finally, on the afternoon of our arrival I stood on the Acropolis and cast my eyes upon the landscape, a surprising thought suddenly entered my mind: 'So all this really *does* exist, just as we learnt it at school.' (Freud, 1936, pp. 240–241; emphasis in original.).

The preceding is a quote from Freud's 1936 Open Letter to Romain Rolland on the occasion of the renowned French author's seventieth birthday (January 29), "A Disturbance of Memory on the Acropolis." In the Open Letter, Freud offers an analysis of his fleeting disbelief in the material reality of the Acropolis. This 'analysis' is actually a smoke screen to keep Freud's readers, including Rolland, from knowing what

---

[*]This essay was previously published in *The Psychoanalytic Review* (95:3, June 2008), and appears here with the requisite rights and permissions of that journal, and those of of the National Psychological Association for Psychoanalysis.

he is about. For, as I intend to show, at the time of his momentary astonishment, Freud's secret ambition to topple and replace Moses, both as lawgiver and as deliverer of the Jews, was stirred up on the Acropolis. According to Freud, that summer he and his brother Alexander, ten years his junior, hadn't intended to visit Athens. On their way to the Greek island of Corfu they stopped off at Trieste, where a business acquaintance of Alexander's advised them "strongly" to change their plans: rather than go to Corfu, which "would be too hot . . . to do anything," it'd be "far better to go to Athens instead." Though perturbed by this "quite impracticable" proposal, Freud and Alexander booked passage for Athens.

At the time of his disbelief in the objective reality of the Acropolis he was, Freud (1936) states, overwhelmed by a "feeling of derealization":

> . . . the whole psychical situation, which seems so confused and is so difficult to describe, can be satisfactorily cleared up by assuming that at the time I had (or might have had) a momentary feeling: *'What I see here is not real.'* Such a feeling is known as 'a feeling of derealization' [*Entremdungsgefuhl,* literally, a "feeling of alienation"] (p. 244; italics in orginal).

Asserting that all derealizations "aim at keeping something from the ego, at disavowing it," Freud (1936, p. 245), in the Open Letter's last few sentences, states that his standing on the Acropolis in Athens signified the fulfillment of a forbidden wish, the wish to excel one's father, and that the derealization or his fleeting disbelief in the Acropolis kept him from acknowledging that this impious wish has been realized:

> I might that day on the Acropolis have said to my brother: 'Do you still remember how, when we were young, we used day after day to walk on the same streets on our way to school, and how every Sunday we used to go to the Prater or on some excursion we knew so well? And now, here we are in Athens, and standing on the Acropolis! We really *have* gone a long way!'. . . . It must be that a sense of guilt was attached to the satisfaction in having gone such a long way: there was something about it that was wrong, that from earliest times had been forbidden. . . . It seems as though the essence of success was to have got further than one's father, and as though to excel one's father was still something forbidden.
> . . . The very theme of Athens and the Acropolis in itself contained evidence of the son's superiority. Our father had been in business, he had had no secondary education, and Athens could not have

meant much to him. Thus what interfered with our enjoyment of the journey to Athens was a feeling of *filial piety* ... (pp. 247–248; italics in original.)

It is here that Freud is holding back: the "feeling of *filial piety*" which interfered with his enjoyment on the Acropolis pertained not only to his deceased father, Jakob, whom he has excelled, but also to Moses, whom Freud, since before the turn of the century, has been secretly bent on surpassing

After relating the derealization on the Acropolis, Freud refers to "a marginal case" of derealization, the Moorish King Boabdil's refusal to acknowledge a portent of the end of his kingdom Granada, the fall of the fortified city of Alhama:

> You remember the famous lament of the Spanish Moors '*Aye de mi Alhama*' [Alas for my Alhama], which tells how King Boabdil received the news of the fall of the town of Alhama. He feels that this loss means the end of his rule. But he will not "let it be true," he determines to treat the news as '*non arrive*'. The verse runs:
>
>> 'Letters had reached him telling that Alhama was taken. He threw the letters in the fire and killed the messenger' (James Strachey's translation; in Freud, 1936, p. 246).

The fall of Granada in 1492 brought to an end 800 years of Muslim dominion on the Iberian Peninsula. From this significant triumph of Christendom—following which the victorious Catholic sovereigns, Ferdinand and Isabella, banished the Jews from Spain—Freud turns to a symbolic vanquishing of the Church, Napoleon's self-coronation in Notre Dame as Emperor of France on Sunday, December 4, 1804:

> ... if I may compare such a small event [Freud standing with Alexander on the Acropolis] with a greater one, Napoleon, during his coronation as Emperor in Notre Dame, turned to one of his brothers—it must no doubt have been the eldest one, Joseph—and remarked: 'What would *Monsieur notre Pere* have said to this, if he could be here today?' .. (p. 247).

During the ceremony, just as Pope Pius VII was about to place the Bourbon crown on his head, Napoleon "took care to put the crown on his head himself" (Butterfield, 1966, p. 62), thereby, symbolically castrating the Holy Father (hats, accoring to Freud, symbolize male genital organs). This allusion to Napoleon's 'castration' of the Pope suggests strongly that at the time of the derealization a similar 'castration' was evoked, that of his father, Jakob, by the Christian in the small Catholic city of Freud's birth, Freiberg in Moravia. Again, it was on one of their Sunday walks, when Freud was "ten or twelve," that Jakob related the incident which occurred on the Jewish sabbath:

> When I was a young man . . . I went for a walk one Saturday . . . . A Christian came up to me and with a single blow he knocked off my [new fur] cap from my head into the mud and shouted, "Jew! get off the pavement!" "And what did you do?,"I asked. "I went into the roadway and picked up my cap," was his quiet reply. This struck me as unheroic conduct on the part of the big, strong man who was holding the little boy by the hand. I contrasted this situation with another which fitted my feelings better: the scene in which Hannibal's father . . . made his boy swear to take vengeance on the Romans. Ever since that time Hannibal has had a place in my fantasies (Freud, 1900, p. 197).

In the Open Letter Freud refers to his Sunday walks with his father, Jakob ("how every Sunday . . ."). So, it is reasonable to assume that Jakob's 'castration' on the Jewish sabbath was evoked during the derealization, as well as Freud's 'Hannibal' phantasy "to take vengeance on the Romans"—that is, the new Romans, the Catholic Church.

According to legend, when Boabdil burst into tears while casting his eyes one last time at his palace-fortress, the Alhambra, his mother, the Sultana, reproached him: "You do well to weep like a woman for what you do not defend like a man." Like the Sultana, Amalie Freud too had given birth to a "Moor": " (. . . It appears that I came into the world with such a tangle of black hair that my young mother declared I was a little Moor)." (Freud, 1900, p. 337, n.1).

But unlike the Sultana's Moor, who "weeps and does not defend," Amalie's Moor, her "*Goldener Sigi,*" who was born in a caul and so is destined to become "a great man" (Freud, 1900, p. 192), would not only "defend," he would destroy their common enemy, Christianity. And thereby avenge—according to the *lex talionis* ("an eye for an eye, a tooth for a tooth ")—the humiliation of his beloved papa, for he will have perpetrated the ultimate castration on the papacy, the killing off of the papal line.

Essay V: Freud's "Disturbance of Memory on the Acropolis" Revisited

Introducing the Open Letter's subject matter, the derealization on the Acropolis, Freud states: "*During the last few years* [an odd experience] . . . which I had never understood, has kept on returning to my mind" (p. 239, my emphasis). But why—after three decades—the "returning to [Freud's] mind" of the derealization? This reasonable question—"Why now? . . . "—the father of psychoanalysis does not address, as though it had never entered his mind, which is hard to believe, as is his claim that he "had never [before] understood" the derealization. "During the last few years" Freud had been writing and researching *Moses and Monotheism* (1939), a draft of which he had completed in 1934, and which he, moreover, had seriously considered writing since at least as early August 1933 (Schur, 1972, p. 91). Because it is intimately related to his secret messianic ambition, Freud secretly understands that the surfacing or "returning" of the three-decades-old derealization was instigated by his preoccupation with this ongoing work which would be his last major assault on religion—and in which he asserts that Christianity and the scourge of anti-Semitism are inextricably linked:

> The [Christians] have not got over a grudge against the new religion which was imposed on them; but they have displaced the grudge on to the source from which Christianity reached them. The fact that the Gospels tell a story which is set among Jews, and in fact deals only with Jews, has made this displacement easy for them. Their hatred of Jews is at bottom a hatred of Christians. . . (Freud, 1939, pp. 91–92).

In other words, the good Christian, not having the moral courage to acknowledge his hatred for his religion which obliges him to renounce his aggressive and illicit sexual impulses, displaces this disavowed hatred on to the people who had made his life miserable by shackling him with his chains, the Jews. This hostility, Freud adds, can be traced back to Moses: ". . . we venture to declare that it was the one man Moses who created the Jews. It is to him that this people owes its tenacity of life and also much of the hostility it has experienced and still experiences." (Freud, 1939, p. 106). Hence it follows: In order to annihilate anti-Semitism, it is essential that the Jews' Tree of Life, the Torah—and their Great Man Moses—be sacrificed. Or to paraphrase the Boabdil verse: He [Amalie's Moor] threw the letters [the Law] in the fire and killed [Yahweh's] messenger [Moses]. This then is Freud's secret solution to the Jewish Problem: no Law, no Judaism, no Christianity, no miserable anti-Semitism.

Which brings us to the essential premise or speculation of *Moses and Monotheism*: Jewish monotheism can be traced back to a patricide, the killing of Moses by the Jews [Deuteronomy 34:7–8 notwithstanding ("Moses was an hundred and twenty years old when he died . . .")]: the Jews rose up and killed the stern and demanding Moses; it is from the corresponding filial sense of guilt and remorse vis-a-vis this (alleged) patricide that Judaism arose. Universal acceptance of this 'patricide' theory regarding Judaism's beginnings would eliminate Judaism's miserable offshoot, Christianity—albeit, again, at a great double cost, the Law and Moses. After completing the book two years later, Freud in an unguarded moment will show his hand:

> Neither in my private life nor in my writings have I ever made a secret of my being an out and out unbeliever. Anyone considering the book [then at the printer's] from that point of view will have to admit it is only Jewry and not Christianity which has reason to feel offended by its conclusions. For only a few incidental remarks, which say nothing that hasn't been said before, allude to Christianity. At most one can quote the old adage: *"Caught together, hanged together!"* (letter of October 31, 1938, to Charles Singer, a professor of history of science; in Freud, 1960, p. 453; emphasis added.)

Years earlier, in *The Future of an Illusion*, Freud (1927) alluded to his enlightened Promised Land:

> . . . New generations, who have been brought up in kindness and taught to have a high opinion of reason, and who have experienced the benefits of civilization at an early age . . . . will feel it as a possession of their very own and will be ready for its sake to make the sacrifices as regards work and instinctual satisfaction that are necessary for its preservation. They will be able to do without coercion from their leaders. If no culture has so far produced human masses of such a quality, it is because no culture has yet devised regulations which will influence men in this way, and in particular from childhood onwards (p. 8).

Later in the book, Freud (1927) continued:

ESSAY V: Freud's "Disturbance of Memory on the Acropolis" Revisited

As honest smallholders on this earth they will know how to cultivate their plot in such a way that it supports them. By withdrawing their expectations from the other world and concentrating all their liberated energies into their life on earth, they will probably succeed in achieving a state of things in which life will become tolerable for everyone and civilization no longer oppressive to anyone. Then, with one of our fellow-unbelievers [Heine], they will be able to say without regret:

["We leave Heaven to the angels and the sparrows." Translation, James Strachey.] (p. 50).

Sandwiched between these two 'Promised Land' passages, Freud refers to his derealization experience on the Acropolis:

I was already a man of mature years [48] when I stood for the first time on the hill of the Acropolis of Athens, between the temple ruins, looking out over the blue sea. A feeling of astonishment mingled with my joy . . . [M]y astonishment . . . has to do with the special character of the place (1927, p. 25).

And what better setting than the preceding scene—Freud, standing for the first time "between the temple ruins" of the Acropolis in Athens, the fountainhead of Western Civilization—to excite this striver's vast ambition to institute his boundless Promised Land, a socially just world grounded in Reason, wherein all abide freely by his one law, the Delphic precept, "Know thyself," and for whose realization it is essential that this hero annihilate religion, leave it in the dust?

Bearing in mind the preceding scenario, please consider this partial reconstruction of Freud's derealization experience: Standing on the Acropolis, Freud is initially in a state of exaltation ("my joy"), which is instigated by a subconscious delusion: his passionately longed-for peaceable kingdom—his boundless, harmonious Promised Land in which at long last the seed of Abraham are truly at home—is now within range or on the horizon (cf. "looking out over the blue sea"), for he has destroyed Christianity, the seedbed for anti-Semites like the good Christian who had knocked off Jakob's new *shabbes* hat. But in a flash, before Freud can fully savor this passionately longed-for moment, the delusion disappears—owing to his filial sense of guilt ("a feeling of *filial piety*") vis-a-vis his Promised Land's great double cost: the Law ("the temple ruins") and that great man, Moses. Consequently, to paraphrase this impious striver, "a feeling of astonishment [is now] mingled with my joy." Here it is worth noting: the Freud family Bible, the illustrated German-Hebrew Phillipson Bible, whose frontispiece depicts Moses holding the Tablets of the Law (with rays of light emanating upward from both sides of his forehead), contains a picture of the Acropolis (Vitz, 1988, p. 196).

Now, behind Freud's pleasure-sabotaging "feeling of astonishment" not only is there "a feeling of *filial piety.*" There is also, Freud's closing words betray, his fear of Yahweh, of His terrible Justice:

> ... what interfered ... was a feeling of *filial piety*. And now you will no longer wonder that the recollection of this incident [*erlebnis*, experience] on the Acropolis would have troubled me so often [*mich ... so oft heimsucht*] since I myself have grown old and stand in need of forbearance [*nachsicht*] and can travel no more. (pp. 237–238; emphasis added.)

Pertinent here is S.S. Prawer's (1983) comment on James Strachey's rendering of *heimsucht* as "troubled" above):

> "Heimsuchen" is the verb Luther's Bible uses as its equivalent for God's "visiting" the sins of the fathers on future generations [2 Moses 20:5] and any appropriate German dictionary will furnish plenty of examples in which "heimsuchen" has to do with "smiting", "afflicting", "being stricken", and "suffering", as well as "being favored with benefits" . . . .There *is* something troubling about the sudden irruption, the "Auftauchen," of the memory image.... (p. 812).

When writing the Open Letter, Freud, whose writings contain many references to Luther's Bible, probably suspects that Yahweh's visitations have already begun. And with a vengeance! On January 25, 1920, Freud's middle daughter, Sophie Halberstadt, died at the age of 26 after a bout with the grippe. Two and one-half years later, and just two months after Freud had undergone the first of 33 surgical procedures for cancer of the mouth and jaw (April 20, 1923), Sophie's 4½-year-old son Heinele, who was his favorite grandchild, died from an acute miliary tuberculosis on June 19, 1923. Almost five years after his beloved Heinele's death, Freud wrote the following in his letter of March 11, 1928, to Ernest Jones who had just lost his daughter, an exceptionally brilliant little girl:

> ... Only when ... little Heinele died did I become weary of life

Essay V: Freud's "Disturbance of Memory on the Acropolis" Revisited

for good. He . . . was of superior intelligence and indescribable spiritual grace, and repeatedly said that he would die soon! How do these children come to know those things? (Schur, 1972, p. 406).

Despite fearing that he is to blame for the deaths of his beloved "Sunday child" Sophie and his precious "little Heinele," Freud to the very end (he will die three years later on Yom Kippur, September 23, 1939) sticks to his rebellious path, hoping against hope that his mighty weapon, his theoretical knowledge about God's humble beginnings, is not itself what he asserts God to be, a hollow wish fulfillment, that his other little ones "unto the third and fourth *generation* . . ." (Exodus 20:5) won't suffer Yahweh's vengeance, won't pay for their father's rebellion. How then can we account for Freud's staying on this potentially calamitous path?

After Jakob passed away at the age of eighty-one on October 23, 1896, Freud, feeling uprooted, began to study himself in depth. In 1897, several months into his detailed self-analysis, Freud discovered to his horror that he is a Cain, a brother-killer: "I welcomed my one-year-younger brother (who died within a few months) with ill wishes and real infantile jealousy, and . . . his death left the germ of guilt in me." (Letter dated October 3, 1897; Freud and Fliess, 1954, p. 219). Oppressed by his fratricidal sense of guilt, Freud secretly resolved to redeem himself by making the world a better place for future Juliuses (and Sarahs), a world without anti-Semitism. This, then, vis-á-vis his messianic ambition, is the determinative factor: Freud's need to make an atonement for having 'killed' his rival, baby Julius.

(On April 15, 1908, the fiftieth anniversary of Julius's death, the six-year-old Psychological Wednesday Society, as per Freud's carried motion, was re-named the Vienna Psychoanalytic Society (Nunberg and Federn, 1962, p. 373). In this manner Freud dedicated to the memory of Julius the psychoanalytic movement, which would, were all to go according to plan, institute his brotherly world, an enlightened and healed socially just world in which reason overrides passion—or to paraphrase Freud, "Where id was, ego reason is." At any rate, this is his secret game plan.)

With death near and dreading Yahweh's retribution, Freud closes the Open Letter with an apt plea, "I . . . stand in need of forbearance [*nachsicht*]." According to *The New Cassell's German Dictionary*, nachsicht means "indulgence, forbearance, leniency, clemency, pity, respite." But undeterred, this tormented and weary freedom fighter, his Job-like cancerous sores ravaging his mouth and jaw, continues on his impious and perilous path, penning the last sentence of *Moses and Monotheism* in his temporary London home (39 Elsworthy Road, N.W. 3) on Sunday, July 17, 1938—or the civil date of the Fast of Tammuz, the day of mourning commemorating both the Chaldean breach (586 B.C.E.) and Roman breach (70 C.E.) of the walls of Jerusalem, which led to the destruction of the First and Second Temples (Spier, 1986). And this is fitting, for to repeat: universal acceptance of the book's essential premise—Judaism stems from a patricide—would result in destruction of the Jews' 'stone' fortress, the Torah.

After writing the last sentence of *Moses and Monotheism* and placing his pen on his antiquities-covered desk, did this lonely and unknown fighter for the human rights of his beseiged nation lift his precious "Athene," and to that virgin goddess of wisdom and of war make a silent prayer?

REFERENCES

BUTTERFIELD, H. (1966). *Napoleon*. New York: Collier Books.

CASSELL'S GERMAN DICTIONARY, THE NEW (1962). New York: Funk and Wagnalls.

FREUD, S. (1900). The Interpretation of Dreams. In J.S. Strachey, ed. and Trans. *The Standard Edition of the Complete Psychological Works of Sigmund Freud.* 24 vols. London: Hogarth Press.

——— (1927). The Future of an Illusion. *Standard Edition* 21.

——— (1936). A Disturbance of Memory on the Acropolis. *Standard Edition* 22.

——— (1939). Moses and Monotheism. *Standard Edition* 23.

——— & Fliess, W. (1954). *The Origins of Psycho-Analysis: Letters to Wilhelm Fliess, Drafts and Notes, 1887–1902.* (M. Bonaparte, A. Freud, & E. Kris, eds.; J. Strachey & E. Mosbacher, trans.) New York: Basic Books.

——— (1960). *The Letters of Sigmund Freud*. Selected and edited by E. Freud. New York: Basic Books.

——— & Zweig, A. (1970). *The Letters of Sigmund Freud and Arnold Zweig.* (E. Freud, ed. E. & W. Robson-Scott, trans. New York: Harcourt Brace and World.

JONES, E. (1955, 1957). *The Life and Work of Sigmund Freud.* New York: Basic Books.

NUNBERG, H., & FEDERN, E., eds. (1962). *Minutes of the Vienna Psychoanalytic Society, Vol. I, 1906–1908,* New York: International Universities Press.

PRAWER. S.S. (1983). The Psyche in Transition. In *Times Literary Supplement.* 29 July.
SCHUR, M. (1972). *FREUD: Living and Dying.* New York: International Universities Press.
SPIER, A. (1986). *The Comprehensive Hebrew Calendar.* New York: Feldheim Press.
VITZ, P. (1988). *Sigmund Freud's Christian Unconscious.* New York: Guilford Press.

AUTHOR'S OTHER RELEVANT PAPERS

1. January, 2000. Is Freud in the Dates? *Midstream,* 36, No. 1.

2. July/August, 2001. Freud's Hypothesis that the Jews Killed Moses. *Midstream,* 37, No. 5.

3. November/December, 2002. Sigmund Freud Avoids His Double, Theodor Herzl. *Midstream,* 38, No. 7.

4. January, 2003. Freud, the Law, and Michelangelo's Moses. *Midstream,* 39, No. 1.

5. July 17, 2008. Freud's Failure to Recall the Name of Luca Signorelli. http://internationalpsychoanalysis.net/2008/07/17.
(Revised version on the internet site *Researchgate: https://www.researchgate.net/publication/228382542_Freud%27s_failure_to_recall_the_name_of_Luca_Signorelli*.)

6. November 18, 2009. Freud, Minna, and Schliemann's *Ilios*. http://internationalpsychoanalysis.net/2009/11/18.

7. September 15, 2011. Freud's Gruesome Dream, Dissecting My Own Pelvis. http://internationalpsychoanalysis.net/2011/09/15.

8. July 12, 2012. The Classical Psychoanalytic Technique Revisited. http://internationalpsychoanalysis.net/2012/07/12.

SELECTED BIBLIOGRAPY

ABRAHAM, H.C. & Freud, E.L. (1965). *A Psycho-Analytic Dialogue: The Letters of Sigmund Freud and Karl Abraham, 1907–1926*. B. Marsh & H.C. Abraham, trans. London: Hogarth Press.
AGNON, S.Y. (1948). *Days Of Awe*. New York: Schocken.
ALTER, R. & KERMODE, F. (1990). *The Literary Guide to the Bible*. Cambridge: Harvard.
ANZIEU, D. (1986). *Freud's Self-Analysis*. P. Graham, trans. London Hogarth Press.
AUDEN, W.H. (1979). In Memory of Sigmund Freud. (1939). In *W.H. Auden, Selected Poems*. (E. Mendelson, ed.) New York: Vantage Books.
AUGUSTINE. (1943). *The Confessions of St. Augustine*. J.G. Pilkington, trans. New York: Liveright.
———— (1958). *City of God*. G.G. Walsh, D.B. Zema, G. Monahan, & D.J. Honan, trans. Garden City: Image Books.
BAEDEKER, K. (1909). *Baedeker's Italy: From the Alps to Naples*. Leipzig: Karl Baedeker Publishers.
BALZAC, H. (1897). *The Wild Ass's Skin; La Grande Breteche; A Passion In The Desert*, Volume V. E. Marriage, trans. Preface by G. Saintsbury. The Review of Reviews Co. (1940). Online edition at: https://ia902205.us.archive.org/22/items/wildassskinother00balziala/wildassskinother00balziala_bw.pdf.
BELLER, S. (2004). Theodor Herzl and Austria: A Century Later. *The Austrian Federal Ministry for Foreign Affairs*.
BEN-SASSON, H., ed. (1976). *A History of the Jewish People*. Cambridge: Harvard University Press.
BERGSTEIN, M. (2010). Freud's Michelangelo, The Sculptural Meditations of a Hellenized Jew; in *The Jewish World of Sigmund Freud: Essays on Cultural Roots and the Problem of Religious Identity*, Arnold D. Richards, ed.: Jefferson, North Carolina: McFarland and Company.
BETTELHEIM, B. (1983). *Freud and Man's Soul*. New York: Alfred A. Knopf.
———— (1989). *Freud's Vienna and Other Essays*. New York: Knopf.
BETTERIDGE, H.T., & BREUL, K. (1962). *The New Cassell's German Dictionary* (German-English, English-German). New York: Funk & Wagnalls.
BERKELEY, G. (1988). *Vienna and Its Jews: The Tragedy of Success, 1880-1980s*. Boston: Abt Books.
BILLINSKY, J.M. (1969). Jung and Freud (The End of a Romance). *Andover Newton Quarterly* (November):39-43.
BINSWANGER, L. (1957). *Sigmund Freud: Reminiscences of a Friendship*. New York and London.

Selected Bibliography

BLUM, H. (1994). Freud and The Figure of Moses: The Moses of Freud. *Journal of the American Psychoanalytic Association* 39:513–535.

BLUMENTHAL, R. (2006). Hotel Log Hints at Illicit Desire That Dr. Freud Didn't Repress. *The New York Times*, December 24.

BRANDES, G. (1967). *Michelangelo: His Life. His Times. His ERA.* H. Nodern, ed. New York: Federick Ungar Publ.

BREDIN, J. (1986). *The Affair: The Case of Alfred Dreyfus.* J. Mehlman, trans. New York: George Braziller.

BREUL, K. (1906, Rev., 1914). *A New German and English Dictionary.* New York: Funk & Wagnalls.

BROME, V. (1968). *Freud And His Early Circle.* New York: William Morrow & Co.

BUBER, M. (1947). *Tales of Hasidim: The Early Masters.* O. Marx, trans. New York: Farrar, Straus and Young.

BUTLER, Rev. A. (1955). *Lives of the Saints.* New York: Benziger Brothers, Inc.

BUTTERFIELD, H. (1966). *Napoleon.* New York: Collier Books.

CAROTENU, A. (1982). *A Secret Symmetry: Sabina Spielrein Between Jung and Freud.* A. Pomerans, J. Shepley, J., & K. Winston, trans. New York: Pantheon Books.

CLARK, R. (1980). *Freud, The Man and the Cause.* London: Jonathan Cape.

COHEN, M. (1950). Freud's *Moses and Monotheism.* In *Reflections of a Wandering Jew.* Boston: Beacon Press.

COTTRELL, L. (1953). *The Bull of Minos: The Discoveries of Schliemann And Evans.* New York; London: Fact On File Publications.

DANTE, A. (1952). *The Divine Comedy.* C.E. Norton, trans. Chicago: Great Books.

DERFLER, L. (1963). *The Dreyfus Affair: Tragedy of Errors.* Boston: D.C. Heath.

DONIN, Rabbi H.H. (1972). *To Be a Jew.* New York: Basic Books.

FALK, A. (1977). Freud and Herzl, *Midstream* 23:3–24, January.

FREUD, E. FREUD, L. & GRUBRICH-SIMITIS, I. (1985). *Sigmund Freud: His Life in Pictures and Words.* New York: W.W, Norton & Company.

FREUD, S. (1896). The Aetiology of Hysteria. *Standard Edition of the Complete Psychological Works of Sigmund Freud.* 24 vols. London: Hogarth Press. 1953–1974. 3.

——— (1898). The Psychical Mechanism of Forgetfulness. *Standard Edition* 3.

——— (1899). Screen Memories. *Standard Edition* 3.

——— (1900). *Die Traumdeutung.* Vienna, G.W. II/III.

SELECTED BIBLIOGRAPHY

——— (1900). The Interpretation of Dreams. *Standard Edition* 4–5.
——— (1901). The Psychopathology of Everyday Life. *Standard Edition* 6.
——— (1905 [1901]). Fragment of an Analysis of a Case of Hysteria. *Standard Edition* 7.
——— (1910). Leonardo da Vinci and a Memory of His Childhood. *Standard Edition* 11.
——— (1912). Recommendations to Physicians Practising Psycho-Analysis. *Standard Edition* 12.
——— (1912–1913). Totem and Taboo. *Standard Edition* 13.
——— (1914). *Der Moses des Michelangelo*. G.W. X.
——— (1914). The Moses of Michelangelo. *Standard Edition* 13.
——— (1916–1917). Introductory Lectures on Psycho-analysis. *Standard Edition* 15–16.
——— (1919). The "Uncanny." *Standard Edition* 17.
——— (1919). The "Uncanny." In *Collected Papers*, Volume 4. New York: Basic Books, 1925.
——— (1919). *Das Unheimlich*. G.W. XII.
——— (1921). *Massenpsychologie und Ich-Analyse*. G.W. XIII.
——— (1921). Group Psychology and the Analysis of the Ego. *Standard Edition* 18.
——— (1924). The Dissolution of the Oedipus Complex. *Standard Edition* 19.
——— (1925). An Autobiographical Study. *Standard Edition* 20.
——— (1927). The Future of an Illusion. *Standard Edition* 21.
——— (1930). Address delivered in the Goethe House at Frankfurt, *Standard Edition* 21.
——— (1933). New Introductory Lectures on Psycho-Analysis. *Standard Edition* 22.
——— (1936). A Disturbance of Memory on the Acropolis. *Standard Edition* 22.
——— (1939). Moses and Monotheism. *Standard Edition* 23.
——— (1940–1968). *Gesammelte Werke, Chronologisch Geordnet*. A. Freud, E. Bibring, W. Hoffer, E. Kris, & O. Isakower, eds., in collaboration with M. Bonaparte. 18 Volumes. London: Imago (Vol. II/III; Vol. X; Vol. XIII.)
——— (1954). *The Origins of Psycho-Analysis: Letters to Wilhelm Fliess, Draft and Notes, 1887–1902*. M. Bonaparte, A. Freud & E. Kris, eds.; E. Mosbacher & J. Strachey, trans. London and New York, Basic Books and Imago.
——— (1959). *Collected Papers*. Authorized translation under the supervision of Joan Riviere, Edited by Ernest Jones. London: Hogarth Press.

——— (1960). *The Letters of Sigmund Freud*. Selected and Edited by E. Freud. New York: Basic Books.

——— (1965). *A Psycho-Analytic Dialogue: The Letters of Sigmund Freud and Karl Abraham*. 1907–1926, eds. Hilda C. Abraham & Ernst L. Freud; B. Marsh & H.C. Abraham, trans. New York: Basic Books.

——— (1985). *The Complete Letters of Sigmund Freud to Wilhelm Fliess, 1887–1904*. J. M. Masson, ed. and trans. Cambridge: Harvard University Press.

——— (1992). *The Diary of Sigmund Freud 1929–1939*. Translated, annotated, and introduced by M.Molnar. New York: Charles Scribner's Sons.

——— (1993). *The Correspondence of Sigmund Freud and Sandor Ferenczi, Volume 1, 1908–1914*. E. Brabant. E. Falzeder, P. Giampieri-Deutsch, eds.; P.T. Hofer, trans.; A. Haynal, intro. Cambridge: Belknap Press of Harvard University.

——— & JONES, E. (1995). *The Complete Correspondence of Sigmund Freud and Ernest Jones 1908–1939*, ed. R.A. Paskauskas; intro. R. Steiner. Cambridge: Belknap Press of Harvard University.

——— & JUNG, C. (1974). *The Freud/Jung Letters: the Correspondence Between Sigmund Freud and C.G. Jung*. William McGuire, ed. R. Manheim & R.F.C. Hull, trans. Bollingen Series XCIV. Princeton: Princeton University Press.

——— & ZWIEG, A. (1970). *The Letters of Sigmund Freud and Arnold Zweig*. Freud, E., ed. E. & W. Robson-Scott, trans. New York: Harcourt Brace and World.

FROMM, E. (1963). *The Dogma of Christ*. New York: Holt, Rhinehart and Winston.

GAY, P. (1987). *A Godless Jew: Freud, Atheism and the Making of Psychoanalysis*. New Haven: Yale University.

——— (1988). *FREUD: A Life for Our Times*. New York: Norton.

GIFFORD, G.E., Jr. (1972). Freud and the Porcupine. *Harvard Medical Alumni Bulletin* March/April: 28–33.

GILMAN, S.L. (1993). *The Case of Sigmund Freud*. Baltimore: Johns Hopkins.

GINSBURG, L.M. & GINSBURG, S.A. (1992). Paradise in the Life of Sigmund Freud: An Understanding of its Imagery and Paradoxes. *International Review of Psychoanalysis* 19:285–308.

GREGORY. (1967). *Dialogues, Book II, Saint Benedict*. M.L. Uhlfelder, trans. Indianapolis: Bobbs-Merrill.

GRESSER, M. (1994). *Dual Allegiance: Freud as a Modern Jew*. Albany: SUNY.

GRINKER, R. (1940). Reminiscences of a Personal Contact with Freud. In H.M. Ruitenbeek, ed., *Freud as we knew him*. Detroit: Wayne State University Press.

HALASZ, N. (1955). *Captain Dreyfus: The Story of A Mass Hysteria*. New York: Simon and Schuster.

HERZL, T. (1896, 1988). *The Jewish State*. Based on S.D'Avigdor's 1896 translation; introduction by Louis Lipsky, biography by A. Bein. New York: Dover.

HIRSCHMULLER, A. (2007). Evidence for a Sexual Relationship between Sigmund Freud and Mirna Bernays? *American Imago*, 64:125–129.

HOGENSON, G.B. (1983). *Jung's Struggle With Freud*. Notre Dame: University of Notre Dame Press.

HOMANS, P. (1989). *The Ability to Mourn*. Chicago: University of Chicago.

ISBITER, J. (1985). *Freud An Introduction to His Life and Work*. Cambridge: Polity Press.

JONES, E. (1953, 1955, 1957). *The Life and Work of Sigmund Freud*. New York: Basic Books.

JONES, R. & Penny, N. (1983). *Raphael*. New Haven: Yale University Press.

JUNG, C.G. (1963). *Memories, Dreams, Reflections* (A. Jaffe, recorder/editor; R. & C. Winston, trans.) New York: Pantheon Books.

KLEIN, D. (1985). *Jewish Origins of the Psychoanalytic Movement*. Chicago: University of Chicago.

KRULL. M. (1986). *Freud and His Father*. A.J. Pomerans, trans. Preface by H. Stierlin. New York: Norton.

KUBIE, L. (1975). *Practical and Theoretical Aspects of Psychoanalysis*. New York; International Universities Press.

LOTHANE, Z. (2007). Sensation-Mongering Among Historians: A Response to: "Did Freud Sleep with His Wife's Sister: an Expert Interview with Franz Maciejewski, Ph.D." *Medscape Psychiatry News* (June 13).

MACIEJEWSKI, F. (2007). Did Freud Sleep With his Wife's Sister: An Expert Interview with Franz Maciejewski, Ph.D, *Medscape Psychiatry News*, May 4.

MCGRATH, W.J. (1986). *Freud's Discovery of Psychoanalysis: The Politics of Hysteria*. New York: Cornell Univ. Press.

MAIMONIDES, M. (1946). *The Guide for the Perplexed*. M. Friedlander, trans. Haifa, Israel: Pardes Publishing House.

MAKARI, G. (2008). *Revolution in Mind: The Creation of Psychoanalysis*. New York: Harper Collins.

MENNINGER, K. (1958). *Theory of Psychoanalytic Technique*. New York: Basic Books.

Selected Bibliography

NUNBERG, H. & FEDERN, E. (1962). *Minutes of the Vienna Psycho-analytic Society.* Volume I, 1906–1908. New York: International Universities Press.

O'HARA, D. (2000). Not 'Too Good to Be True': A late Freudian phantasy of self-education. *Boundary,* Spring 27:1; Research.

PALOMBO, S. (1988). Day Residue and Screen Memory in Freud's Dream of the Botanical Monograph. *Journal of the American Psychoanalytic Association* 36:881–904.

PATAI, R. (1960). Herzl's School Years. *Herzl Yearbook* 111:53–75.

PAWEL, E. (1989). *The Labyrtinthe of Exile: A Life of Theodor Herzl.* New York: Farrar, Straus, & Giroux.

PETERS, U. (1985). *Anna Freud: a life dedicated to children.* New York: Schoken.

PHILIPPSON, L. (1858). *Die Israelitische Bibel.* 4 vols. Leipzig: Baumgartners Buchhandlung.

PRAWER, S.S. (1983). The Psyche in Transition. In *Times Literary Supplement,* 29 July.

PRESCOTT, H. (1838). History of the Reign of Ferdinand and Isabella the Catholic. In *The Alhambra,* D. Stewart, 1974. New York: Newsweek Books.

REICH, W. (1967). *Reich Speaks of Freud.* Edited by Mary Higgins and Chester Raphael, M.D. Interviewer, K. R. Eissler. New York: Farrar Straus.

REIK, T. (1949). *Listening with the Third Ear.* New York: Farrar Straus.

RICE, E. (1990). *Freud and Moses: The Long Journey Home.* Albany: SUNY.

——— (1994). The Jewish Heritage of Sigmund Freud, *Psychoanalytic Review,* Vol. 18:2.

RIZZUTO, A. (1979). *The Birth of the Living God.* Chicago: University of Chicago Press.

ROAZEN, P. (1975). *Freud and His Followers.* New York: Alfred A. Knopf.

ROTH, C. (1954). *A Bird's-Eye View of Jewish History.* New York: Union of American Hebrew Congregations.

SACHS, H. (1944). *Freud, Master and Friend.* Cambridge: Harvard University Press.

SELTZER, R. (1980). *Jewish People, Jewish Thought: The Jewish Experience in History.* New York: Macmillan.

SCHAUSS, H. (1970). *Guide to the Jewish Holy Days.* S. Jaffe, trans. New York: Schocken Books.

SCHOLEM, G. (1971). *The Messianic Idea in Judaism.* New York: Schocken Books.

Selected Bibliography

SCHORSKE. C.E. (1973). Politics and Patricide in Freud's Interpretation of Dreams. *American Historical Review* 78:328–347. Reprinted in Schorske's *Fin-de-siecle Vienna: Politics and Culture*. New York: Knopf. (1980); pp. 181–207.

SCHULZ, B. (1990). *Letters and Drawings of Bruno Schulz*. W. Arndt; V. & J. Ficowski, eds.; V. Nelson, trans. New York: Fromm International Publishing Corp.

SCHUR, M. (1966). Some Additional "Day Residues" of the Specimen Dream of Psychoanalysis. In *Psychoanalysis, A General Psychology: Essays in Honor of Heinz Hartmann*. R.M. Lowenstein, L.M. Newman, M. Schur, & A.J. Solnit, eds. New York: International Universities Press.

―――― (1972). *FREUD: Living and Dying*. New York: International Universities Press.

SELTZER, R.M. (1980). *Jewish People, Jewish Thought: The Jewish Experience in History*. New York: Macmillan Publishing Company.

SHAPIRO, E.R. (1996). Grief in Freud's Life: Reconceptualizing Bereavement in Psychoanalytic Theory. *Psychoanalytic Psychology: A Journal of Theory, Practice, Research, and Criticism*, 13(4):547–566.

SPIER, A. (1986). *The Comprehensive Hebrew Calendar*. New York: Feldheim Press.

STEWART, D. (1974). *Theodore Herzl: Artist and Politician*. London: Quartet Books.

SWALES, P.J. (1982). Freud, Minna Bernays, and the conquest of Rome. New light on the origins of psychoanalysis. *New American Review* 1:1–23.

TORAH, THE (1962). *The Five Books of Moses: A New Translation of the Holy Scriptures According to the Masoretic Text*. Philadelphia: The Jewish Publication Society of America.

TURNER, M. (2007/2008). Ashes to Ashes: The Riddle of Sigmund Freud's Death. *The AAIA Bulletin* 5:29–39 (The Australian Archeological Institute: Athens).

VASARI, G. (1978). *Artists of the Renaissance: A Selection from Lives of the Artists*. G. Bull, trans. New York: Viking.

VIRGIL. (1983). *The Aeneid*. R. Fitzgerald. New York: Random House.

VITZ, P. (1988). *Sigmund Freud's Christian Unconscious*. New York: Guilford Press.

VON UNWERTH, M. (2005). *Freud's Requiem: Mourning, Memory, and the Invisible History of a Summer Walk*. New York: Riverhead.

VON WEIZSACKER, V. (1957). Reminiscences of Freud and Jung, in *Freud and the 20th Century*. Benjamin Nelson, ed. Cleveland and New York:

Selected Bibliography

The World Publishing Company.

WAAGENAAR, S. (1974). *The Pope's Jews.* La Salle, IL: Open Court.

WAT, A. (1988). *My Century: The Odyssey of a Polish Intellectual.* R. Lourie, ed. and trans. C. Milosz, Foreword. New York: Norton.

WEISEL, E. (1972). *Souls on Fire: Portraits and Legends of Hasidic Masters.* New York: Random House.

WISTRICH, R.S. (1991). *Antisemitism: The Longest Hatred.* New York: Schocken Books.

YERUSHALMI, Y.H. (1991). *Freud's Moses: Judaism Terminable and Interminable.* New Haven: Yale University Press.

ZIEGLER, P. (1971). Germany: The Flagellants and the Persecution of the Jews. In *The Black Death: A Turning Point in History?* (W.H. Bowsky, ed.) New York: Holt, Rinehart and Winston.

ZILBOORG, G. (1964). *Freud and Religion: A Restatement of an Old Controversy.* Westminster, Maryland: The Newman Press.

ZOLA, E. (1925 [1899, *Fecondite*]). *Fruitfulness.* Vizetelly, trans. London: Chatto and Widus.

But for the support of my lovely wife, Hiroko, and my sometimes contentious children, Susan and David, this book would have remained an unrealized dream.

www.ingramcontent.com/pod-product-compliance
Lightning Source LLC
Chambersburg PA
CBHW071153300426
44113CB00009B/1185